THE PROFESSIONAL CHEF'S

ART OF
GARDE MANGER

THIRD EDITION

THE PROFESSIONAL CHEF'S

ART OF
GARDE MANGER

THIRD EDITION

**FREDERIC H.
SONNENSCHMIDT**

JEAN F. NICOLAS

A CBI Book

Published by Van Nostrand Reinhold Company

ॐ ॐ

*To the Student of Culinary Arts
and the Future Chef*

ॐ ॐ

Production Editor: Becky Handler
Text Design and Composition: Arabesque Composition
Cover Designer: Charles G. Mitchell

A CBI Book
(CBI is an imprint of Van Nostrand Reinhold Company Inc.)
Copyright © 1973, 1976, 1982 by the Culinary Institute of America

Library of Congress Catalog Card Number 81-15451

ISBN 0-8436-2223-7

Printed in the United States of America

Published by Van Nostrand Reinhold Company Inc.
135 West 50th Street
New York, New York 10020

Van Nostrand Reinhold Company Limited
Molly Millars Lane
Wokingham, Berkshire RG11 2PY, England

Van Nostrand Reinhold
480 La Trobe Street
Melbourne, Victoria 3000, Australia

Macmillan of Canada
Division of Canada Publishing Corporation
164 Commander Boulevard
Agincourt, Ontario M1S 3C7, Canada

16 15 14 13 12 11 10 9 8 7 6 5 4

Library of Congress Cataloging in Publication Data

Sonnenschmidt, Frederic H., 1935–
    The professional chef's art of garde manger.

    Includes index.
    1. Quantity cookery.   2. Cookery (Cold dishes)
3. Cookery (Garnishes)   4. Buffets
I. Nicolas, Jean F.   II. Title.
TX820.S64   1982   641.5′72   81-15451
ISBN 0-8436-2223-7   AACR2

CONTENTS

FOREWORD

The *Art of Garde Manger* is no doubt one of the most complete and best-researched documents focusing solely on the artistry and creativity that today are such important components of a chef's function. The fact that this new edition has been revised to incorporate the modern trends of garde manger presentations shows that the authors have recognized the changing environment and have seen fit to accommodate this change. They have updated concepts and introduced new ideas that make this book even more meaningful to the reader and to the practitioners of cooking.

This new edition further demonstrates the fact that garde manger, as well as any type of cooking, is based on the fundamentals often linked to the classical cuisine. It also realizes that in today's economy, and with today's concern for nutrition and health, certain modifications will occur in the preparation and presentation of food that we consume every day.

As we look over the lavish buffets, which at one time were dominated by an abundance of various foods prepared with different flavors and combinations of spices, we can very clearly see a trend that goes toward a clean and simple line of presentation. This new trend not only places greater importance on the exactness and neatness of the garde manger's work habits as he or she prepares the platters; it also recognizes the beauty that can be found in the simplicity of food in its natural colors, shapes, and flavors. The new garde manger concept, as incorporated in this book, also recognizes the fact that no matter how beautifully a buffet may be prepared, it is virtually worthless unless it is affordable. Consequently, the many hints and ideas that this book introduces to any culinarian, in terms of simple but effective garnishes, will become helpful guides toward creating buffets that not only look good but also taste good and are within today's economic means. The recipes in this volume were developed and tested in the instructional kitchens of The Culinary Institute of America, where the *Art of Garde Manger* is now used as the text for buffet catering courses. The *Art of Garde Manger* has established itself as one of the most desirable additions to any culinary library.

Since the last edition, Mr. Sonnenschmidt has further enhanced his culinary reputation by having most successfully competed as a member of the 1976 United States Culinary Olympic Team where he personally was awarded two gold medals in the World Class Competition. These honors no doubt recognize his creative designs and his simple, practical, yet beautiful presentations which have today become the highlight of many buffets prepared by those influenced by the teaching of Mr. Sonnenschmidt.

Ferdinand E. Metz
President
The Culinary Institute of America
Hyde Park, New York 12538
September 1981

ACKNOWLEDGMENTS

The authors would like to express their appreciation to the following people who helped in the preparation of this book:

Franz K. Lemoine, then Facilities and Organization Instructor, The Culinary Institute of America, for consultation on planning layouts for the garde manger

Alfred Natale, Chef-Instructor, C.C.E.

Steve Beno, Chef-Instructor

James Heywood, Chef-Instructor

J. De Chanteloup, Chef-Instructor

Bill Reynolds, Chef-Instructor

Lyde Buchtenkirch, Chef-Instructor

Wm. Brandt Cutlery Company, Inc.

Rougie-Vivies and Cie, Souillac, France, black and white photographs

Clement A. Gareri, Jr., black and white photographs

John Thos. Grubel, black and white and color photographs

John Hugelmeyer, black and white and color photographs, and

Many helpful students at The Culinary Institute of America.

CHAPTER ONE

WHAT IS THE ART OF GARDE MANGER?

Reputations for fine food in many eating places are dependent on the performance of the garde manger department. In smaller operations, although there may be no formal department, the same food specialties usually created in a garde manger department must be prepared using the techniques that have been developed over centuries by masters of garde manger work. These are the methods and techniques presented in this book. However, the garde manger work shown and described here has been updated. Modern methods for garde manger work have been developed that are adapted to today's menu requirements, food products, and equipment.

Garde manger tasks were so-called because in French the term *garde manger* meant food storage space; the work that was done in that location also was described by the term *garde manger.*

In France, the garde manger area was located next to the kitchen and it was here that foods required for preparation of meals were stored. All preparatory work on meat, poultry, game, and other provisions also took place in this area.

Since the area was located in a cool, airy spot that usually had some kind of food chilling provisions, cold food specialties were also prepared, decorated, and arranged for service there. This is how the work known as garde manger developed.

Since the basis of fine cuisine continues to include the preparation of specialties using aspic, chaud-froid, forcemeat, pate, mousse, marinades, sauces, and dressings, the art of garde manger work is essential to culinary expertise.

The work done in the garde manger department starts with the preparation of basic ingredients—meat, poultry, fish and seafood, fruits, and vegetables. Larding, trussing, and the creation of fruit and vegetable decorations are among the skills to be learned.

The creation of a display piece such as a roast turkey is a process involving many steps. The turkey must be properly prepared for roasting; when roasted, the breast must be properly carved out; a mousse must be prepared to fill the cavity; the breast must be sliced and arranged over the mousse. The decorative touches needed must be selected, created, and put in place both on the bird and on the platter used in its presentation. All of these tasks require skills and methods learned in the garde manger department.

Garde manger output is also the foundation of such showcase items as canapes, hors d'oeuvre, salads, galantines, and all of the cold food presentations that highlight the buffet. Knowledge of the use of the ingredients essential to these presentations is indispensable.

An operation does not have to be large, formal, or committed to high food costs to profit from the art of garde manger. Preparation of a sizable number of specialties is not necessary; actually, it takes only one or two unique presentations to gain extra attention for a buffet or a special menu. Because garde manger specialties can be tailored to match menu requirements, the mastery of garde manger skills is an invaluable asset in food preparation for foodservice operations of every size and style.

CHAPTER TWO

BUFFET PRESENTATION

In a period of changing foodservice requirements, the buffet has proved to be a device for pleasing the public that can be used 24 hours a day. It can be styled as a formal presentation of elaborate food displays or it can offer a choice of favorite foods in casual array for the speedy service of roadside travelers or the weekly luncheons scheduled to meet the minimum time requirements of service club members.

Whatever the level of presentation, it is important that buffet foods be planned and necessary preparations completed well in advance so that the presentation for final service can be done speedily and without difficulty.

To plan a buffet effectively the following information should be received well in advance:

1. Number of covers (persons to be served)
2. Price per cover
3. Time of serving
4. Location where the buffet tables are to be displayed
5. Menu and zoning arrangement
6. Number of serving lines (based on the number of covers and zones)
7. Number, sizes, and shapes of sectional tables available
8. Type of cloth (and color) desired
9. Nonedible pieces (ice carving, tallow, etc.) that will be needed based on the theme, or as requested by the guests
10. Other artifacts that might be needed to enhance the theme, or atmosphere, or as requested by the guests

A buffet table in the desired size and shape can be constructed by assembling collapsible sectional tables that have been specially designed for this use. These sectional tables come in six basic shapes:

- Oblong (6-ft. × 30-in.; 6-ft. × 36-in.; or 8-ft. × 30-in.; 8-ft. × 36-in.)
- Round (60 in. in diam. or 72 in. in diam.)
- Half-round
- Quarter-round
- Serpentine (built to fit with the above dimensions)
- Trapezoid (built to fit with the above dimensions)

What kinds of tops can be used in assembling buffet tables?

Tops come in six basic shapes:

OBLONG (6- or 8-ft., 30 in. wide)

ROUND (60 in. across)

HALF-ROUND (60 in. across)

QUARTER-ROUND (30-in. radius)

SERPENTINE (cut out of a "doughnut-shaped" table: inner arc, 2-1/2-ft. radius; outer arc, 5-ft. radius)

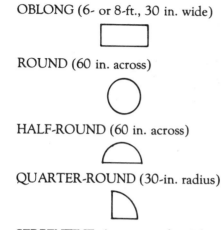

TRAPEZOID (cut out of a 30-in.-sided-hexagon, giving a trapezoid measuring 5 ft. at the base and 30 in. on each of the three remaining sides)

The most popular shapes for buffet tables are the first four. The other two types are sometimes necessary in setting up buffets that are to be presented on tables in special shapes.

The size of a buffet table should be calculated first, its shape second. To calculate the size, allow 1 linear foot of table per piece or arrangement of food (bowl or platter) to be displayed. Thus, a buffet menu having 36 pieces on display would require a table that measured at least 36 ft. for the full presentation.

When counting the number of pieces to be included in the display, do not forget to include the number of pieces that are not edible, i.e., centerpieces, stacks of plates, pepper mills, floral arrangement, and similar items.

The shape of the buffet table will be determined by one or more of the following factors:

1. Number of serving lines
2. Size and shape of the room
3. Seating arrangement
4. Occasion
5. Preferences of the guests

Before the tables are to be assembled, a sketch should be made by the chef indicating the number of zones and courses. Each zone, or table area, contains a complete selection of the buffet items being offered. The number of times the selection is repeated depends on the number of persons to be served. This must be determined before the number, size, and shape of the buffet tables can be settled. In the illustration on the facing page only two zones were needed.

The zoning must be correlated with the number of serving lines, and the number of serving lines will depend on the number of covers to be served. If there is more than one serving line, the guests will be served more efficiently and quickly.

Each zone would be divided into course areas; these will be duplicated in each zone. For example, the type of food displayed in Course Area No. 4 in Zone I should be identical to that displayed in Course Area No. 4 in Zone II.

In an a la carte dining room (as differentiated from banquet rooms), the buffet table should be placed preferably in the center of the dining room; this is often done in restaurants that feature a smorgasbord. Such a centrally located table will discourage guests from forming a line, and the operation will benefit from increased turnover. When a centrally located buffet table is not possible, the table can be built against a

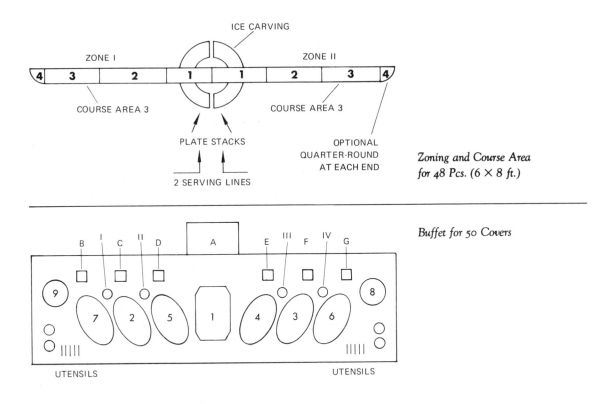

Zoning and Course Area for 48 Pcs. (6 × 8 ft.)

Buffet for 50 Covers

wall in a zigzag fashion (like teeth on a saw). This will generate a "scrambled" serving line that will speed and ensure the proper turnover.

BUFFET FOR 50 COVERS

1. Roast Beef Platter, Texas style (Rib of Beef as centerpiece and Roast Beef Roulades)
2. Roast Capon with Canadian Bacon and Asparagus
3. Poached Salmon cut into slices with stuffed eggs and cucumbers
4. Stuffed Eggs Spring Style
5. Pate de Foie Volaille (Garnish: poached apple rings and chopped pineapple). Flavored with Kirschwasser
6. Medaillons of Veal with liver pate and black cherries
7. Roulades of Beef Tongue with creamed horseradish (Garnish of artichoke bottoms stuffed with Ham Mousse)

A. Ice Carving
B. German Potato Salad
C. String Bean Salad
D. Vegetable Salad
E. Italian Salad
F. Fish Salad
G. Prosciutto Ham and Melon
H. Prosciutto Ham and Pears

I. Creamed Horseradish Sauce
II. Sauce Verte
III. Sauce Chantilly
IV. Sauce Cumberland

NOTE: Hot foods and desserts should be on separate tables.

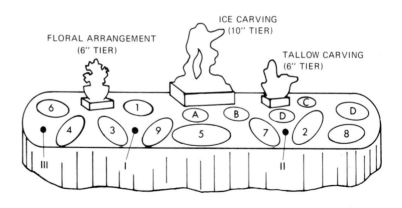

Buffet for 100 to 150 Covers

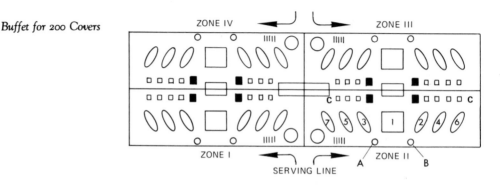

Buffet for 200 Covers

BUFFET FOR 100 to 150 COVERS

1. Prawn Salad or Langostino Salad
2. Smoked Salmon, Smoked Eel, and Brisling Sardines
3. Tea Sandwiches and Canapes
4. Stuffed Eggs and Watercress and Stuffed Tomatoes
5. Rooster baked in a crust (See Pate)
6. Boiled Ham with bone in and ham roulades
7. Roast Sirloin Roulade (slice Roast Beef and spread sweet relish mixed with mayonnaise over slices, then roll slice around a piece of celery)
8. Stuffed Roast Chicken in Madeira Gelee
9. Saddle of Venison stuffed with liver pate and decorated with grapes

A. Tomato Salad
B. Swiss Salad
C. Asparagus Vinaigrette
D. Cucumber Salad, English style
I. Sauce Cumberland
II. Creamed Horseradish Sauce

For this buffet extra platters of food should be ready to make speedy replacements.

NOTE: Hot food should be set on separate tables.

BUFFET FOR 200 COVERS

1. Roast Turkey with Pineapples and Truffles
2. Westphalian Ham and Canned Ham with Pickled Vegetables

3. Pate of Pheasant with Orange Salad in Port Wine
4. Smoked Fresh Trout with Frozen Horseradish
5. Roast Duck with Bananas
6. Roast Veal with Tunafish Sauce
7. Stuffed Dover Sole with Lobster Mousse and Stuffed Eggs

A. Sauce Cumberland
B. Sauce Raiford (Horseradish)
C. String Bean Salad – Beet Salad – Coleslaw – Waldorf Salad – Salad Nicoise – Mousse of Salmon garnished with cucumbers – Parfait of Chicken Liver in Port Aspic

NOTE: Hot foods and desserts should be on separate tables.

PRINTEMPS A PARIS
French Classical Buffet

HORS D'OEUVRE

Barquettes de mousse de foies
Champignons farcis au foie gras

Oeufs poches varies
Concombres Dijonnaise

POISSONS

Homard a la Parisienne

Pate de truite saumonee
Quenelles de brochet et de homard
Chaud-froid a l'Armoricaine

ENTREES FROIDES

Galantine de chapon
Pate de campagne en croute
Souffle de jambon de Strasbourg

Cervelles de veau vinaigrette
Longe de veau a ma facon
Filet de boeuf en gelee
Rillettes de Tours
Jambon Persille de Bourgogne

ENTREES CHAUDES

Turbot souffle sauce Banquise

Saute de veau Marengo
Cassoulet
Boudin de Mortagne

Cuisses de grenoilles
    poulette at frites
Croustades de morilles a la creme
Nouilles fraiches
Pommes Mousseline
Tripes a la mode de Caen

SALADES

Salade Nicoise

Salade d'endives
Celery remoulade

ENTREMETS

Souffle glace au praline
Sorbet a l'ananas
Patisseries Francaises

Tarte aux fraises
Tarte aux pommes
Gateau moka

FROMAGES DE FRANCE

Brie
Boursin aux fines herbes
Saint Paulin

Fromage fondu parfume au Kirsch
Camembert
Roquefort

(Tallow displays: Eiffel Tower or Coats of Arms of provinces of France or bust of Escoffier)
(Ice carving displays: basket with handles filled with flowers, or Arc of Triumph.)

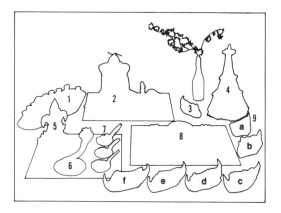

PRINTEMPS A PARIS: *On this classical French buffet: (1) sliced Galantine of Capon, with mushrooms made of stuffed eggs, topped with tomato slices; (2) Homard a la Parisienne (salad of carrots, peas, potatoes, lobster in mustard mayonnaise) with sliced Galantine of Lobster; (3) ravier of pickled cucumbers; (4) Eiffel Tower in tallow; (5) Fleur de Lis butter sculpture; (6) Filet de Boeuf en Gelee; (7) marinated vegetables in pans shaped from pate dough; (8) Souffle de Jambon de Strasbourg, cherry tomato border, sliced, mousse-filled tomatoes; (9) raviers— (a) pickled mushrooms, (b) marinated sausage slices, (c) marinated cauliflower, (d) cherry tomatoes, (e) artichokes, (f) marinated squash slices.*

BARQUETTES DE MOUSSE DE FOIES

The barquettes (p. 94) are freshly baked and filled with a mousse of chicken livers. Use either recipe on p. 145 or the following recipe, which is typically French.

MOUSSE DE FOIES DE VOLAILLE

Yield: 1-1/2 pt.

Ingredients

Chicken Livers, deveined, cleaned	1 lb.
Butter	4 oz.
Onion	2 oz.
Brandy	1 oz.
Salt	1 tsp.
Pate Seasoning	1/4 tsp.
Cream, heavy	2 oz.

Method

Broil livers to remove excess blood, which may give meat a bitter taste. In a saute pan, melt 2 oz. butter; add chopped onion; cook until transparent. Add livers and seasonings. Cook for about 5 min. Allow livers to cool. Then put through chopper or blender with 2 oz. raw butter and brandy. Whip cream and fold into liver mousse. Refrigerate.

NOTE: Decorate filled barquettes with finely chopped hard-cooked eggs, chopped aspic, chopped parsley, or capers.

CHAMPIGNONS FARCIS AU FOIE GRAS

Method

Peel freshest mushroom caps available and simmer in melted butter and lemon juice. Drain. Mushrooms should retain whiteness when cooked.

Open the can or terrine of foie gras (p. 101). Take truffles out of goose liver; chop finely. Make a paste of liver and pipe with pastry bag into drained mushrooms. Sprinkle chopped truffles over stuffed mushrooms.

OEUFS POCHES VARIES

An appealing choice might include:
OEUFS POCHES A LA LUCULLUS
   (Poached Eggs Gourmet Style), (p. 99)
OEUFS POCHES A LA SICILIENNE
   (Poached Eggs Sicilian Style), (p. 99)
OEUFS POCHES A LA JEANNETTE
   (Poached eggs in aspic with puree of liver garnish), (recipe follows)

OEUFS POCHES A LA JEANNETTE

Yield: 6

Ingredients

Eggs, poached, chilled	6
Chaud-Froid Sauce	2/3 cup

| Aspic | 1-1/2 cups |
| Goose or Chicken Liver Puree | 2/3 cup |

Method

Trim edges of egg whites to shape eggs uniformly. Coat eggs with chaud-froid sauce. Place each in custard cup; chill to allow chaud-froid to set. When aspic is consistency of heavy syrup, pour over eggs to coat but do not fill cups. Using pastry bag and fluted tube, use puree of goose or chicken livers to garnish each dish. Chill for 1/2 hour. Unmold cups on a serving platter and garnish with cut out truffle pieces.

NOTE: If using silver platters or trays, coat bottom of trays with aspic before placing eggs on them. Silver tarnishes in direct contact with egg dishes.

CONCOMBRES DIJONNAISE

Yield: 10 to 12 portions

Ingredients

Cucumbers	4
Olive Oil	4 tbsp.
Wine Vinegar	2 tbsp.
Salt	1/2 tsp.
Paprika	1/4 tsp.
Dijon Mustard	2 tbsp.
Sour Cream	1 tbsp.

Method

Peel the cucumbers; cut in half lengthwise; remove all seeds and cut into 2-in. sticks. Simmer in boiling water for 10 to 12 min. Cool under cold water to retain crispness.

Combine remaining ingredients and mix well with drained cucumbers. Marinate for 1/2 hour in refrigerator. Place in serving dish; sprinkle with chopped parsley; serve chilled.

HOW TO PRESENT THE HORS D'OEUVRE

Prepare a bouquet of vegetables as described in chapter on Food Decoration (p. 167). Coat large silver tray with a thin layer of aspic and place bouquet in the center. Arrange the barquettes, stuffed mushrooms, and poached eggs attractively around the bouquet of vegetables.

HOMARD A LA PARISIENNE

Lobster a la Parisienne is boiled lobster garnished with hard-cooked eggs, sliced tomatoes, and Russian Salad. It is one of the various elaborate presentations that make lobster a dramatic display.

Method

Buy lobsters preferably weighing 4 to 5 lbs. Lobsters of this size show to best advantage, and medallions of the desired size can be sliced from the tail of a 4- to 5-lb. lobster. Follow standard procedures in cooking the lobsters.

Since a high arrangement will be made with the lobsters, a bread socle or rice socle should be placed in the center to support the lobsters.

Before arranging the lobsters on platter, remove tails and all meat from claws. The tails are easily removed by cutting under the shell with scissors. Be careful not to damage the meat. Using a meat saw, cut out a 2-sq.-inch piece of shell under each claw. Remove all meat. The carcass of the lobster will remain intact when displayed on the platter.

Prepare Russian Salad following recipe on p. 202. Dice lobster meat from the claws and mix with Russian Salad; use pieces of truffle and pimento aspic sheet (p. 72) to decorate an appropriate mold that has been coated with aspic jelly. Blend a small amount of cold liquid aspic with the Russian Salad. Pour into decorated mold and refrigerate for 1 hour.

Slice lobster tails into small medallions. Decorate with truffle cut-outs and glaze with cold liquid aspic. Unmold aspic mold on platter and surround with medallions. Garnish platter with slices of lemon, whole cherry tomatoes, and slices of hard-cooked eggs.

The lobster shell is first glazed with a clear aspic, then decorated with cut-outs made from aspic sheets of various colors. Pipe some chopped aspic around medallions and Russian Salad mold. Serve lobster with Vincent Sauce (p. 181).

NOTE: For a less elaborate display, the Russian Salad may be set on artichoke bottoms.

✢ ✢

PATE DE TRUITE SAUMONEE

A truite saumonee is a salmon trout that has pink, tender meat with a delicate flavor. Salmon trout are found in salmon rivers, mostly in Canada, and weigh from 8 oz. to 10 lb. or more. They are caught during the salmon fishing season, from June to August. Although salmon trout are not sold commercially, a pate of salmon trout can be prepared successfully, by using a mixture of half each fresh salmon and brook trout.

Method
Prepare a quenelle forcemeat (p. 110), using half fresh salmon, half fresh brook trout. Marinate a few strips of salmon filets, if available. Prepare the pate, following recipe for Galantine of Salmon (p. 110). Slice the cold salmon trout pate, saving one larger piece that can be decorated to provide a focal point for the platter. Place slices on a rack and glaze with aspic jelly (p. 69). Garnish platter with cubed aspic jelly and tomatoes stuffed with shrimp salad. A Sauce Andalouse is the perfect accompaniment for the pate of salmon trout.

✢ ✢

QUENELLES DE BROCHET ET DE HOMARD, CHAUD-FROID A L'ARMORICAINE

This dish—quenelles of pike coated with green chaud-froid and lobster with pink Armoricaine Chaud-Froid Sauce—will be one of the most appealing on the buffet if it is executed with proper care. The pike quenelles, covered with light green chaud-froid, and the lobster quenelles, coated with rich, pink lobster chaud-froid, present an unusually effective contrast that will inevitably attract the attention of the guests. A socle (base) will enhance the presentation and is surrounded by a colorful display of vegetables.

QUENELLES OF PIKE
Yield: 8 portions
Ingredients

Butter	3 oz.
Flour	4 oz.
Milk	1 pt.
Egg Yolks	6
Salt	1/2 tsp.
Pepper	1/4 tsp.
Nutmeg, grated	2–3 gratings
Filet of Pike, chilled	1 lb.
Beef Kidney Suet	1 lb.
Egg Whites	2

Method
Melt butter, add flour, and mix. Heat milk to boiling point, pour into butter-flour mixture and mix until it forms a paste. Remove from heat and add egg yolks; season with salt, pepper, and nutmeg. Set aside to cool. This is called a flour panada.

Finely grind chilled pike filet with suet. Add the flour panada and gradually mix in the egg whites. The mixture should remain cold and thick.

Shape oval dumplings with two tablespoons and simmer in salted boiling water for 12 to 15 min. Drain the quenelles and allow to cool for 1 hour.

QUENELLES OF LOBSTER
Yield: 8 portions
Ingredients

Lobster, raw	10 oz.
Sole or Flounder Filets	6 oz.
Egg, whole	1
Cream, heavy	1 cup
Cayenne Pepper	1/8 tsp.
Nutmeg, grated	2–3 gratings

Salt	1/2 tsp.
White Pepper, ground	1/8 tsp.

Method

Peel and devein lobster; wash; drain. Cut fish filets into 1-in. pieces. Place the lobster and fish into a chopper. Grind finely and add the egg, cream, seasonings, salt, and pepper to taste. Butter a flame-proof cooking utensil that is large enough to accommodate the quenelles when shaped. Shape the quenelles following procedure used for quenelles of pike. Put quenelles in boiling salted water and poach for 10 min. Drain and cool for 1 hour.

To Coat Quenelles

Coat the quenelles of pike with green chaud-froid (p. 76). Glaze with cold liquid aspic. Coat quenelles of lobster with Armoricaine Chaud-Froid Sauce. Glaze with cold liquid aspic.

Arranging Presentation

Shape cooked cream of wheat and corn meal into a fan and chill for use as socle. The socle should be large enough to hold both quenelles. Place socle on a mirror if one is available. Alternate socles on fan for maximum color contrast.

Make small, round, raw carrot and turnip balls, using a small parisian scoop. Poach in salted boiling water; cool and use as garnish around edge of socle. Stuff small tomatoes with French Cucumber Salad (p. 199) and arrange on platter. If mirror is used, decorate edge with aspic croutons; this can also be used to frame display on tray. Pipe chopped aspic around stuffed tomatoes.

ARMORICAINE CHAUD-FROID SAUCE

Yield: about 4 cups

Ingredients

Lobster Meat, frozen	2 cans
Olive Oil	1/4 cup
Butter	1 tbsp.
Mirepoix	1 cup
Shallots, chopped	2
Dry White Wine	1/2 cup
Brandy, warmed	1/4 cup
Tomato Sauce	1/2 cup
Fish Stock	2 cups
Parsley, fresh sprigs	6
Tarragon, fresh	1 branch
Garlic Clove, crushed	1
Tomatoes, peeled, seeded, chopped	3
Beurre Manie	to thicken
Cream, heavy	1/2 cup
Aspic Jelly, chilled, full strength	1/2 cup

Method

Saute lobster meat in hot oil for 2 min.; in a separate pan, melt the butter, add mirepoix and shallots and cook over low heat for 5 min. Add sauteed lobster and white wine to mirepoix. Pour brandy over mixture and ignite. Add tomato sauce, fish stock, parsley sprigs, fresh tarragon branch, garlic, and peeled, seeded, and chopped tomatoes. Cover tightly; simmer 20 to 25 min. Strain and thicken with small bits of beurre manie. Add cream and bring to boiling point. Cool sauce on ice, stirring occasionally. Add heavy cream and aspic jelly.

GALANTINE DE CHAPON

Follow recipe for Galantine de Volaille (p. 135). Decorate galantine as shown in illustration.

PATE DE CAMPAGNE EN CROUTE

Make a pate en croute following procedure (p. 117). For the filling, use recipe on p. 129 for Ham and Veal Pate; however, for the garnish for the pate, substitute a marinated filet of pork for ham and veal.

SOUFFLE DE JAMBON DE STRASBOURG

Follow recipe for Ham Mousse, Strasbourg Style (p. 143).

To Prepare Cold Souffle

Fold wax paper around the outside of a 5-1/2-cup souffle dish leaving 2 in. above the rim. Make sure that paper overlaps at least an inch. Secure it with string or paper clips. Pour ham mousse in the prepared dish and refrigerate for 2 hours. Before placing on the buffet table, remove wax paper and decorate ham mousse with cut-outs of attractive design from aspic sheets in two complimentary colors.

✣ ✣

CERVELLES DE VEAU VINAIGRETTE
(Calves' Brains, Vinaigrette)

Although calves' brains are not frequently served to Americans, they are considered a delicacy in France where they are prepared in many ways. One well-known recipe is "au beurre noir" (in brown butter); they can also be fried, served in aspic, with chaud-froid, or vinaigrette, as in the following recipe:

Method

Soak calves' brains in cold water for 24 hours. Trim away fat and sinews, if any. Blanch in salted, boiling water for 4 min. Cook brains in veal stock for about 5 min. Cool in cooking liquid. Drain brains; cut into slices and pat dry.

Prepare a basic French dressing and add chopped, hard-cooked eggs, chopped gherkins, and chopped parsley. Marinate brains in sauce for a few hours. Serve chilled with sauce.

✣ ✣

LONGE DE VEAU A MA FACON *(Loin of Veal, Homemade Style)*

Trim loin of veal; season with salt and pepper. Cover entire surface of veal with thin layer of chicken forcemeat (p. 111). Wrap pate dough (p. 117) around veal. Make a chimney as for pate en croute. Bake in oven at 350°F. 12 to 15 min. per lb. Cool veal completely. Slice one half; glaze slices with aspic jelly. Place remaining half on serving platter in one piece; arrange veal slices around it. Garnish with saffron rice molds, chopped Madeira aspic, and artichoke bottoms stuffed with green beans that have been seasoned with an oil and vinegar dressing. Serve with a sauce that combines tunafish puree, lemon juice, and Worcestershire sauce with mayonnaise.

✣ ✣

FILET DE BOEUF EN GELEE

Trim a large tenderloin of beef and lard it (follow procedure on p. 154). In larding, insert large julienne slices of truffles in the filet for additional flavor as well as color contrast when meat is sliced. Season with salt and pepper. Roast to medium doneness. Allow the filet to cool completely, then slice half of it into slices about 1/2 in. thick. Glaze slices with aspic and decorate with truffles. Place remaining half in a narrow dish of desired size; fill with aspic jelly and allow to set for 1 hour. Unmold on a silver platter and arrange slices of filet around large piece. Place chopped aspic that has been mixed with chopped truffles around display. Appropriate garnishes for the platter include green and white asparagus tips, stuffed green and ripe olives. Serve the slices of the filet with Remoulade Sauce (p. 180).

NOTE: A decorative skewer called a hatelet is an eye-catching addition to filet of beef presented in this manner.

✣ ✣

RILLETTES DE TOURS

Rillettes can be prepared weeks in advance and will even improve in taste during the holding period. To make rillettes, follow recipe on p. 132.

The rillettes are served in the terrine in which they are stored after the top layer of fat has been removed. Decorate terrine with a tomato rosette or other vegetable flower decoration. French bread should be available to serve with rillettes.

Filet de boeuf en gelee with marinated vegetables in pans of baked pate dough.

NOTE: Some restaurants in Tours use 1/2 rabbit and 1/2 pork shoulder when making rillettes.

✣✣

JAMBON PERSILLE DE BOURGOGNE

Jambon Persille is a specialty from Burgundy. Originally, the ham was smoked, washed, desalted, blanched, drained, skinned, and cut into large, uniformly sized chunks. The ham was then cooked in white wine with chervil, tarragon, thyme, bayleaves, and peppercorns. Calves' feet were cooked with the ham to gelatinize the cooking liquid. The ham was flaked with pieces of calves' feet, pressed into a mold, covered with the jellied liquid, and held until firm and chilled.

Chopped parsley was sometimes added to the ham. The following recipe simplifies the original lengthy preparation of the ham, yet gives perfect results.

Yield: about 2 lb.

Ingredients

Boiled or Baked Ham, chilled	2 lb.
Parsley, finely chopped	1 cup
Unflavored Gelatin	1 envelope
Water, cold	1/4 cup
Beef or Chicken Bouillon, clarified	1-1/2 cups
White Wine, dry	1/2 cup

Method

Ham used in this recipe should be of good quality; canned Polish or Danish hams are excellent. Remove all fat from ham; cut meat into coarse julienne. Mix chopped parsley with ham; place in a suitable rectangular mold. Dissolve gelatin in water, then combine with 1/2 cup of boiling bouillon. Cool; combine with remaining bouillon and wine. Pour over the ham and parsley mixture. Chill in the refrigerator. Unmold on platter, and garnish with cornichons (tiny French sour pickles). Serve with mustard and mustard mayonnaise.

꒷꒦

TURBOT SOUFFLE, SAUCE BANQUISE

Turbot Souffle, Sauce Banquise is a great classic preparation that requires time and service with "savoir faire." The following recipe represents the typical image of the great French classical cuisine. To make the Turbot Souffle, the fish must be boned without separating the filets, to form a pouch for the stuffing. The boning process is laborious and requires patience.

Yield: 10 to 12 portions

Ingredients

Turbot, 10- to 12-lb.	1

FOR MOUSSE

White Fish (Dover sole, lemon sole, or pike)	3 lb.
Egg Whites	6
Cream, heavy	1-1/2 cups
Salt	1/2 tsp.
Pepper	1/4 tsp.
Nutmeg	1/8 tsp.
Alaska King Crab, diced	1 cup

FOR COOKING FISH

Bacon Slices	6
White Wine, dry	1/2 bottle
Bourbon	4 oz.
Fish Fumet (stock)	to cover

FOR SAUCE

Cream, heavy	1 qt.
Beurre Manie	2-3 oz.
Salt	to taste
Pepper	to taste

FOR ASSEMBLING TURBOT

Mushrooms, fluted	10 to 12
Truffle Stars	10 to 12
Croutons, fried, heart-shaped	10 to 12

Method

BONING FISH

Use scissors to trim off fins, leaving tail intact. On the dark skin side, using a sharp, flexible boning knife, cut along backbone of turbot. Slice through flesh along lateral bones, leaving filet attached at outer edge of fish. Clip off end of lateral bone. Proceed in the same manner on other side of fish. Lift backbone out of fish, starting at the end and cutting under the flesh. Remove gills; wash fish carefully.

PREPARING MOUSSE

Finely chop filets of selected fish; put fish through a fine sieve for best results. Place container of fish on ice and gradually stir in egg whites and cream. Season mixture to taste, then combine with diced crabmeat. Stuff turbot with mousse.

COOKING FISH

A specially constructed pan called a turbotiere is used to cook the fish. Lay the turbot, stuffed side down, on the rack. Place rack holding fish in pan. Cover surface of turbot with bacon slices. Add white wine and bourbon.

Bring enough fumet (fish stock), to barely cover fish, to the boiling point on top of stove. Put cover on turbotiere; bake fish in moderate oven for approximately 50 min. Lift turbot out of the pan and slide it on a serving platter or tray. Discard bacon slices.

SAUCE BANQUISE

Strain the cooking liquid and reduce to about 3/4. Add heavy cream and reduce further, until sauce starts thickening. Mix in a few bits of beurre manie as the sauce should be thick enough to coat the back of a spoon. Season to taste with salt and pepper.

PRESENTATION OF TURBOT

Remove all cooking liquid from platter. Place a row of fluted, cooked mushrooms along center of turbot. Cover with sauce. Serve remaining sauce in a sauceboat. Place croutons around platter and use truffle stars to highlight arrangement. Serve hot.

❧❧

SAUTE DE VEAU MARENGO

Yield: 10 to 12 portions

Ingredients

Veal, cubed	2 lb.
Oil	4 tbsp.
Onion, small, chopped	1
Garlic Clove, crushed	1
White Wine, dry	1 cup
Tomato Sauce	2 cups
Brown Sauce	1 qt.
Bouquet Garni (thyme, bayleaf, and parsley sprigs)	1
Pearl Onions, peeled, blanched	12
Mushroom Caps, peeled	12
Parsley, chopped	1 tbsp.
Croutons, fried, heart-shaped	12

Method

Sear veal in oil until brown; add onion and garlic; mix well. Pour out excess fat; deglaze with wine. Add tomato sauce and brown sauce. Make a bouquet garni of thyme, bayleaves, and parsley sprigs tied in cheesecloth. Cook for 45 min. to 1 hour. Saute peeled, blanched pearl onions until golden brown. Fry peeled mushroom caps in butter. Add onions and mushrooms to veal. Simmer veal mixture for 15 min. Arrange in a serving dish; sprinkle with parsley and surround with croutons.

❧❧

CASSOULET

Yield: 10 to 12 portions

Ingredients

Roast Goose (save gravy)	1
Garlic Sausage	2 lb.
Pastrami	2 lb.
Bouquet Garni (parsley sprigs, bayleaves, thyme)	1
Carrots	3
Celery Stalks	2
Flageolets (green kidney beans)	3 cans

SAUCE

Onion, large	1
Garlic Clove	1
Tomatoes, peeled, seeded, chopped	3
Brown Gravy	1/2 cup

Method

Carve roast goose into slices; leave skin on slices. Cook the fresh garlic sausage in boiling water. Wash pastrami and cook with the bouquet garni, carrots, and celery. Slice sausage; trim pastrami and cut into 1/2-in. cubes. Mix flageolets, goose meat, sausage, and pastrami.

SAUCE

Lightly brown finely chopped onion in goose fat. Add crushed clove of garlic, tomatoes, and brown gravy. Add goose gravy and boil for a few minutes. Mix beans, goose, sausage, and pastrami thoroughly. Add sauce. Bake in a bean pot for 1 hour at 325°F.

❧❧

BOUDIN DE MORTAGNE

Mortagne is a small French town where the best blood sausage (boudin) is made. Blood sausage can be purchased in German butcher shops that specialize in the making of a large variety of sausages. Blood sausage should be fried very slowly in a frying pan; be sure to cook sausage as directed because if cooked at higher temperatures it may burst. Mousseline Potatoes are the usual accompaniment for this dish.

꒰ ꒱

CUISSES DE GRENOUILLES POULETTE
(Frog Legs Poached with Mushrooms and White Wine)

Yield: 8 portions

Ingredients

Frog Legs, medium	16
Salt	to taste
Pepper	to taste
Mushrooms, sliced	1 cup
Shallots, chopped	1-1/2 tbsp.
White Wine, dry	1 cup
Cream, heavy	1 cup
Sweet Butter	2 oz.
Flour	1-1/2 oz.
Lemon Juice	1/2 lemon
Parsley, chopped	1 tbsp.

Method

Trim and wash frog legs; season with a little salt and pepper. Sprinkle the mushrooms and shallots in a suitable pan; arrange frog legs on top. Pan should be a small one, just large enough for frog legs. Add enough wine and heavy cream to cover frog legs. If liquid does not cover, add a little water. Cover and poach 10 min. or until frog legs are done. Transfer frog legs to serving dish. Bring sauce to a boil and reduce to about 2 cups. Blend butter with flour and drop small lumps into boiling sauce until sauce thickens to proper consistency. Add lemon juice and parsley to thickened sauce and pour over frog legs.

꒰ ꒱

CUISSES DE GRENOUILLES FRITES
(Frog Legs Fried in Batter)

Yield: 8 portions

Ingredients

Frog Legs, small	16
Lemon Juice	1/2 lemon
Parsley, chopped	1 tbsp.
Salt	to taste
Pepper	to taste
Garlic Clove, crushed	1
Oil	for frying
Flour	for dredging

BATTER

Flour	1 lb.
Salt	1 tsp.
Olive Oil	4 tbsp.
Egg, whole	1
Beer	1/2 cup
Water, lukewarm	1 cup
Egg Whites	4

Method

Trim and wash frog legs; marinate in mixture of lemon juice, parsley, salt, pepper, and garlic. Mix thoroughly all batter ingredients except egg whites. When ready to fry frog legs, beat egg whites until stiff and fold into beer batter. Flour frog legs; dip into batter; fry in deep fryer at 350°F. until golden brown. Garnish with fried parsley. Serve, preferably with tomato sauce.

꒰ ꒱

CROUSTADES DE MORILLES A LA CREME *(Patty Shells Filled with Creamed Mushrooms)*

Method

PATTY SHELLS

The croustades (patty shells) are made of puff paste dough (see p. 404 *Professional Chef,* 4th Edition, for recipe). Roll out a piece of dough about 1/2 in. in thickness. Cut out rounds using a 3-in. cutter with scalloped edges. Make a round incision in center of each round, using a 2-in. scalloped cutter. Place rounds one on top of the other to desired height. Brush rounds with egg wash; allow to stand 30 min. before baking. Place on baking sheet and bake for about 20 min. at 375°F. If greased paper is placed over the top of patty shells before baking, they will not topple over. Be careful that paper does not burn. As soon as croustades are baked, cut out the tops with a sharp knife. Reserve for later use. Remove any uncooked dough from the croustades.

MUSHROOMS

It is imperative that the best quality of morels be used for this recipe. Dehydrated morels are far better than canned morels. Small, pointed, French, dehydrated morels are preferable, although Swiss morels are of good quality. Soak morels in cold water for 30 min.; cut into small pieces; wash twice in cold water. Saute some chopped shallots in butter, add drained morels, and cook for 5 min. Add Madeira wine, reduce to half, and mix with cream sauce. Season to taste with salt and pepper.

TO SERVE

Fill the croustades with creamed morels; place on a platter. Place tops on croustades and serve at once so filling is hot.

❦ ❦

NOUILLES FRAICHES (Fresh Noodles)

Yield: 10 to 12 portions

Ingredients

Bread Flour	1 lb.
Eggs, medium, beaten	5
Salt	2 tsp.

Method

Make a well in the middle of the flour. Put beaten eggs and salt in well. Mix flour into eggs until dough is stiff. Knead for several minutes. Allow to rest for 1/2 hour. Divide dough into 7 or 8 pieces. Roll each piece on a floured board until very thin. If available, use a dough machine. Fold the rolled-out dough in half, then in half again; cut into thin strips. Separate into noodles. Cook in salted, boiling water for 6 to 8 min. Drain noodles in strainer, then saute in butter. Serve with Saute of Veal Marengo.

❦ ❦

POMMES MOUSSELINE (Mousseline Potatoes)

Method

Peel, quarter, and cook potatoes in salted boiling water. Drain potatoes when cooked and dry in oven for a few minutes. Rice potatoes; mix in some butter and dry riced potatoes over medium heat. Scald a mixture of half milk and half cream; beat liquid into potatoes until they are light and fluffy.

❦ ❦

TRIPES A LA MODE DE CAEN

Yield: 10 to 12 portions

Ingredients

Calves' Feet	2
Beef Kidney Suet, chopped	4 oz.
Onions, sliced	2
Carrots, sliced	2
Celery Stalks, cut into slices	2
Tripe, blanched, cut into 2-in. squares	3 lb.
Parsley Sprigs	4
Thyme	1/4 tsp.
Bayleaves	2
Garlic Cloves	2
Mace Leaf	1
Peppercorns	6
Cloves, whole	2
Salt	1 tsp.
Beef Stock	to cover
Brandy	1/4 cup
Applejack	1/2 cup

Method

Split calves' feet lengthwise. Arrange ingredients in a heavy oval pan (called brazier; has handles at either end). Place them in the following order: suet, vegetables, tripe, calves' feet, seasonings, and spices. Cover with beef stock. Bring to boil, cover tightly, and bake 10 to 12 hours at 300°F. Remove tripe to a serving casserole; remove meat from calves' feet; cut into pieces and mix with tripe. Strain cooking liquid; skim off fat and reduce to 1/2. Add brandy and applejack; mix with tripe. Bake for 1/2 hour at 325°F. Serve hot; accompany with small, boiled potatoes.

🙰 🙰

SALADE NICOISE

Yield: 12 to 15 portions

Ingredients

Tunafish, canned in oil	7 oz.
Anchovy Filets, flat can	1
Green Peppers	2
Cucumber, small	1
Green Olives	2 oz.
Nicoise Olives, in oil	4 oz.
Artichokes, marinated	1 jar
Scallions, bunch	1
Romaine, head	1
Cherry Tomatoes, small box	1
Hard-cooked Egg	1
Avocado	1
Endive	1
Radishes	3

Method

Break up tunafish with a fork, mixing in the oil. Chop anchovy filets, mixing with oil. Cut up green peppers, cucumber, and olives. Quarter marinated artichokes, chop scallions, and break lettuce into 2-in. pieces. Cut tomatoes in half. Combine all ingredients and toss together. Place in a salad bowl. Garnish with sliced, hard-cooked eggs, sliced avocados, endive leaves, and sliced radishes. Pour a small amount of French dressing over salad. Serve chilled.

NOTE: An alternate recipe for Nicoise Salad appears on p. 202.

🙰 🙰

SALADE D'ENDIVES *(Endive Salad)*

Method

Trim and wash endive. Cut crosswise into 1-in. pieces; wash pieces in cold water; drain well. Place in a salad bowl, sprinkle with chopped wal-nuts. Serve with Roquefort dressing or Green Goddess Dressing (p. 194).

🙰 🙰

CELERY REMOULADE

Method

The type of celery used for this recipe is the celeriac or celery roots. Celeriac may be purchased in cans or jars already shredded. When using fresh celeriac, it should be peeled, sliced, and cut into julienne strips. Celeriac is not cooked. The dressing for this dish is made of mayonnaise, Dijon mustard, and lemon juice. Toss celeriac in dressing. Add salt and pepper to taste. Arrange in a salad bowl and sprinkle chopped parsley over mixture.

NOTE: Always use firm celeriac; discard any spongy portions.

🙰 🙰

SOUFFLE GLACE AU PRALINE

Yield: 10 portions

Ingredients

Milk	1 cup
Egg Yolks	4
Sugar	4 oz.
Vanilla Extract	1/2 tsp.
Praline Paste	7 oz.
Egg Whites	4
Sugar	4 oz.
Water	2 oz.
Cream, heavy	1 cup
Instant Vanilla Pudding Mix	1 tsp.

Method

Boil milk. Beat egg yolks and sugar until light and creamy; add vanilla. Pour milk over mixture and blend well. Cook over medium heat until mixture reaches boiling point but do not let it boil. Whip in the praline paste. Cool mixture.

Cook sugar and water to a temperature of 230° to 235°F. Whip egg whites; as they start to mound, pour whites over hot sugar syrup and continue beating until meringue cools. Whip cream and blend in the instant pudding mix. Fold meringue and whipped cream into custard mix. Wrap wax paper around a 5-cup souffle dish, using a large enough piece to extend about 2 in. above the rim. Fasten paper wrapping with a string or paper clips. Pour praline mix in souffle dish; freeze for at least 4 hours. Before serving, remove wax paper.

❧ ❧

SORBET A L'ANANAS (Pineapple Sherbet)

Yield: approx. 1 qt.

Ingredients

Pulp from Pineapple, large, fresh	2 lb.
Water	2 cups
Sugar	10 oz.
Lemon Juice	1 oz.

Method

Cut the top off large, fresh, ripe pineapple; reserve top. Remove all pulp from shell, keeping shell intact. Bring water and sugar to boil; remove from heat, let cool to room temperature; add lemon juice. Puree pineapple pulp and strain through a chinois (French-type strainer). Mix syrup with pulp and freeze in an ice cream freezer. The sherbet should be white and creamy. Fill pineapple shell with sherbet. Place top over sherbet on shell. Decorate with spun sugar on the top and outside of pineapple.

NOTE: Sherbet is usually served with petits fours.

❧ ❧

PATISSERIES FRANCAISES

One of the most striking dessert displays for the French buffet can be an arrangement of French pastries with a centerpiece such as the Arc de Triomphe made of pastillage (gum paste), or decorations made of pulled sugar. A large variety of French pastries can be prepared. With puff paste make:

NAPOLEONS
CREAM HORNS
TURNOVERS

With cream puff paste make:

CREAM PUFFS
CHOCOLATE ECLAIRS
COFFEE ECLAIRS
PROFITEROLES
TARTELETTES with many different fillings can be part of a display for a French buffet although they would not be appropriate for this French buffet as two different tarts have been planned for it.

❧ ❧

TARTE AUX FRAISES (Strawberry Tart)

A pie crust filled with a rich custard, then fresh strawberries that have been topped with a strawberry glaze is one of the most popular desserts in France.

Yield: 9-in. pie

Ingredients
PIE CRUST DOUGH

Flour	9 oz.
Butter, at room temperature	6 oz.
Egg Yolk	1
Water, cold	1 oz.
Sugar	1 oz.
Salt	1/4 tsp.

Method

Put flour in large bowl. Make a well in flour and add remaining ingredients. Work mixture to form a smooth dough, kneading for a few minutes on a floured surface. Refrigerate dough for 1/2 hour before rolling it out. Line a 9-in. pie plate with the rolled-out dough. Place a sheet of wax paper on dough; place a few small stones or dried beans on paper so that dough will not puff while baking. Bake 20 min. in oven at 350°F. Take out paper and weights. Bake 5 more min. to brown the crust.

CUSTARD CREAM

Milk	1 cup
Sugar	1-1/2 oz.
Egg Yolks	2
Flour	3/4 oz.

Method

Scald milk. Beat sugar and egg yolks until light and creamy. Add flour and mix thoroughly. Pour milk over egg yolk mixture and blend well. Cook over medium heat until custard boils. Flavor with strawberry liqueur; cool; cover with buttered wax paper until ready to use. Refrigerate unless custard is scheduled for immediate use.

Assembling Tart

Cover the bottom of the cooked pie shell with a layer of custard cream. Arrange fresh cleaned strawberries on top of cream; glaze with strawberry jelly.

❧

TARTE AUX POMMES (French Apple Pie)

Yield: 11-in. pie

Ingredients

Pie Crust Dough (use recipe for Strawberry Tart)	1 pie
Apples, Baking	2 lb.
Apricot Jam	4 oz.
Kirsch	1 tbsp.

Method

Butter an 11-in. pie plate and line with dough that has been rolled out to fit pan. Make applesauce with 1 lb. of apples. Bake the pie crust for 30 min.; follow directions used in strawberry tart recipe. Spread cooled applesauce in bottom of pie shell. Peel 1 lb. of apples and cut each apple in half. Slice apple halves into thin slices and arrange slices on top of layer of applesauce, covering it completely. Bake at 400°F. for 10 min.; reduce oven temperature to 350°F. and bake for 20 min. or until apple slices are tender. Melt apricot jam; add kirsch and strain. Brush the top of tart with apricot-kirsch mixture.

❧

GATEAU MOKA (Mocha Cake)

This is a sponge cake, cut into layers and filled with a coffee-flavored buttercream.

Yield: 10 portions

Ingredients

SPONGE CAKE

Eggs, whole	8
Sugar	9 oz.
Cake Flour	9 oz.
Butter, melted	2 oz.

MOCHA CREAM

Sugar	10 oz.
Eggs, beaten	4
Butter, soft	1 lb.
Coffee Extract	2 tsp.

Method

SPONGE CAKE

It is preferable to use an electric mixer for this cake; it will be lighter and will have a better yield. Combine eggs and sugar in small container and beat at high speed over warm, not boiling, water. When mixture is lukewarm, remove from heat and beat until thick and cool. Fold in sifted flour, adding butter slowly. Butter and flour two 9-in. round molds. Divide cake mixture between the 2 molds. Bake at 350°F. for 20 min. or until top of cake is golden brown.

MOCHA CREAM

Dissolve sugar in 1/2 cup water and cook syrup to 238°F. Pour syrup over beaten eggs and whip until mixture is cool. Mix in butter and coffee extract.

To Prepare Gateau Moka

Cut each cake into two layers. Spread mocha cream over each layer, and place one on top of other to make one cake. Decorate the sides and top of cake. French pastry chefs decorate mocha cakes with coffee bean candies.

❧

Tallow bust of August Escoffier

FROMAGES DE FRANCE (*Cheese from France*)

France produces over 400 varieties of cheese, each as distinctive as a fingerprint. Store cheese in the refrigerator. The cheeses listed on the French buffet menu are among the varieties of soft-ripened cheese (brie, camembert) and semi-hard cheese (St. Paulin, fondu au kirsch). There are also two others, different in taste and flavor: Boursin aux fines herbes and the famous Roquefort.

Cheese is at its best at room temperature. Take out of refrigerator one or two hours before serving. Serve thinly sliced French bread or un-salted crackers with cheese. Different kinds of cheese may be displayed on the buffet. Arrange them on a board or a platter decorated with a few green and red grapes and grape leaves.

Use cheese markers to identify the cheeses. Guests can then be more knowledgeable about what they are eating or tasting.

NOTE: The display on p. 223 would also be most appropriate for a cheese-tasting buffet or as a part of the classical buffet.

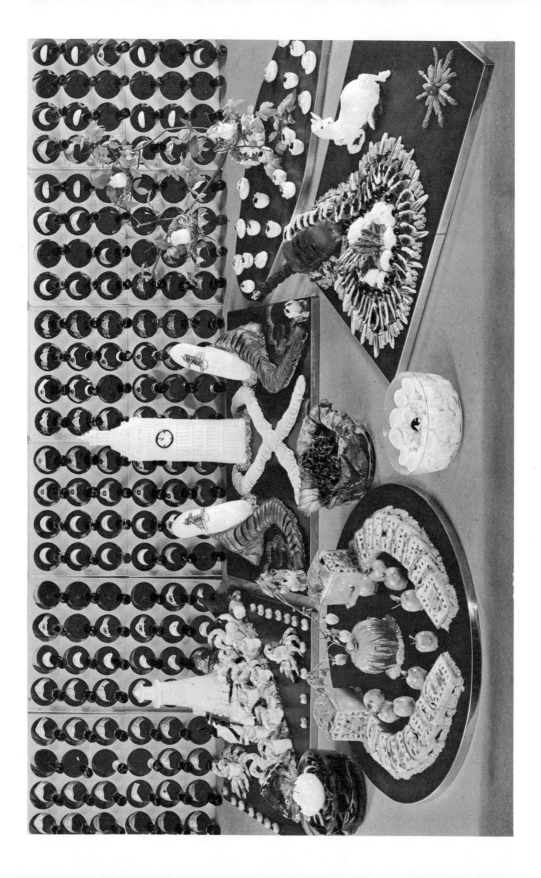

YE OLDE BRITISH BUFFET

HORS D'OEUVRE: Pickled onions and mushrooms
Welsh pickled fruit
Marinated cucumbers
Anchovy stuffed eggs
Pickled cabbage

FISH: Potted shrimp
Galantine of Scottish salmon
Soused mackerel in white wine
Filet of Dover sole "Domino"

COLD ENTREES: Beef tongue "Jockey club"
Baked loin of pork, applesauce
Ham and veal pie

SALADS: Lentil salad
Red beet salad
Watercress Mimosa

HOT ENTREES: Kedgeree
Roast sirloin of beef, Yorkshire pudding
Beef and kidney pie
Toad in the hole

DESSERTS: Treacle tart
Trifle
Blackberry and apple pie
Burnt cream
Gingerbread
Fresh fruit salad

CHEESES: Cheddar cheese
Stilton and Gorgonzola
Caerphilly
Lancashire
    served with scones

Nonedible displays:
London Tower, Big Ben,
Coat of Arms, Flags, etc.

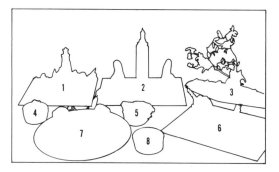

YE OLDE BRITISH BUFFET: (1) Potted Shrimp with Dover sole timbales stuffed with forcemeat around light-house (butter sculpture); (2) Big Ben on Tower, in center; left, Beef Tongue Jockey Club; right, Baked Loin of Pork, whole and slices; (3) Anchovy Stuffed Eggs around tree of anchovies on base holding potato nest with birds made of hard-cooked eggs; (4) Red Beet Salad; (5) Pickled Cabbage; (6) Roast Saddle of Lamb London Style with "picallily" arrangement of marinated asparagus, minia-ture ears of corn, pickled carrots, cherry tomatoes, pickled mushrooms and cauliflower with unicorn in butter sculpture; (7) Ham and Veal Pie with slices circling squash holding branch of tiny liver pate apples; larger apples have truffle stems; (8) Marinated cucumbers.

PICKLED ONIONS AND MUSHROOMS

Yield: 3 cups

Ingredients

Pearl Onions	1 lb.
Mushrooms, fresh, tiny	1 lb.
Salt	1/2 cup
Malt Vinegar	3 cups
Sugar	1/2 cup
Cloves, whole	3
Mixed Pickling Spices	2 tbsp.

Method

Pour boiling water over pearl onions; allow to stand for 5 min., then drain and cool under cold water. This procedure makes it easy to peel onions. Cut off mushroom stems; wash mush-rooms in cold water. Drain. Mix onions and mushrooms and sprinkle with the salt. Mix well. Marinate in refrigerator for 5 to 6 hours. Wash onions and mushrooms in cold water; drain well. Combine remaining ingredients and boil until sugar is dissolved. Add onions and mushrooms; boil briskly for 5 min. Transfer vegetables to a serving dish. Add enough liquid to cover; chill for several hours before serving. This hors d'oeuvre may be prepared 2 to 3 days ahead.

❧❧

WELSH PICKLED FRUIT

Yield: 10 to 12 portions

Ingredients

Tomatoes, large, ripe, peeled	5
Peaches	3
Pears	3
Onions, White, medium	2
Green Pepper, large	1
White Vinegar	1 cup
Coarse Salt	1 tbsp.
Sugar	2-1/2 cups
Pickling Spices, in cheesecloth	1 tsp.

Method

Quarter tomatoes, peaches, and pears. Peel and slice onions. Cut green pepper in half; remove seeds; slice crosswise into thin slices. In a large saucepan, boil vinegar, salt, and sugar; add pickling spices and all other ingredients; bring to a boil; simmer for about 1-1/2 hours or until mixture has thickened. Remove spices. Transfer to serving bowl; cool at room temperature and chill for several hours before serving.

❧❧

MARINATED CUCUMBERS

For recipe, see p. 199 (English Cucumber Salad).

❧❧

ANCHOVY STUFFED EGGS

Yield: 2 doz.

Ingredients

Eggs	1 doz.
Butter	4 oz.

Cream Cheese	4 oz.
Salt	1/2 tsp.
Mayonnaise	1 tbsp.
Liquid Hot Pepper Sauce	dash
Anchovy Paste	1 tbsp.
Anchovy Filets	1 doz.

Method

For best results, eggs should be at room temperature. Place eggs in boiling water; return water to boil and simmer for 10 min. Chill eggs in cold water or on ice. Peel eggs, cut in half lengthwise. Remove yolks and press through a sieve. Mix with butter, cream cheese, salt, mayonnaise, liquid hot pepper sauce, and anchovy paste. Blend mixture until it is smooth. Pipe egg yolk mixture into whites and top with strips of anchovy filets. Cover platter with shredded lettuce and arrange stuffed eggs on top of it.

PICKLED CABBAGE

Yield: 10 to 12 portions

Ingredients

Cabbage, Green, small	1
Cabbage, Red, small	1
Salt, coarse (kosher)	1 cup
Malt Vinegar	2 tbsp.
Sugar	2 tbsp.
Pickling Spices, in cheesecloth	1 tbsp.

Method

Remove outer leaves from cabbages. Wash, quarter, and cut out cores of both cabbages. Shred cabbage and combine with salt. Allow to stand for one day in a cool place. Boil vinegar with sugar and spices. Squeeze shredded cabbage dry and pour the vinegar mixture over it. Let marinate for 2 to 3 days under refrigeration. To serve, remove cabbage from marinade and place in salad bowl.

POTTED SHRIMP

Yield: 10 to 12 portions

Ingredients

Lobster Butter (p. 184)	8 oz.
Shrimp (under 40 count), shelled	2 cups
Mace	1/4 tsp.
Cayenne Pepper	1/4 tsp.
Lemon Juice	2 tbsp.

Method

Melt lobster butter in saucepan. Add shrimp and seasonings; simmer for 10 to 15 min. Stir in lemon juice and pour mixture into a souffle mold or individual ramekins. Chill for 2 hours before serving.

GALANTINE OF SCOTTISH SALMON

Follow recipe on p. 141. Garnishes on platter include Pickled Eggs (p. 100) with olive centers, pickled shrimp, and chopped aspic. Serve with Andalouse Sauce.

SOUSED MACKEREL IN WHITE WINE

Yield: 10 to 12 portions

Ingredients

Mackerel, fresh, 1 lb.	4
Onion, large, sliced	1
Parsley, chopped	1 tbsp.
Bayleaves	2
Peppercorns	1 tsp.
Salt	1 tsp.
White Wine, dry	2 cups
Lemon Juice	2 tbsp.

Method

Eviscerate fish; discard heads; wash thoroughly. Place fish in baking pan; sprinkle with onion slices, parsley, bayleaves, peppercorns, and salt.

Pour wine and lemon juice over fish; bring to a boil over medium heat. Cover and bake in oven at 350°F. for 15 to 20 min. Cool to room temperature, then allow to cool for several hours in the refrigerator. Debone mackerel and arrange on serving platter. Strain cooking liquid; pour over filets; garnish platter with sprigs of parsley.

FILET OF DOVER SOLE "DOMINO"

Yield: 12 portions

Ingredients

Dover Sole	3
Salt	1/3–1/2 tsp.
Pepper, whole	2–3 grinds
Fish Stock	1 cup
White Wine, dry	1 cup
Truffle Sheet	1
Mayonnaise Chaud-Froid	1 qt.

Method

Reserve one Dover sole to decorate and present whole on buffet platter. To filet remaining sole, follow standard procedure. Flatten filets; fold them over. Place filets in buttered baking dish; season with salt and pepper; cover with fish stock and white wine. Bake for about 15 min. or until done. Cool the fish at room temperature.

Trim each cooked filet to form a rectangle. Coat whole fish and filets with mayonnaise chaud-froid sauce. Decorate whole fish. Decorate each filet with dots and pieces cut from black truffle sheet to resemble a domino. Arrange fish and filets on a silver platter; garnish with chopped aspic jelly.

BEEF TONGUE JOCKEY CLUB

Yield: 25 to 30 portions

Ingredients

Smoked Beef Tongues	3
Brown Chaud-Froid Sauce (p. 77)	1 qt.
Truffle Sheet	1

Method

Select two beef tongues about the same size. Curve tongues so they can be shaped like a pair of boots for presentation. Cook tongues in salted, boiling water until meat is tender. Remove all outer skin. Allow to cool in cooking liquid.

Trim the two curved tongues and shape them like a standing pair of boots. Coat boot-shaped tongues with brown chaud-froid sauce. Decorate them using a truffle sheet to create effect of shoe-laces and eyelets. Arrange two decorated tongues in the middle of a large platter or mirror. Slice remaining tongue into thin slices and arrange around boot-shaped tongues on platter. Decorate platter with aspic jelly croutons and chopped aspic.

BAKED LOIN OF PORK, APPLESAUCE

Yield: 12 portions

Ingredients

Prunes, dried	16
Pork Loin, boneless, 4 lb.	1
Oil	1/4 cup
Salt	1/2 tsp.
Black Pepper, ground	1/4 tsp.
Brown Chaud-Froid Sauce	2 cups

Method

Pit prunes; place in mixing bowl. Add enough boiling water to cover and let stand for one hour. Make a pocket in the pork loin by running a sharp knife through the center of the meat. It may be necessary to insert the knife first from one end and then the other to complete pocket. Trim excess fat from loin. Drain prunes and insert to fill pocket in pork; tie loin with string so it retains shape while roasting. Place meat in roasting pan; pour oil over it and season with salt and pepper. Bake in oven at 400°F. for 1 hour, 45 min. Turn meat every half hour. Cool the pork at room temperature.

Slice half of cooled pork into 1/4-in. slices. Reserve remaining half. Glaze both piece and slices with brown chaud-froid sauce. Coat bottom of serving platter with thin layer of brown chaud-froid sauce. Place piece of loin in center of platter; arrange glazed pork slices around it. Garnish platter with a bunch of watercress and stuffed green olives. Serve with applesauce.

HAM AND VEAL PIE

Yield: 15 to 20 portions

Ingredients

Pate Dough (p. 117)	5 lb.
Veal, lean, 1/4-in. cubes	2 lb.
Smoked Ham, lean, 1/4-in. cubes	2 lb.
Brandy	1/2 cup
Parsley, chopped	1/4 cup
Chicken Stock, full-flavored	1/2 cup
Black Pepper, ground	1/4 tsp.
Sage, ground	1 tsp.
Lemon Juice	1 tbsp.
Hard-cooked Eggs	4

Method

Use rectangular mold for pie. To line mold with dough, follow procedure on p. 117. Combine veal, ham, brandy, parsley, stock, pepper, sage, and lemon juice. Mix well. Spoon mixture into lined mold until it is about half full. Place peeled, whole, hard-cooked eggs down the middle in a row. Fill mold with remaining mixture, covering eggs. Cover top of mold, following procedure on p. 117, steps 7 and 8. Bake in oven at 350°F. for 1-1/2 hours. Cool to room temperature, then chill in refrigerator for 3 to 4 hours. Fill pie with cold aspic jelly and allow to set, about one hour in the refrigerator. Unmold pie and cut half of it into 1/2-in. thick slices. Present on a platter that has been coated with a thin layer of aspic. Garnish with aspic croutons and chopped aspic.

NOTE: Bars cut from blanched veal and canned ham can be arranged in alternate layers to make red and white checkerboard pattern when pie is cut.

LENTIL SALAD

Yield: 10 to 12 portions

Ingredients

Lentils	1 cup
Smoked Ham, piece (or one ham hock)	4 oz.
Vinaigrette Sauce (p. 182)	1/2 cup
Parsley, chopped	2 tbsp.
Pimento, diced, small can	1
Onion Rings, thinly sliced	2 oz.
Green Pepper Rings, thinly sliced	2 oz.

Method

Soak lentils for 12 hours. Cook with ham over medium heat until lentils are tender. Drain; cool thoroughly. Season with vinaigrette, blending thoroughly. Add chopped parsley and pimento. Place in serving dish; alternate slices of onion and green pepper rings over the lentils in attractive pattern.

RED BEET SALAD

Use recipe on p. 89.

WATERCRESS MIMOSA

Yield: 8 to 10 portions

Ingredients

Watercress	3 bunches
Hard-cooked Eggs	4
Green Goddess Dressing, (p. 194)	1 cup

Method

Wash watercress; make sure to clean thoroughly. Break off stems and drain well to remove any excess water. Toss watercress with dressing. Sprinkle chopped eggs over salad.

KEDGEREE

Yield: 10 to 12 portions

Ingredients

Converted Rice	1 cup
Haddock, smoked	2 lb.
Hard-cooked Eggs	6
Parsley, chopped	2 tbsp.
Butter	2 tbsp.
Curry Powder	2 tsp.

Method

Cook rice according to directions on package. Poach fish in court bouillon made with half water and half milk. Chop eggs and mix with parsley. Flake cooked fish and combine with rice, melted butter, curry, and 1/2 of the egg-parsley mixture. Heat and toss together. Place in an oven-proof serving dish. Sprinkle remaining egg-parsley mixture over fish. Heat in oven for a few minutes before serving.

ROAST SIRLOIN OF BEEF, YORKSHIRE PUDDING

Yield: 15 to 20 portions

Ingredients

Shell Strip of Beef, boneless	1
Salt	to season
Black Pepper, ground	to season

Method

Place beef in roasting pan; season with salt and pepper. Roast in oven at 375°F. about 10 min. per lb. for rare and medium rare or 15 min. per lb. for medium. Turn meat after 30 min. When roast beef is done, transfer to heated platter and let it rest for 30 to 40 min. Save the fat for the Yorkshire Pudding.

YORKSHIRE PUDDING

Ingredients

Eggs, whole	6
Milk	3 cups
Salt	1 tsp.
Flour	3 cups

Method

Beat eggs with milk. Add salt and gently mix in flour. Strain mixture to remove lumps. Pour about 1/2-in. fat in a 12- to 14-in. iron skillet. Heat pan in the oven at 400°F. When oil starts smoking, pour mixture in skillet and bake in oven at 350°F. for 40 to 45 min. Yorkshire Pudding should be brown and crisp. Remove from pan and keep warm until ready to serve. Cut pudding into portions of desired size.

To Serve

Carve roast beef in slices of desired size; serve with its own juices and a piece of Yorkshire Pudding.

BEEF AND KIDNEY PIE

Yield: 10 to 12 portions

Ingredients

Veal Kidneys	2 lb.
Sirloin or Top Round of Beef, cubed	3 lb.
Salt	1 tsp.
Black Pepper, ground	1/2 tsp.
Flour	1/2 cup
Onion, chopped	1/2 cup
Mushrooms, sliced	2 cups
Water	3 cups
Parsley, fresh, chopped	1 tbsp.
Worcestershire Sauce	1 tsp.
Puff Paste Dough	2 lb.
Egg, beaten with 1 tbsp. milk	1

Method

Trim fat off kidneys; peel off skin and cut into 1-in. cubes. Mix cubed beef and kidneys and season with salt and pepper. Heat a small amount of oil in a 14-in. skillet. Brown half of meat over high heat; repeat process with remaining half. When all has been browned, transfer meat to a heavy casserole; add flour and brown over medium heat. Add onion and mushrooms; stir well and cook a little longer. Add water and mix well to make sauce. Season with parsley and worcestershire sauce. Transfer stew to a rectangular pan about 2 in. deep. Cover stew with puff paste dough using an extra strip of dough to seal the edges completely. Brush with egg and milk mixture. Make decorative cut-outs from leftover dough and arrange on dough cover for stew. Bake in oven at 350°F. for 30 to 40 min. until crust is golden brown.

᧩ ᧩

TOAD IN THE HOLE

Yield: 12 portions

Ingredients

Flour	3 cups
Eggs, whole	6
Milk	3 cups
Salt	1 tsp.
Fresh Pork Sausages	3 lb.

Method

Mix flour, eggs, milk, and salt to make batter as described in the method of preparation for Yorkshire Pudding (p. 30). Brown sausages in a 14-in. iron skillet. Transfer sausages to a medium-sized rectangular pan. Arrange them at least 1 in. apart in a single layer. Heat pan of sausages in the oven, then pour batter over the sausages. Moisten batter with 2 to 3 tbsp. of drippings. Bake in oven at 375°F. 30 to 40 min. until the pudding is brown and crisp.

᧩ ᧩

TREACLE TART

Yield: 10 to 12 portions, 1 9-in. pie

Ingredients

Pie Shell	1
English Golden Syrup	1-1/2 cups

OR

Corn Syrup, 1/2 light and 1/2 dark	1-1/2 cups
Fresh Bread Crumbs	1-1/2 cups
Lemon Juice	1 tbsp.
Ginger, ground	1/2 tsp.
Eggs, whole, beaten	2

Method

In a large bowl, combine syrup, bread crumbs, lemon juice, ginger, and eggs. Mix ingredients together well. Pour into pie shell and bake for 20 to 25 min. in oven at 350°F. The tart should be golden brown when done. Treacle Tart is usually served with a Custard Sauce.

᧩ ᧩

TRIFLE

Yield: 10 to 12 portions

Ingredients

Pound Cake	14 oz.
Raspberry Jam	1/2 cup
Almonds, sliced	1 cup
Brandy	1/2 cup
Sherry, dry	1/2 cup
Sugar	3/4 cup
Cream, heavy	2 cups
Sugar, superfine	2 tbsp.
Raspberries, fresh or frozen	2 cups
Custard Sauce	3 cups

Method

Cut pound cake into 1/2-in. slices. Spread jam over slices. Arrange slices in a glass serving bowl. Sprinkle almonds over each layer. Dissolve sugar in brandy and sherry; heat until sugar is completely dissolved. Cool the syrup and pour over cake. Whip cream until stiff, fold in superfine sugar. Scatter raspberries over cake, saving a dozen berries to use in decorating finished dish. Next spread custard sauce over top of cake. Pipe whipped cream around cake and decorate with the remaining raspberries.

BLACKBERRY AND APPLE PIE

Yield: 8 to 10 portions

Ingredients

Apples, cooking	3 large
Butter, melted	2 tbsp.
Sugar	1/2 cup
Blackberries, fresh	1 qt.
Pie Crust Dough, for 9-in. pie	1
Egg Yolk, beaten with 1 tbsp. sugar	1

Method

Peel, core, and slice apples. In heavy saute pan, melt butter and cook apples over medium heat. Sprinkle with 2 tbsp. sugar; stir well. Apples should retain shape after cooking; do not over-cook. Combine remaining sugar with black-berries; add more sugar, if necessary. Spread blackberries in a 2-in. deep pie dish. Spoon apples over the top. Roll out pie crust dough on floured surface. Cover entire surface of pie, seal-ing edges with extra strips of dough. Brush top with egg yolk and sugar mixture. Bake in oven at 400°F. for 20 to 25 min., until crust is golden brown. Cool pie at room temperature; serve with heavy cream.

BURNT CREAM

Yield: 8 to 10 portions

Ingredients

Milk	2 cups
Cream, heavy	2 cups
Eggs, whole	3
Egg Yolks	4
Sugar	3/4 cup
Vanilla Extract	1 tsp.
Sugar	1/2 cup

Method

Scald milk and cream in saucepan. Combine whole eggs and egg yolks in mixing bowl; add sugar; beat for 4 to 5 min. Pour milk and cream into egg mixture; stir well; mix in vanilla extract. Strain custard into a 1-qt. souffle dish. Bake in a water bath for 40 to 45 min., at 350°F. Cool at room temperature.

Prepare a dark caramel syrup by putting sugar into hot pan over high heat and stirring constantly until it becomes a light brown syrup. Pour syrup over top of custard cream. Refrigerate Burnt Cream before serving.

GINGERBREAD

Yield: about 20 portions

Ingredients

Water	1 lb.
Honey	1 lb.
Salt	1/8 tsp.
Aniseed	1/8 tsp.
Cinnamon	1/8 tsp.
Baking Powder	1 tsp.
Flour	2 lb.
Rum	4 oz.
Milk	6 oz.

Method

Heat water, honey, salt, and spices. Cool. Sift baking powder into flour; add rum. Add to first mixture. Combine ingredients, preferably mix-ing with an electric mixer. Add milk to mixture; stir well. Fill two rectangular molds lined with greased wax paper half full. Bake in oven at 350°F. for 45 min. to 1 hour.

NOTE: Before baking, gingerbread can be given extra flavor by adding:

Angelica, diced	4 oz.
Cherries, glace	4 oz.
Lemon Peel	4 oz.

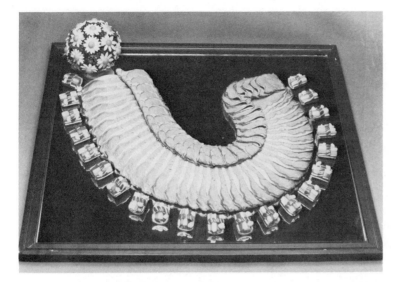

Sliced Roast Sirloin of Beef
Centerpiece: Turnip Daisies
Garniture: Zucchini basket with
marinated stick vegetables

FRESH FRUIT SALAD

The fruit salad should combine:

gooseberries	blackberries
raspberries	blueberries
strawberries	

Wash and drain fruit. Sprinkle generously with sugar and mix gently. Arrange the fruit salad in glass bowl; refrigerate mixture for 1 to 2 hours.

GERMAN BUFFET

SOUP

Kirschen Kaltschale
(Cold Cherry Soup)

SALADS

Wurst Salad, Bavarian Style
Cucumber Salad with Sour Cream
Potato Salad with Apple
Knob Celery Salad (Celeriac)

APPETIZERS

Big Steak Tartare with Schinken Haeger
Smoked Eel with Horseradish and Pumpernickel
Herring in Mustard Sauce
Marinated Beef Tongue Bavarian Style

COLD PLATTER

Saddle of Venison Schloss Seefeld
German Cold Cuts with Pumpernickel, Callenberger Style
Parfait of Chicken Livers, Bayerischer Hof

HOT PLATTER

German Bratwurst with Sweet Mustard
Smoked Pork Loin with Wine Kraut
Southern German Noodles with Brown Butter
Venison Sausage

DESSERTS

Zuger Kirsch Torte
Bavarian Cream Bombe
Blatterteig Geback
Fruit Compote

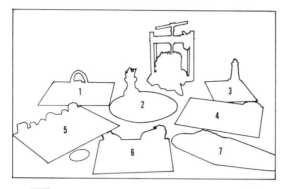

GERMAN BUFFET: (1) Tray of roast beef slices framed with dried beef rolls, tallow basket of pickled vegetables in center; (2) Parfait of Chicken Livers, Bayerischer Hof; (3) Smoked Trout with Horseradish, lighthouse butter sculpture; (4) smoked salmon slices, circles of galantine of striped bass, pickled egg halves, Sauce Verte; (5) Pate of Smoked Ham slices and ham slices with poached apple baskets filled with currant jelly and raspberry frambois liqueur; (6) smoked whole chicken and whole roast capon with slices; (7) Whole Striped Bass decorated with chaud-froid and whole shrimp, sliced poached bass.

KIRSCHEN KALTSCHALE (Cold Cherry Soup)

Yield: 24 5-oz. portions

Ingredients

Sour Cherries, frozen	4 cups
Water	1 qt.
Red Wine	1 pt.
Lemon Juice	2 oz.
Sugar	1/2 cup
Cloves, whole	2
Cinnamon Stick, small	1
Cornstarch	1 tsp.

Method

Bring cherries, water, wine, lemon juice, sugar, and spices to boiling point. Remove enough cherries to use as garnish when serving. Thicken soup with cornstarch. Strain through food mill. Chill well and serve with reserved cherries and lemon slices.

NOTE: Orange juice added to the cherry soup heightens flavor.

WURST SALAD, BAVARIAN STYLE

Yield: 2-1/2 lb.

Ingredients

Knockwurst, peeled, thinly sliced	2 lb.
Onion, thinly sliced	1/2 lb.

MARINADE

Water	12 oz.
Vinegar, white	4 oz.
Olive Oil	2 oz.
Prepared Mustard	1 tsp.
Black Pepper, ground	1/2 tsp.

Method

Mix marinade well; combine with sliced knockwurst and onion; reserve onion rings for garnish. Arrange mixture in salad bowl. Garnish around edge of bowl with sliced onion rings and parsley.

CUCUMBER SALAD WITH SOUR CREAM

Yield: 4 lb.

Ingredients

Cucumbers, 10 to 11 oz.	6
Coarse Salt	2 tbsp.
Vinegar, white, distilled	1 tsp.

MARINADE

Vinegar, white, distilled	1/2 cup
Onion, medium, diced	1
Dill, finely chopped	4 tbsp.
Sugar	1 tsp.
Sour Cream	1-1/2 cups
Oil	1/2 cup

Method

Peel cucumbers and slice thinly; mix with salt and vinegar. Marinate for 30 min.; drain through sieve and dry thoroughly.

Combine all remaining ingredients except oil. Add cucumbers and mix well, taste, and add more salt if needed. Then add oil and toss. Marinate for 2 to 3 hours or overnight.

ALTERNATE SOUR CREAM DRESSING FOR CUCUMBERS

Yield: 1 pt.

Ingredients

Hard-cooked Eggs	5
Dusseldorf Mustard	1-1/2 tsp.
Sour Cream	2/3 cup
Vinegar, white	3 tsp.
Sugar	1/2 tsp.
Dill, fresh, chopped	1-1/2 tbsp.
White Pepper	1/3 tsp.
Lettuce Leaves, washed, dried	6-8

Method

Separate yolks from whites of hard-cooked eggs. Cut whites into thin strips and stir into cucumbers. With a spatula, press egg yolks through a fine sieve into a small bowl; beat in mustard, sour cream, vinegar, sugar, dill, and white pepper. When dressing is smooth, pour it over cucumbers and toss together. Taste for seasoning. Arrange salad leaves in bowl and top with salad.

POTATO SALAD WITH APPLE

Yield: about 2 lb.

Ingredients

Potatoes	2 lb.
Oil	1/4 cup
Vinegar, white	1/4 cup
Chicken Stock, hot	1/4 cup
Onion, medium, sliced	1/2 cup
Salt	1 tsp.
Pepper	1/2 tsp.
Sugar	1/3 tsp.
Apple, diced	1

Method

Wash potatoes and cook in jackets. When done, let potatoes cool at room temperature and peel while still warm. Dice or slice, as preferred. Mix potatoes with oil, vinegar, stock, onion, salt, pepper, sugar, and apple; marinate for 2 hours. Serve at room temperature.

KNOB CELERY SALAD (*Celeriac*)

Yield: about 2 lb.

Ingredients

Knob Celery	2 lb.
Lemons	2
Vinegar	2 oz.
Sugar	1 oz.
Olive Oil	3 oz.
Prepared Mustard	1 tsp.
Salt	to taste
Pepper	to taste

Method

Brush, wash, and cook knob celery; peel when cold; slice thinly. Combine remaining ingredients for marinade. Place sliced celery in a suitable bowl, cover with marinade. When celery slices have marinated for several hours, drain and arrange in bowl; garnish with fresh watercress.

BIG STEAK TARTARE WITH SCHINKEN HAEGER (*Steak Tartare the German Way*)

Yield: 2 portions

Ingredients

Lean Boneless Beef, from filet, top or eye round	1/2 lb.
Egg, whole	1
Salt, coarse	to taste
Black Pepper, Malabar,* crushed	to taste
Schinken Haeger (Gin)	1/2 oz.
Onion, chopped	2 tbsp.
Pickles, chopped	2 tbsp.
Anchovy Filets, flat	3
Vinegar, white, distilled	1/2 tsp.

(continued)

Big Steak Tartare with Schinken Haeger
(continued)

Hungarian Paprika, sweet	1/2 tsp.
Mustard	1/2 tsp.

Method

Blend all ingredients thoroughly; serve on pumpernickel.

*Malabar black pepper, which comes from the southwestern Malabar Coast of India, has excellent aroma, flavor, and pungency and adds a unique touch to this version of Steak Tartare.

SMOKED EEL WITH HORSERADISH AND PUMPERNICKEL

Remove skin and bones from smoked eel; cut into 1/2- to 1-in. pieces. Serve with Frozen Horseradish Sauce (p. 181).

HERRING IN MUSTARD SAUCE

Yield: 4 lb. 5 oz.

Ingredients

Schmaltz Herring	10

MARINADE

Vinegar, white, distilled	1 qt.
Sugar	8 oz.
Dill Stalks	15
Pickling Spices	1 tbsp.
Carrots	4 oz.
Horseradish, fresh	1 oz.
Onion, medium	1
Juniper Berries	10
Cloves	2
Peppercorns	20
Mustard Seeds	1 tsp.

Method

Combine all ingredients for marinade and boil for 5 min. Then cool. Filet Schmaltz Herring; soak in water overnight. Place filets in a crock and pour cold marinade over them. Marinate for 4 to 5 days. Remove herring filets from marinade and cut into 1-in. pieces. Drain well and mix with mustard sauce. Garnish serving dish with fresh dill and pimentos.

MUSTARD SAUCE

Yield: 3/4 pt.

Ingredients

White Wine	1/2 cup
Shallots, chopped	1 tsp.
Mustard Seeds	1 tbsp.
Mayonnaise	1 cup
Dijon or Dusseldorf Mustard	1-2 tsp.

Method

Combine wine, shallots, mustard seeds and heat to boiling. Reduce liquid by 3/4 and cool. When cool mix into mayonnaise. Add mustard; after 5 to 10 min., strain through cheesecloth.

NOTE: Herring can also be used for Herring Salad, Bismarck Herring, Rollmops, and similar dishes.

MARINATED BEEF TONGUE BAVARIAN STYLE

Yield: 2-1/2 to 3 lb.

Ingredients

Smoked Beef Tongue	1
Black Pepper, crushed	
Mustard	
Oil	

MARINADE

Vinegar, white	4 parts
Stock, from tongue	4 parts
Onion, finely diced	1 part

Method

Simmer beef tongue for 2 to 3 hours. Cool overnight; slice paper thin. Bring marinade ingredients to boil; remove from heat and while still warm pour over sliced tongue. After marinating for several hours, drain and season with coarsely

Saddle of Venison Schloss Seefeld

crushed black pepper, mustard, and oil. Garnish serving dish with thinly cut raw onion rings.

✿✿

SADDLE OF VENISON SCHLOSS SEEFELD

Yield: 6 to 8 portions

Ingredients

Saddle of Venison, 3-1/2 lb.	1

MARINADE

Water, slightly salted	3 cups
Carrots	2
Knob Celery	1
Parsnip	1
Onions, medium	2
Peppercorns	6
Juniper Berries	6
Bayleaf	1
Thyme	pinch
Marjoram	pinch
Vinegar, plain, distilled	1 cup
Red Wine	2 cups

(Peppercorns, Juniper Berries, Bayleaf, Thyme, Marjoram) for sachet bag

FOR LARDING

Slab Bacon	7 oz.
Salt	to taste
Pepper	to taste
Butter, for browning	1-1/2 oz.

FOR ASPIC

Carrots, Onion, Celery, diced	6 oz.
Tomato Paste	1 tsp.
Stock or Water	2 qt.
Unflavored Gelatin	1–2 oz.

FOR GARNISH

Pears	6
Poaching Liquid (see recipe, p. 52)	2 qt.
Lemon, peel in one strip	zest
Cinnamon Stick	1/2
Red Currant Jelly	4 oz.
Raspberry Brandy	1/2 oz.

Method

Rinse saddle of venison; dry well; remove skin.

Prepare marinade. Bring slightly salted water to a boil; add diced carrots, knob celery, parsnip, and onion. Simmer for 30 min. While cooking, add sachet bag (of peppercorns, juniper berries, bayleaf, thyme, and marjoram); add vinegar and red wine. Bring to a fast boil and cool.

When cool, pour marinade over saddle of venison; marinate for 2 days. Remove from marinade and dry well.

Cut smoked slab bacon in small strips and lard saddle with it (for larding procedure, see p. 156). Sprinkle salt and pepper over surface. Heat butter; brown meat. Roast saddle of venison for 15 to 20 min. in oven at 400°F. The meat should be pink. Remove; cool. Add to pan meat that was roasted in mirepoix of diced carrots, onion, and celery and the saddle trimmings. Brown mixture for 15 to 20 min., stirring as needed; add tomato paste, stir well, and add water or stock; simmer for 1/2 to 1 hour and strain. Add gelatin and clarify (see method, p. 71). Strain and cool.

Remove both filets from saddle of venison, slice thinly and put slices back in place on carcass. Coat with aspic (for method, see p. 79). Decorate with oranges, grapes, and walnuts or hazelnuts. Garnish with chilled pears filled with red currant jelly. Pears for a garnish are peeled, cut in half, the core removed with parisian cutter, and poached. Follow method in American Buffet, on p. 51. Poaching liquid should be flavored with cinnamon stick and lemon peel. Mix red currant jelly with raspberry brandy; fill pear cavities. Decorate pears with fresh mint leaves and place around saddle of venison. A melon filled with grapes, dates, and nuts can be an eye-catching addition to this presentation.

ᚷᚦᚲ

GERMAN COLD CUTS WITH PUMPERNICKEL, CALLENBERGER STYLE

Usually six or seven different kinds of sausage and meats are offered in this buffet item. The sausage or "Wurst" (the German word for sausage) can be made in an operation's own kitchen and requires neither extra equipment nor expense. The garnish for this display is created with pickle sticks, radishes, pumpernickel rolls filled with cream cheese. Several sausage recipes follow.

JAEGERWURST

Yield: 11 lb.

Ingredients

Lean Beef ⎱ ground together	4-1/2 lb.
Pork Butt, fat ⎰ on medium	4-1/2 lb.
Fresh Pork Fat, skinless, 1/8-in. dice	2 lb.
Salt	1-1/2 oz.
Curing Salt or Saltpeter	1/8 oz.
White Pepper	2 tsp.
Garlic, finely chopped	2/3 oz.
Potato Starch or Cornstarch	8 oz.
Water, ice cold	1 qt.
Monosodium Glutamate	2 tbsp.
Beef Casing	1

Method

Place all ingredients in bowl of mixer; beat very slowly with the arm or paddle for 30 sec. Place mixture in beef casing. Smoke for 6 hours, then poach for 45 min. in liquid at 180°F. Chill. Serve cold.

ROLLED PORK SHOULDER

Yield: 7 to 8 lb.

Ingredients

Pork Shoulder, boneless, medium-sized	1
Brine	2 gal.
Bouquet Garni	1
Onions, whole, each holding 4 cloves	2
Carrots	3
Fat from Pate, melted	for rubbing
Breadcrumbs, very dry	for coating

Method

Using a special brine pump, inject brine into meat, being sure to reach all of thick parts. Soak meat in brine overnight.

The next day, after rinsing meat in clear water, roll it in a clean cloth. Tie both ends loosely and place meat in a deep pan. Cover with water; bring to boiling point. If the water becomes too salty, remove the pork to fresh water. Add bouquet garni, onions, and carrots. Bring to boiling point again; lower heat; simmer about

25 min. per pound of meat. Cool off in the bouillon for 24 hours and then unwrap and wipe dry. Rub thoroughly with a good pate fat, and roll in very dry breadcrumbs.

Rolled pork shoulder is usually served cold as a buffet item.

NOTE: If no special brine pump is available, pierce meat all over and soak in brine for 2 to 3 days.

KASSLER LIVERWURST

Yield: 4-1/2 lb.

Ingredients

Pork Shoulder	1-1/2 lb.
Pork Liver	1 lb.
Fresh Pork Fat	1/2 lb.
Tongue, cooked, diced	1 lb.
Onion, chopped	1/4 cup
Salt	2 tbsp.
Ground Pepper	1/2 tsp.
Pate Spice	1/2 tsp.
Truffle Peelings, chopped (optional)	1 oz.
Pistachio Nuts, blanched, peeled	2 oz.
Potato Flour, diluted in white wine	2 oz.
Eggs, whole	3
Yellow Food Coloring	2 drops
Large Pork Casings	as needed

Method

Grind together pork, liver, fresh pork fat, tongue, and onion, using fine blade. Add spices and seasonings; place in mixer bowl and beat slowly in mixer for about 2 min. Add all remaining ingredients, except food coloring and casings. Fill pork casings; tie each end and all around with butcher twine. Poach very slowly for about 45 min. Remove from casing; rub with yellow food coloring; smoke in a warm smoke box for about 2 hours. Chill. Serve cold.

NOTE: If no smoked tongue is available, poach for 1-1/2 hr. only.

CHICKEN SAUSAGE

(For grilling, sauteing, or boiling)

Yield: 6 lb.

Ingredients

Chicken Leg Meat	4.4 lb.
Fatback or Pork Belly	24.7 oz.
Salt	2 oz. or to taste
Pepper	to taste
Nutmeg	to taste
Curry	to taste
Eggs, whole	4
Shaved Ice	1/2–1 lb.

Method

Grind chicken leg meat through medium plate. Grind fatback through medium plate. Season chicken meat with salt and spices. Puree half of the chicken meat in a food processor or robot coupe together with ice, fine. Fold in second half of chicken meat and fatback. Mix well. Fold in garnish. Fill into pork casing, tie into ring, and poach in 170°F. water until 150°F. internal temperature. Chill in ice water.

Garnish variations: small Titi shrimps, chopped truffle, pistachio nuts, walnuts, or herbs.

PRESSED HEAD or SULZE

Yield: 5 lb.

Ingredients

Pork Snouts	2 lb.
Pork Ears	3 lb.
Pork Tongues	2 lb.
Curing Brine	2 gal.
Bouquet Garni	1
Onions, whole, each holding 4 cloves	2
Carrots	2
Shallots	3
Parsley, chopped	as needed
Peppercorns, crushed	1/2 tsp.
Bouillon	to cover
Powdered Gelatin, 1 tbsp. per pt. of bouillon	as needed
Butter	to saute

Method

Soak meat in curing brine for about 3 hours. Rinse and place in a deep pan; cover with a good unsalted bouillon; add bouquet garni, onions, carrots, and peppercorns. Bring to a boil, then simmer until the meat is very tender (approx. 1-1/2 to 2 hours).

Remove bouquet garni, onions, carrots, and any skin and bones from meat; reserve the bouillon.

Spread a piece of cloth the size of a napkin on the table; arrange the meat on it so it can be rolled into a cylinder, putting the ears next to the cloth and the meat and tongues in the center. Saute the chopped shallots and parsley in butter and sprinkle over meat; then roll into cylinder on cloth, tying both ends of cloth tightly. Place cylinder of meat in bouillon that has been strengthened with gelatin. Cool overnight.

Unwrap and slice thinly to serve. Serve either plain or with vinaigrette sauce and thinly sliced onions.

CHICKEN LIVER, ORTRERER

Yield: 1 lb. 10 oz.

Ingredients

Fresh Pork Fat, chopped	8 oz.
Chicken Livers	1 lb.
Shallots, finely chopped	2
Mushroom Trimmings, chopped	1/2 cup
Salt	to taste
Pepper	to taste
Pate Spice	1/3 tsp.
Thyme	1/3 tsp.
Bayleaf	1

Method

Melt pork fat in saute pan; use to saute chicken livers. *Do not* cook chicken livers well done; livers should be pink. Remove; saute shallots and mushrooms to desired consistency in same pan; add seasoning and herbs. Combine all ingredients and cool. Blend in blender.

PARFAIT OF CHICKEN LIVERS, BAYERISCHER HOF

Yield: 2 lb.

Ingredients

Chicken Liver, Ortrerer	22 oz.
Brandy	1 oz.
Aspic	6–8 oz.
Cream, heavy	4–5 oz.
Truffles, diced	as desired

Method

Mix all but truffles in a blender. Pour into mold and chill. Garnish with truffles.

GERMAN BRATWURST WITH SWEET MUSTARD

Yield: 20 lb.

Ingredients

White Bread, trimmed	3 lb.
Pork, lean	2 lb.
Fresh Pork Fat	3 lb.
Milk	5 qt.
Eggs, beaten	25
Salt	to taste
Pepper	to taste
Port Wine	1 pt.
Burgundy	1 jigger
Pork Casing	1

Method

Dice bread, dice pork and fresh pork fat. Bring milk to a boil and pour over bread. Combine all ingredients except casing; mix thoroughly; put through fine grinder.

Fill casing with mixture and shape sausage of desired size. Drop sausage into boiling water, lowering heat immediately to prevent bursting. Use a ladle or small pot to keep the water constantly in motion while simmering (20 min.).

To test for doneness, pierce sausage using a needle or sharp skewer. If the sausage rises to the surface, it is ready. When sausage is cooked, remove from water and place on sheet pan; use a

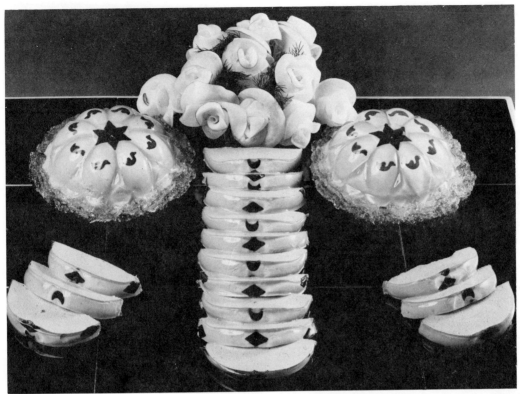

Liver mousse from aspic-lined molds flanks bouquet of turnip roses (made like potato roses but not deep fried). Mousse molds are framed with chopped aspic and deco-rated with designs cut from truffle sheets. Slices have been carefully cut from similar molds so that truffle designs remain whole.

cloth to smooth cooked sausage into even shape. To serve, dip in milk and brown in hot fat.

✥ ✥

SMOKED PORK LOIN WITH WINE KRAUT

Yield: 20 4-oz. portions of meat; 20 2.5-oz. sauerkraut

Ingredients

Loin of Smoked Pork, 6 lb.	1
Onion, medium, diced	4 oz.
Oil	2 oz.
Sauerkraut	3 lb.
White Wine	1 pt.
Stock	1 pt.
Caraway Seeds	2 tbsp.
Applesauce	4 oz.
Salt	to taste
Pepper	to taste
Juniper Berries	2 tbsp.
Potato, raw, grated	4 oz.

Method

Saute onion until transparent. Combine onion, sauerkraut, wine and stock, caraway seeds, apple-sauce, salt, and pepper; add juniper berries in sachet bag. Place in bottom of large roasting pan or brazier. Place smoked loin of pork on top of sauerkraut; cover pan and cook in preheated oven at 375°F. for 1-1/2 hours, or until meat is tender.

Remove loin of pork and stir grated raw potato into sauerkraut; bring to a boil. Slice pork loin and arrange on top of sauerkraut for service.

❧ ❧

SOUTHERN GERMAN NOODLES WITH BROWN BUTTER

Yield: 28 oz. or 14 2-oz. portions

Ingredients

Eggs, whole	3–4
Flour	10 oz.
Milk	8 oz.
Butter, for sauteing	2 oz.
Salt	to taste
Pepper	to taste
Nutmeg	to taste

Method

Combine eggs, milk, flour, salt, pepper, and nutmeg. Beat well until dough is smooth. Use either a spoon or spaetzle machine to shape dumplings or spaetzle. Drop dumplings in boiling water. As soon as dumplings or spaetzle float on top of water, remove to cold water; drain well. Saute in brown butter before service.

❧ ❧

VENISON SAUSAGE

Yield: 68 oz. or 34 2-oz. patties

Ingredients

Venison, fresh, lean	2 lb.
Pork, lean	3/4 lb.
Pork Fat	1 lb.
Water, cold	5 oz.
White Wine (optional)	1 oz.
Salt	1-1/8 oz.
Poultry Seasoning	1/3 oz.
White Pepper	1/2 oz.

Method

Mix liquids and seasonings with the venison, pork, and pork fat. Refrigerate for about 10 min.

Then grind, using a medium 1/4-in.-size plate. Next, grind using a small 1/8-in.-size plate. Shape ground mixture into patties weighing about 2 oz. Fry patties in a small amount of oil, until done.

❧ ❧

ZUGER KIRSCH TORTE

Yield: 1 torte

Ingredients

Old White Bread	4-1/2 oz.
Milk	1/2 pt.
Almond Paste *or* Macaroon Paste	3-1/2 oz.
Butter	3-1/2 oz.
Sugar	3-1/2 oz.
Egg Yolks	6
Egg Whites, beaten stiff	4
Cinnamon	1/3 oz.
Lemon Peel, grated	from 1/8 lemon
Cherries, fresh, pitted	18 oz.

Method

Soak bread in milk and mash it by hand. Whip almond paste, butter, sugar, spices, and egg yolks to a creamy, fluffy mixture. Add soaked bread and fold beaten egg white slowly into the mixture. Grease a high cake mold and line with parchment paper. Sprinkle with cake crumbs and pour in half the mixture. Sprinkle half the amount of cherries over the mixture and add rest of the mixture and rest of the cherries. Press the cherries into the mixture and smooth with a palate knife. Bake in a preheated oven at 350°F. for 60 min. or until firm. Cool and dust with powdered sugar.

❧ ❧

BAVARIAN CREAM BOMBE

Yield: 8 to 10 portions

Ingredients

Strawberries	1 qt.
Orange *or* Cherry Liqueur	1 cup

Water	1/2 cup
Ladyfingers, split	16
Sweet Butter	1/2 lb.
Superfine Sugar	1 cup
Almond Extract	1/4 tsp.
Almonds, finely ground	1-1/4 cups
Heavy Cream, for whipping	2 cups

Method

Select ripe strawberries, wash and dry with a paper towel. Put 1/2 cup liqueur with the water into a bowl. Dip ladyfingers into the mixture and drain on a wire rack. Line the bottom and sides of a 7-in. mold with about half of the ladyfingers. Cream butter and sugar until light and fluffy. Beat in the remaining liqueur and the almond extract. Stir in the almonds and fold in the cream. Spread 1/3 of the mixture in the lined mold. Cover with half the strawberries, then add a layer of ladyfingers. Repeat the layers of whipped cream, berries, and ladyfingers. Then finish off with a layer of whipped cream and ladyfingers. Cover the top with a piece of parchment paper and weight down with a small plate. Chill overnight, then carefully unmold. Serve with additional whipped cream.

AMERICAN BUFFET

RELISHES and SALADS

Pickled Mushrooms, Onions, Carrots, Red Peppers, Green Beans
Eggplant and Tunafish Salad
Wild Turkey Salad Teddy Roosevelt
Black Beans with Ham
Known in the south as "Hopping John."
Succotash
The Indians called it Misiquatash and Henry Hudson never had it this good!

APPETIZERS

Stuffed Cucumber, "Trapper Style"
Early settlers found many ways to prepare simple garden vegetables.
This one is stuffed with cucumber and smoked trout.
Dried Beef with Pears
The Indians smoked the dried meat and called it "jerky."
Served with plump, ripe pears, it's called delicious.
Pork Pie with Eggs
Woodsmen often took a repast of cold pies with them as they
set off for a day's logging in the mountains.
Hudson Valley Apples
Red and ripe and stuffed with the riverman's delight—crawfish.
Celery, Carrots, Olives
Served on a clean, icy floe of Hudson River ice.

MAIN COURSE

Marinated Duck Cornelius Vanderbilt
Deftly seasoned with local herbs.
Beef Stew "Settlers Style"
Headed west in the wagon trains, buffalo was used for this dish.
Whole Smoked Pheasant
Preserved game of local hunters.
Barbequed Fresh Ham
Innkeepers usually had a whole fresh ham ready on the spit for travelers
coming by coach up the old Albany Post Road.

DESSERTS

Dutch Apple Crumb Pie
The Pennsylvania Dutch housewife turned the simple apple
into an All-American dessert.
Peg Leg Peter Stuyvesant's Poundcake
Beaten with an old wooden spoon.
Strawberry Shortcake
Wild strawberries, small and sweet, grew in the meadows of
New York. With dollops of freshly whipped cream it's as traditional
as a picnic on the 4th of July!
Baskets of Bearfoot Bread will be on each table.
Made with cornmeal, or maize, it represents the American
Indians' gift to the first white settlers.

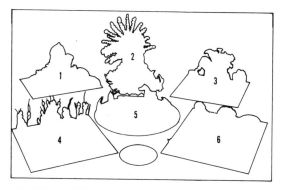

AMERICAN BUFFET: *Dishes equally appropriate for celebration of any American historical holiday: (1) Cheese Tray—Monterey Jack, Wisconsin Brie, Port Salut, fruit, french bread, squash bird; (2) Turkey created from whole watermelon with outspread tail of honeydew, canteloupe, and watermelon balls alternated with strawberries; (3) rows of sliced chicken liver pate and veal and pork pate curved around bouquet of Chinese cabbage leaves, radish roses, leek flowers, and turnip daisies, with butterflies cut from parsnips decorated with truffle sheet designs and feelers. A row of stuffed eggs is final touch; (4) Whole Smoked Pheasant in circle of galantine slices, whole quail, and deviled egg chicks on potato nests among ripe olive trees; (5) seahorse butter sculpture presides over Eggplant and Tunafish Salad, whole poached trout and bass each filled with seafood forcemeat; (6) Rib of Beef, with slices around decorated mold of chopped beef, with horseradish sauce.*

PICKLED MUSHROOMS

Yield: 2 lb. 8 oz.

Ingredients

Mushrooms, sliced	3 lb.
Carrots, 1-1/2-in. julienne strips	1 pk.
Pimento, strips, 1 in. by 1/2 in.	1 can
Oregano	1 tsp.
Garlic Powder	1 tsp.
Vinegar, Cider	1/2 cup
Salt	to taste
Pepper	to taste

Method

Boil mushrooms until tender; remove from heat and drain. Cook carrots until tender; remove from heat and drain. Saute carrots in oil for 3 min.; add mushrooms and continue cooking for another 3 min. Add pimento, oregano, garlic powder, cider vinegar, salt, and pepper. Cook until all ingredients are hot; remove from heat and refrigerate for 24 hours. Serve.

ﺷ ﺷ

MARINATED ONIONS

Yield: 1 lb.

Ingredients

Pearl Onions	1 lb.

MARINADE

White Wine, dry	3/4 cup
Vinegar, white	3/4 cup
Water	4 cups
Oil	6 tbsp.
Garlic Cloves	2
Parsley	small bunch
Sugar	1 tsp.
Salt	1 tsp.
Cayenne Pepper	pinch
Basil, finely chopped	1 tsp.
Prepared Dijon Mustard	1 tsp.

Method

Heat marinade. When it comes to a boil, remove from heat and pour over onions. Cool. Refrigerate for 48 hours. When ready to serve, sprinkle with chopped parsley.

ﺷ ﺷ

MARINATED CARROTS

Yield: 2 lb. 10 oz.

Ingredients

Carrots, tender, young	1 No. 10 can

MARINADE

White Wine, dry	3/4 cup
Vinegar, white	3/4 cup

Water	4 cups
Oil	6 tbsp.
Garlic Cloves	2
Parsley	small bunch
Sugar	1 tsp.
Salt	1 tsp.
Cayenne Pepper	pinch
Basil, finely chopped	1 tsp.
Prepared Dijon Mustard	1 tsp.

Method

Heat marinade. When it comes to a boil, remove from heat and pour over carrots. Refrigerate for 48 hours. When ready to serve, sprinkle with chopped parsley.

༈

MARINATED FRIED PEPPERS

Yield: 1 lb. 7 oz.

Ingredients

Green Peppers	2 lb.
Pimento	1 can

MARINADE

Vinegar, cider	1/2 cup
Oil	2 cups
Garlic Cloves, chopped	2
Oregano	1 tsp.
Salt	to taste
Pepper	to taste

Method

Boil or deep fry green peppers until skins turn white. Remove from heat. Peel skin from each green pepper and also remove core and seeds. Slice lengthwise into 1/2-in. strips. Heat oil in pot, add green peppers, and cook until tender. Add pimento, sliced into strips the same size as green pepper strips. Cook for 5 min. Add other ingredients. Marinate for 24 hours.

NOTE: If fresh red peppers are available, use instead of pimento. Prepare the same way as fresh green peppers.

༈

MARINATED CUT GREEN BEANS

Yield: 2 lb. 4 oz.

Ingredients

Cut Green Beans	2-1/2 lb.
Italian Dressing*	1 qt.

Method

Cook green beans only to crispness, drain but do not cool. Pour Italian dressing over green beans and marinate for 24 hours.

*ITALIAN DRESSING

Ingredients

Salad Oil	3 cups
Vinegar, cider	1 cup
Garlic Cloves, finely chopped	2
Oregano	1 tbsp.
Salt	to taste
Pepper	to taste

༈

EGGPLANT AND TUNAFISH SALAD

Yield: 1/2 gal.

Ingredients

Eggplant, fresh, medium, cubed	2
Tunafish	1 13-oz. can
Marinara Sauce*	1 qt.
Ripe Olives, sliced	1 small can
Green Olives	1 small jar

Method

Slice eggplant lengthwise 3/4 in. thick, then cut into 3/4-in. cubes. Saute in oil until tender, remove from heat, drain, and cool. When cool combine with all other ingredients and refrigerate for 24 hours. Serve.

*MARINARA SAUCE

Ingredients

Oil	1 cup
Garlic Cloves, chopped	4
Tomato Puree	1 No. 10 can
Crushed Tomatoes	1 No. 10 can

(continued)

Marinara Sauce (continued)

Oregano	1 tbsp.
Salt	to taste
Pepper	to taste

Method

Heat oil in sauce pot, add garlic, and cook until garlic starts to brown. Add tomato puree and cook for 20 min. Add crushed tomatoes and cook for another 20 min. Add oregano, salt and pepper to taste; remove from fire.

NOTE: Only half of the marinade is needed for the above recipe.

WILD TURKEY SALAD TEDDY ROOSEVELT

Yield: 10 lb. 5 oz. to 13 lb. 5 oz.

Ingredients

Smoked Turkey, whole, 12 to 14 lb.	1
Pecans	8 oz.
Celery, diced	1–2 lb.
Lemon, juice of	1
Mayonnaise	3–4 cups
Worcestershire Sauce	1 tsp.

Method

Debone turkey; dice all dark meat and one turkey breast. Save the other breast for use in salad presentation. Mix diced turkey, pecans, celery, and lemon juice. Add mayonnaise and Worcestershire sauce. Mix well. Slice remaining turkey breast as demonstrated on p. 160. Put turkey salad in a bowl and shape mound into a dome; fan slices from turkey breast over dome of salad. Decorate with ripe olives and a tomato rose.

BLACK BEANS WITH HAM

Yield: 8 lb.

Ingredients

Black Beans	2 lb.
Ham Hocks (or 2 lb. ham)	4

Bouquet Garni	1
Onion, large	1
Scallions	1 bunch
Vinegar, white	1–2 cups
Salt	to taste
Pepper	to taste
Oil	2 cups
Hard-cooked Eggs	3

Method

Soak beans in cold water for 24 hours. Pour off water and cover beans with warm water. Add ham hocks and a bouquet garni (carrots, celery, leeks). Boil until beans are soft. Remove water and bouquet garni. Remove ham hocks and cool. Chill and cube and add to beans.

Dice ham hocks, onion, and scallions; mix with black beans. Add 1 cup of vinegar, taste, and if more vinegar is needed, add gradually. Add salt, starting with 1 tablespoon of coarse salt and 1 teaspoon of pepper; add more if needed. Mix well and add oil. Marinate for 2 to 3 hours at room temperature, then put in bowl; shape bean-ham mixture like a dome and decorate with sliced eggs. Serve immediately.

SUCCOTASH

Yield: 5 lb.

Ingredients

Lima Beans, frozen	2-1/2 lb.
Baby Corn, frozen	2-1/2 lb.
Red Onion, diced	1 large
Scallions, diced	1 bunch
Vinegar, white	1-1-1/2 cups
Coarse Salt	1-1-1/2 tbsp.
Black Pepper	1/2 tsp.
Monosodium Glutamate	1/2 tsp.
Oil	1-1-1/2 cups
Red Peppers, chopped	2

Method

Cook lima beans and corn just to crispness. Saute diced onion and scallions and mix with lima beans and corn. Add 1 cup of vinegar and, if needed, add more gradually. Then season with salt, black pepper, and monosodium glutamate. Taste and, if satisfactory, add oil. Marinate for 24 hours; put in a bowl; shape like a dome and decorate with chopped red peppers.

STUFFED CUCUMBER, "TRAPPER STYLE"

Yield: 16 Cucumber Baskets

Ingredients

Cucumbers, medium	4
Coarse Salt	2 oz.

Method

Peel cucumbers and cut into 1- to 2-in. pieces. Remove centers and sprinkle with salt. Let stand one hour. Rinse well and dry.

FILLING

Yield: 16 oz.

Ingredients

Smoked Trout	8 oz.
Hard-cooked Eggs, chopped	2
Horseradish, fresh or frozen	1–2 oz.
Mayonnaise	1 tbsp.

Method

Prepare trout as described on p. 162. Filet trout and remove skin. Puree and add chopped eggs, horseradish, and mayonnaise. Adjust seasoning. Use mixture to fill cucumber baskets and top filled pieces of cucumber with ripe green olive and a sprig of dill.

NOTE: If ready-made horseradish is used, be sure to remove some of its moisture before adding to recipe.

DRIED BEEF WITH PEARS

Yield: 4 lb. 5 oz.

Ingredients

Beef, Eye of Round	6 lb.
Salt Brine*	2 gal.
Pears	8

*SALT BRINE

Water	2 gal.
Coarse Salt	2 lb.
Curing Salt	8 oz.
Sugar	2 oz.
Sachet Bag, filled with bay-leaves, thyme, peppercorn, juniper berries, basil, ginger, marjoram, sage	1

Method

Tie beef and put in brine for 24 to 48 hours. Remove from brine and hang in a cool, dry place for one day to dry. Then smoke for 14 hours with cold smoke and 2 to 3 hours with hot smoke. Cool and slice paper thin. Cut pears into wedges and alternate one slice of beef with one wedge of pear around the edge of a round tray. Decorate center with a vegetable centerpiece.

NOTE: Prosciutto Ham or Bundnerfleisch can be substituted for beef in this recipe.

PORK PIE WITH EGGS

(Jacques de Chanteloup)

Yield: 7 lb. 2 oz.

Ingredients

Pork Liver	1 lb.
Pork, boneless, not too lean	5 lb.
Garlic Cloves, small	2
Onion	1/2 lb.
Parsley	5 or 6 sprigs
Flour	5 oz.
Eggs, whole	4
Table Salt	1-1/2 oz.
Curing Salt or Saltpeter	pinch
White Pepper, ground	1/2 tsp.
Brandy	2 oz.
Cream, heavy	1/2 pt.

Method

Put liver, 1 lb. pork, garlic, onion, and parsley through fine grinder. Grind the remainder of the meat on coarse blade. Beat ground meat in mixing bowl, very slowly adding flour, eggs, seasoning, brandy, and heavy cream. Place mixture in molds or terrines lined with pork fat. Refrigerate for 24 hours. Then bake molds or terrines in oven at 350°F. until done. Before the final 15 min. of baking, remove hot fat from molds or terrines; replace it with a strong, hot aspic. Cool overnight before tasting. Slice pate and decorate with hard-cooked eggs.

❧ ❦

HUDSON VALLEY APPLES

Yield: 3 lb. 4 oz.

Ingredients

Ripe Apples	10
Langoustino	2 lb.
Apples, diced	1 lb.
Dill, chopped	2 tbsp.
Monosodium Glutamate	1/2 tsp.
Lemon, juice of	1
Mayonnaise	1–1-1/2 cups
Salt	if needed

POACHING LIQUID FOR APPLES
Formula:

Water	97 percent
Salt	1.7 percent
Vinegar or Lemon	1.3 percent
Water	2 qt.
Salt	1 oz.
Vinegar	3/4 oz.

Method

Bring poaching liquid to a boil. Peel apples, cut in half, and remove cores with a parisian scoop. Simmer apples in poaching liquid at a temperature of 170° to 180°F. for 10 to 12 min. Remove apples from liquid while still crisp and plunge at once into ice water to cool. Dry before using.

Mix langoustino, diced apple, dill, monosodium glutamate, lemon juice, and mayonnaise well. Let mixture stand for 1 hour; use to fill poached apple halves. Place remaining salad in a small bowl and arrange apple halves around it.

NOTE: Frozen langoustino should be defrosted slowly overnight. When defrosted, they should be squeezed slightly to remove some of the liquid. If langoustino are not available, use tiny, ready-cooked shrimp.

❧ ❦

MARINATED DUCK CORNELIUS VANDERBILT

Yield: 2 lb.

Ingredients

Domestic Duck, whole	1 (3–4 lb.)
Dill, fresh, chopped	4 tbsp.
Parsley, fresh, chopped	3 tbsp.
Whole Black Pepper, crushed	1/2 tsp.
Cardamom Powder	1 tsp.
Egg White Powder (Albumen)	1/2 tsp.

MARINADE

Water, cold	1 gal.
Coarse Salt	1 lb.
Sugar	3 oz.
Saltpeter (optional)	1/5 oz.
Garlic Cloves	2
Pickling Sauce	3/4 oz.

Method

Mix marinade ingredients thoroughly.

Debone duck as for galantine. Remove as much fat as possible. Place duck on a moist cheesecloth, skin side down. Add dill, parsley, pepper, cardamom, and egg white powder to duck. Roll duck into cheesecloth tightly and tie cloth at 1-in. intervals. Place in marinade and marinate no less than 4 days. After two days, boil duck in marinade for 20 min. per pound. Remove and place in stainless steel dish; pour stock over duck, and then place a heavy weight on duck to press it. Cool overnight. When ready to serve, slice duck paper thin.

NOTE: If duck becomes loose in cheesecloth after cooking, open cloth and reroll contents tightly before pressing.

❧ ❦

Marinated Duck Cornelius Vanderbilt is boned duck, placed skin side down, with dill, parsley, cardamom, and egg white powder added, then rolled tightly, wrapped in cheesecloth and marinated for 4 days. Next it is boiled or smoked, placed in bowl to cool, and a heavy weight is placed over it to press it. Then it is sliced.

DUTCH APPLE CRUMB PIE

Yield: 6 to 8 slices

Ingredients

Butter	2-1/2 oz.
Sugar	5 oz.
Egg Yolks	3
Grated Orange Peel	1 oz.
Vanilla	1 drop
Salt	1/8 tsp.
Flour	8 oz.
Baking Powder	1/5 oz.
Milk	1/4 pt.
Currants	1-3/4 oz.
Raisins	1-3/4 oz.
Egg Whites	3
Apple Wedges	18 oz.
Cake Crumbs	2-3 oz.

Method

Whip butter, sugar, egg yolks, grated orange peel, vanilla, and salt until creamy. Add flour, baking powder, milk, currants, and raisins. Whip 3 egg whites until stiff and fold into the mixture. Line a well-greased cake mold with parchment paper. Fill with mixture. Arrange apple wedges over mixture and top with cake crumbs. Bake in a pre-heated oven at 375°F. for 40 min. Remove, cool, and dust with powdered sugar.

POUNDCAKE

Yield: 2 lb. of cake batter

Ingredients

Egg Yolks	4
Sugar	1 cup
Butter *or* Shortening	1 cup
Flour	1 cup
Cream of Tartar	1/2 tsp.
Baking Soda	1/2 tsp.
Salt	1 tsp.
Milk	1 cup
Vanilla	1 tsp.
Egg Whites	4

Method

Beat egg whites until stiff; set aside. Blend sugar and shortening with egg yolks. Add flour, cream of tartar, baking soda, and salt. Add milk and mix well. Flavor with vanilla and fold in egg whites. Line a large tube pan with parchment paper and pour mixture into it. Bake in oven at 350°F. for 1 hour, 30 min.

NOTE: 1/2 tsp. baking powder can be substituted for the combined cream of tartar and baking soda.

STRAWBERRY SHORTCAKE

Yield: 6-1/2 lb.

Ingredients

Cake Flour	1-1/2 lb.
Sugar	1/2 lb.
Salt	3/4 oz.
Baking Powder	3/4 oz.
Emulsified Shortening	10 oz.
Skim Milk	1 cup (8 oz.)

Method

Mix together for 5 to 7 min. at slow speed on mixer.

Ingredients

Eggs	7
Skim Milk	1/2 pt.

Method

Blend and add to first mixture in three parts. Mix 3 to 5 min. at slow speed. Pour into a cake mold and bake in oven at 375°F. for 18 min. Cool and cut into three layers.

Ingredients

Strawberries	2 lb.
Heavy Cream, for whipping	1 qt.
Sugar	2 oz.

Method

Whip cream with sugar, blend with strawberries, reserving the necessary amount for decoration. Place whipped cream and strawberry mixture between layers. Decorate with whipped cream and strawberries that have been reserved.

BEARFOOT BREAD

Yield: 11 lb., 10 oz.

Ingredients

Cake Flour	2 lb. 8 oz.
Yellow Corn Meal	2 lb. 8 oz.
Baking Powder	5 oz.
Shortening	8 oz.
Sugar	3 oz.
Salt	2 oz.
Eggs, whole	15
Buttermilk	4 pt.

Method

Blend together and mix thoroughly cake flour, corn meal, baking powder, shortening, sugar, and salt. Add and mix until smooth the whole eggs and 2 pt. of the buttermilk. Then add rest of buttermilk in three parts, mixing well each time. Using a star tube, pipe mixture into corn stick shapes on a parchment-covered sheet pan. Bake in oven at 400°F. for 15 min. or until golden brown.

Specialties of the Garde Manger

This Austrian-German Buffet focuses attention on the food presentation that can be accomplished in the garde manger department. Chefs F. H. Sonnenschmidt (co-author of this book), B. Ellmer, and J. Heywood with students of The Culinary Institute of America created all elements of this display. Butter sculptures—the mountain goat and Lorelei set the theme. Among the dishes offered: top level: Galantine of Veal; Pate of Pheasant; Poached Salmon with Stuffed Eggs and Cucumbers; Saddle of Venison a la Diane. Lower level: Italian meat salad; carrot salad with mustard seed; chicken salad with pineapple; lobster salad; cucumber salad; Roast Sirloin of Beef circled by blue cheese roses on tomato wedges flanked by bread baskets of marinated vegetables. Chafing dishes hold Noisettes of Venison with mushrooms and Spaetzle in brown butter.

This Danish Buffet was prepared by Chefs S. Arnoldi, E. Kristensen, E. Eliason, and students of The Culinary Institute of America. Ship with figurehead, swan and shields of tallow establish the theme for the buffet. Cold foods arranged on the upper level include: herring, head cheese, smoked turkey, lobster and asparagus salad, Danish lobster tail with dill mousse. Displayed foods on the lower level are flanked by two chafing dishes, one filled with Swedish Meatballs in Dill Sauce, the other with Veal Roulades in Brown Sauce. Tray in foreground holds Smoked Tenderloin of Pork with Ham Mousse, garnished with artichokes holding cones of pureed peas. Other dishes: Pork Liver Pate in Aspic, varieties of imported herring on stand, assorted cheeses, Galantine of Eel.

The Sphinx, sculptured in tallow, reigns over the Middle East Buffet, displayed on native cloths and prepared by Chefs P. Van Erp, C. Cristodlous, and students of The Culinary Institute of America. Top level: Syrian bread; white bean salad; olives; feta cheese; meat-filled pastry triangles; baklava; and Beirut bread. Lower level: hot dishes, stuffed grape leaves; shrimp marinated on a skewer; Couscous Marga and toppings; marinated lamb and sweetbreads on skewers; cold dishes, eggplant appetizer; Arab bread; kibby; spinach-filled pastry triangles; stuffed eggplant; assorted olives; yogurt topped with fresh mint.

The grand finale for any buffet is a dessert display. Prepared by Pastry Chefs W. Schreyer, A. Kumin, and students of The Culinary Institute of America, display has as focal point a pastillage replica of the institute's main building done in a mixture of confectioner's sugar, egg white, and gelatin. Beneath it, shadow boxes frame, at left, a pulled sugar basket filled with sugar flowers and, at right, a nougat basket holding marzipan fruits. Cakes on either side are framed in marzipan and decorated with cocoa painting. Boxes made of chocolate hold pralines. The lower level displays on either end pulled sugar baskets surrounded by petit fours decorated with assorted fruits; next to basket from left—Cream Cheese Torte; Hudson Valley Apple Torte; Marzipan Roulades arranged with sugar basket filled with chocolate truffles and marzipan fruits; torte of fresh California fruits; blueberry cheesecake.

CHAPTER THREE

GARDE MANGER AREA PLANNING

LAYOUT

Arranging the layout for a garde manger department can be a complex task. Unlike other departments that can depend on a basic menu and a basic workload, the garde manger department is unique in its operation. It is often a complete foodservice facility within a larger foodservice facility. On a daily basis, the garde manger department will (or may) handle its own butchering; its own baking; its own sauce making; its own frying; its own smoking of fish, meat, and poultry; all the decorating, perhaps including tallow and ice carvings; plus a complete line of "charcuterie" products (sausages, galantines, pates, and terrines).

How does this department relate to the entire operation?
Knowing exactly how this department relates to the whole foodservice facility makes it easier to select the proper layout. The garde manger department can relate to a foodservice operation in three ways:

1. On a "pick-up" basis

2. On a "distribution" basis
3. On a combination of the two bases

What do "pick-up" and "distribution" basis mean?
When a garde manger department executes the food orders (from the waiters) on an a la carte basis, this is known as *"pick-up,"* since the waiters first place their orders, then later pick them up. This system, of necessity, operates in an unpredictable fashion (since the timing for the orders and the number of guests in the party cannot be known in advance).

This method of operation is often found in "a la carte" restaurants. Where pick-up is the system used, the workloads of the garde manger department will be set on the basis of a predetermined number of dishes that are listed on the menu. Because the menu is approximately the same each day, the "mise en place" or arrangement of the space for preparing the dishes can be determined, and the layout can be worked out properly. (See Fig. 1.)

When a garde manger department executes food orders *in advance*, for a *known quantity*, to be *delivered to a given location at a definite time* (i.e., for group feeding), this is known as the "*distribution*" basis. This situation is often found in hotels, where the garde manger department always knows about banquets, private functions, and room service requests in advance. The only drawback is that the workloads will be different each day since function and room service requests will vary as to kind and amounts of food to be prepared; therefore, it is difficult to establish an appropriate "mise en place." The layout for this kind of operation should be planned with basic preparations in mind, rather than for specific dishes. (See Fig. 2.)

How are "pick-up" and "distribution" combined?
The type of layout needed when pick-up and distribution are both in use in the same operation is shown in Fig. 3. It represents a combination of Figs. 1 and 2. This layout is appropriate when the garde manger department is located *between* an "a la carte" *dining room* and *banquet rooms*, but on the same floor. When the banquet rooms are located on a different floor, the garde manger dept. (Fig. 2) can be located by itself or in conjunction with a separate banquet kitchen on the same floor as the banquet room. When it fills a combined pick-up and distribution function, the garde manger dept. (Fig. 1) can become a part of, or be located close to, the main kitchen on the same floor with the "a la carte" dining room, and may receive some of the bulk preparation from facilities shown in Fig. 2.

REFRIGERATION

After finding out how a garde manger department relates to the whole operation (pick-up basis, distribution basis, or combination of the two), attention can be directed to the equipment needed.

Refrigeration equipment is of prime importance since without refrigeration (refrigerators, freezers, cold bain-marie, refrigerated counter tops, etc.), a garde manger department could not exist, or if it did exist, the output and

the type of dishes would have to be very limited, as foods prepared in such a department would be limited in variety and easily contaminated.

The problems of food preparation in the garde manger department are complicated by the fact that in no other department is food manipulated as often as it is there. Frequent manipulation of foodstuffs accelerates deterioration, detracts from the appearance of the finished product, as well as the odor and taste, and can lead to contamination.

To prevent these developments, it is not enough for workers to be knowledgeable about keeping hands, tools, and garments immaculately clean; there must also be proper refrigeration equipment and the worker must make proper use of it.

Anyone working on food preparation should have a good basic understanding of what refrigeration is all about and how it works. When this is understood, it will be easy to select the appropriate refrigeration or freezing unit where food is to be held and to know how to use and maintain such a unit. A table on p. 67 gives freezing, storing, and defrosting information for basic foods.

There is one basic principle of refrigeration that must be understood: cold is not created, but rather, cold is obtained by removing heat. Therefore, all refrigerators, freezers, and air-conditioning units are equipped with machinery designed for heat removal.

Basically, heat is removed from a refrigerator via the three methods of heat transfer: conduction, radiation, and convection. However, because the first two methods (conduction and radiation) occur in a negligible percentage of equipment, it can be stated that the convection method is responsible almost exclusively for removing the heat.

How does heat come into a refrigerator?
Heat enters a refrigerator in three ways:

1. Because a refrigerator has doors, it cannot be completely insulated; therefore, heat

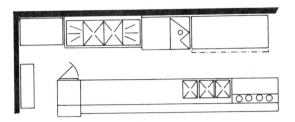

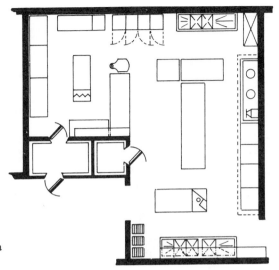

Figure 1. *Layout for garde manger department operating on an a la carte or pick-up basis.*

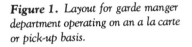

Figure 2. *This is the kind of layout used when the garde manger operates on the distribution system, preparing known quantities of food in advance.*

Figure 3. *This is the layout needed when an operation must operate on both the pick-up and distribution system.*

1. Walk-in cooler
2. Walk-in freezer
3. Sinks for foodstuffs
4. Clam and oyster sinks
5. Cooling sink
6. Pot sinks
7. Work benches
8. Chopper-bench-mixer
9. Meat saw
10. Electric blender—Work bench
11. Slicer
12. Reach-in refrigerators
13. Salad center incl. dressing and bain-marie
14. Dry food storage cabinets
15. Special equipment cabinets (Terrines-molds-etc. . . .)

16. Ice machine—Ice maker
17. Iced bain-marie
18. Steam center with floor curb and hood
19. Ranges with overhead hood
20. Overhead shelving
21. Reach-in refrigerator-freezer

22. Egg-timing machine
23. Waiter pick-up area with plate shelves below (pass-thru)
24. Mobile rackshelves

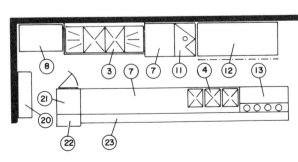

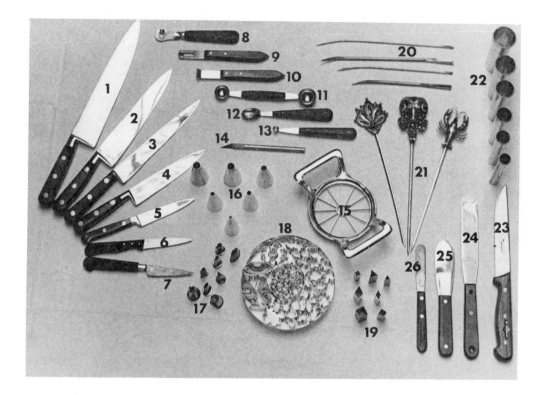

SPECIAL TOOLS AND EQUIPMENT.

In every industry today workers depend on special tools. Such tools have long been important in foodservice. For each item made by the chef or a helper, a tool is needed, and having the proper tool will not only make it easier to work, but actually is essential to proper preparation. For example, to create the various food decorations, a small paring knife is necessary; for chopping parsley, a French knife; when working with melon, a melon ball cutter. Pictured here is a collection of some of the most important tools. After collecting the must protect them as one would the hands. The experienced chef follows the rule: "Respect your working tools as you would respect yourself." The chef knows that the tool that is not properly cared for soon becomes worthless, making work harder rather than easier.

1. French knife (10 in.)
2. French knife (8 in.)
3. Chef's slicer (8 in.)
4. French knife (6 in.)
5. Paring knife, stainless (4-1/2 in.)
6. Paring knife (3-1/2 in.)
7. Paring knife (2-1/2 in.)
8. Zesteur or cester for fruit carving
9. Zesteur or cester for melon carving
10. Zesteur or cester for butter decoration and lemon or orange peeler
11. Parisian scoop (2 sizes)
12. Olivette cutter
13. Tiny parisian scoop for decorative work
14. Scalpel to cut leeks or carrots
15. Applecutter, can be used for radishes
16. Set of pastry tubes, can be used as round cutters and for truffles
17, 18, 19. Fancy aspic cutters, miniature, medium, large
20. Larding and curved sewing needle
21. Hatelets or decorative silver skewers
22. Column cutters
23. Boning knife
24. Spatula (6 in.)
25. Sandwich spreader with flexible blade
26. Spatula (2-1/2 in.), for pates and small timbales

1. *Inside Air*

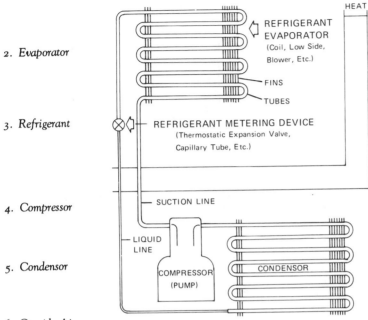

2. *Evaporator*

3. *Refrigerant*

4. *Compressor*

5. *Condensor*

6. *Outside Air*

Figure 4. *Interior of insulated enclosure.*

keeps seeping through around the doors. Although the amount of heat that gets in is not large, it seeps in steadily.

2. When food is placed in a refrigerator, the food itself introduces a certain amount of heat, especially if the food has been stored at temperatures above 72°F.

3. The frequency of door opening is another source by which heat "walks in" the refrigerator.

The Refrigeration Cycle

Heat is removed from a refrigerator through a series of heat transfers; this is known as the refrigeration cycle. Specifically, there are four elements involved in the process of heat transfer:

1. The evaporator
2. The refrigerant
3. The compressor
4. The condensor

The refrigeration cycle goes through the following phases: (See Fig. 4.)

1. Heat present in a refrigerator is dispersed throughout the air in the unit.

2. As it rises, the air then transfers the added heat to the evaporator, which is made out of tubing surrounded by fins. The fins have many surfaces which collect the heat and then transfer it to the refrigerant flowing in the tubing.

3. The refrigerant carries the heat to the compressor. The refrigerant is a gas that expands as it collects the heat.

4. The compressor (which is a pump) removes the heat from the refrigerant by compressing it back to its original volume and, in turn, the compressor transfers the heat to a condensor.

5. The condensor collects the heat in its tubing and it then transfers the heat to the numerous

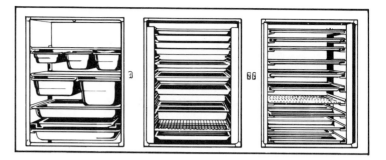

Figure 5. *Refrigerator storage space—for pans (left); for bakery products (center); for varied foods (right).*

surfaces of the fins surrounding the tubing. At that point, a fan blows the heat out of the refrigerator.

6. The now compressed, cold refrigerant returns to the evaporator to collect more heat, and the cycle takes place again and again.

Depending on the type of refrigerator, various engineering methods are used to complete the refrigeration cycle. Some condensors are water-cooled. In this case, heat is transferred to the water which carries the heat along to a drain or, again, back to the evaporator where it evaporates.

What makes a good refrigerator?

A good refrigerator is one that is engineered to keep a:

1. *Constant* appropriate temperature
2. *Constant* relative humidity
3. *Constant* air flow

Constant appropriate temperature is achieved through:

1. Insulation
2. Door gasket or lining
3. Door "hardware," mainly the lock and/or hinges

Providing proper humidity in a refrigerator depends on the following process. Like a sponge holding water, air holds water vapor, or moisture; the warmer the air in a refrigerator, the more moisture it will hold with absolute humidity at 100%. However, the cold air in a refrigerator only holds a certain percentage of moisture and most food will respond well to an 80% to 85% relative humidity. When the relative humidity is too low (below 80%), the dry cold air will begin to absorb humidity from the moisture contained in certain foods, causing these foodstuffs to discolor, dry up, and "crack." When the relative humidity is too high (above 80%), the air in the refrigerator will release some of its moisture, and dry foodstuffs will become soggy or shiny or covered with "sweat" (condensation).

Unless a refrigerator is designated to contain only one type of food, it is difficult to control the relative humidity. Most stored foods, if they are of the heterogeneous type (some dry and some moist), will be affected by the relative humidity. This is why some refrigerators are designed to contain a homogeneous type of food (all dry and/or all moist items—for example, dough or meat, respectively). (See Fig. 5.)

Air flow is important because foodstuffs do not respond well to a "stagnant climate." Natural air movement exists inside a refrigerator but, depending on how the food is being stored, some containers may "block" air movement and prevent other foods from getting proper air circulation. For this reason, modern refrigerators use "forced air" circulation, produced by a fan located in the vicinity of the evaporator. Well-designed air circulation is also found in refrigerators equipped with a louvered vertical "shaft" that can distribute the air through all of the shelves, no matter how the food is stored. (See Fig. 6.)

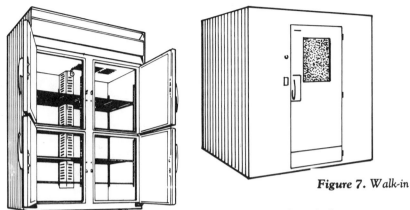

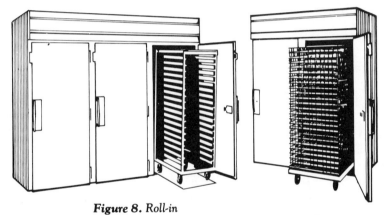

Figure 7. *Walk-in*

Figure 6. *Louvered air shaft*

Figure 8. *Roll-in*

Figure 8. (*alternate view*)

Because there are so many refrigerator designs on the market, only a few basic designs and their suggested purposes can be listed here:

"Walk-ins" (Fig. 7) are excellent for storing food in bulk (usually found in main storage areas).

"Roll-ins" (Fig. 8) are similar to "walk-ins," but are equipped with a small ramp at the door to the area to allow hand trucks and mobile shelves to be wheeled in. These are excellent for quantity storage of pre-portioned food (especially for high-volume operations).

When used for such storage, there should be three compartments (three doors), one for dairy, one for meat, one for vegetable; dairy and vegetable products can be combined, as these products usually are kept at the same temperature.

"Reach-ins" *with full-length doors* (Fig. 9) are excellent for storage in small operations, or as "hold" refrigerators for foods to be held

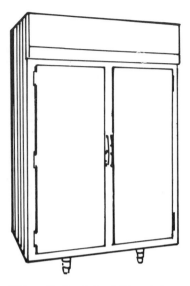

Figure 11. *Pull-out*

Figure 10. *Half-length door*

Figure 9. *Reach-in, full-length door*

in temporary storage awaiting further preparation steps.

"Reach-ins" with half-length doors (Fig. 10) are excellent when heterogeneous types of food are used within the same preparation area, also for heterogeneous portions of prepared foods that have to be located in the immediate vicinity of cooking appliances for processing "to order."

"Pass-throughs" with full- or half-length doors are excellent when located between preparation and service areas.

"Pull-outs" (Fig. 11) are excellent when refrigerator must have mobility from one area to another. This design prevents spillage while in motion as these units are usually portable and travel from the production area to a service area.

All the above-mentioned refrigerators are designed with swinging doors (right- or left-hinged) or sliding doors. Sliding doors, also available in a solid- or glazed-type glass door, make it easy to locate a specified food without having to open the doors unnecessarily.

Storing and Thawing Frozen Foods

Foodstuffs	For Freezing	Storage	Defrosting
BAKERY			
Bread	Very good	2–4 months	At room temperature or in 300°F. oven
Rolls	Very good		Heat in oven (low temperature)
BEEF—Cuts Not			
Listed Below	Very good	Up to 12 months	At room temperature
Bones	Good	6–8 months	Use frozen
Chopped beef	Good	4–6 months	In refrigerator
Liver	Good	3–6 months	Do not defrost; cook frozen
Stew meat	Good	4–6 months	In refrigerator
DAIRY PRODUCTS			
Butter	Very good	8–10 months	Refrigerator
Egg without shell	Good	8–10 months	In refrigerator
Egg yolk	Good	8–10 months	In refrigerator
Egg white	Very good	10–12 months	In refrigerator
FISH			
Fat Fish (Mackerel, Herring, or Salmon)	Good	1–3 months	Whole frozen fish should be defrosted in cold water
Filet of Fish (Sole or Haddock)	Very good	3–4 months	Do not defrost, just wash and cook
Lean Fish (Trout or Cod)	Very good	4–6 months	Defrost in cold water
Smoked Fish		1–2 months	In refrigerator
GAME			
Birds	Very good	8–10 months	Defrost at room temperature
Meat	Very good	Up to 12 months	Put frozen in marinade
HERBS (in an aluminum pouch)			
Fresh	Very good	8–10 months	Use frozen
PATE (Maison)	Good	2–3 months	In refrigerator
PORK—Cuts Not			
Listed Below	Very good	6–8 months (If very fat, not over 4 months)	At room temperature
Fatback	Good	4–6 months	At room temperature
Sausages	Good	4–6 months (If strongly seasoned, not over 3 months)	At room temperature

Storing and Thawing Frozen Foods (*Continued*)

Foodstuffs	For Freezing	Storage	Defrosting
POULTRY			
Broilers	Very good	8–10 months	Remove from wrappings
Capon	Very good	8–10 months	Defrost at room temperature
Duck	Good	4–6 months	Defrost at room temperature
Other	Very good	8–10 months	Defrost at room temperature
VEAL	Good	6–8 months	At room temperature
VEGETABLES			
Asparagus	Very good	10–12 months	In boiling water
Button Mushrooms	Good	6–8 months	While cooking
Cabbage (Savoy)	Good	10–12 months	While cooking
Carrots (sliced)	Very good	10–12 months	While cooking
Cauliflower	Good	8–10 months	In boiling water
Corn	Very good	10–12 months	While cooking
Cucumber (sliced)	Very good	6–8 months	Defrost in marinade
Green Pepper	Very good	6–8 months	At room temperature
Peas	Excellent	10–12 months	In boiling water
Spinach	Excellent	10–12 months	While cooking
String Beans	Excellent	10–12 months	In boiling water

CHAPTER FOUR

ASPIC-GELEE-CHAUD-FROID

Aspic and gelee play an important part in the preparation of many of the cold dishes created in the garde manger department. The glistening coating or sparkling bases supplied by aspic and gelee highlight the ingredients being presented. Proper preparation and application of aspic and gelee is essential to assure maximum impact for a large piece of meat or fish or a whole fowl or fish.

ASPIC AND GELEE

In American cuisine there is usually no distinction between aspic and gelee. In continental cuisine, however, a gelee, or jelly, is a gelatinous meat or fish stock. A gelee becomes an aspic gelee or aspic jelly when it is clarified. The word *aspic* is used to refer to a combination of cold meat, fish, vegetables, eggs, etc. placed in a mold to form a decorative arrangement that is then covered with aspic jelly. When thoroughly chilled, the arrangement is unmolded on a silver platter and surrounded with aspic jelly croutons.

The aspic jelly must always be crystal clear and of a light, golden color. The quantity of

gelatin used in the aspic jelly should be well proportioned so that the jelly, when set, is neither too firm nor too light in consistency. The aspic jelly provides special protection for cold dishes. A display of poultry, fish, game, or other ingredients when covered with aspic jelly will keep its original flavor and freshness for a longer period.

The making of a fresh aspic jelly is elaborate and in modern kitchens is often considered very time consuming. However, aspic jelly can be bought commercially in powdered form and can be used with acceptable results when time does not allow the preparation of fresh aspic jelly.

How do you prepare aspic jelly?
The preparation of an aspic jelly consists of several steps:

1. A stock must be made using gelatinous products, such as veal bones, calves' feet, pork skin, etc.
2. The reduction and clarification of the stock and the addition of aromatic products (vegetables, wines, seasonings) must be accomplished next.

That crimson crustacean, Alaska King Crab, presides
over an arrangement of aspic-coated and framed slices of
crab mousse decorated with a half tip of white asparagus,
sliced lengthwise, with a circle of truffle sheet at the base.
Toast-hatted egg penguins in a row in the middle and crab
claws cleverly arranged on small socles add a humorous
note to this prize-winning display.

3. Finally, the jelly must be tested to determine the consistency when cold.

NOTE: Today's modern chef may use well-known savoury jelly brands.

WHITE ASPIC JELLY

Yield: 1 gal.

Ingredients

Veal Bones, cut into small pieces	3 lb.
Calves' Feet, split in half lengthwise	2
Pork Skin	8 oz.
Veal Shank	1
Beef Chuck	2 lb.
Carrots	3–4
Onions, medium	2
Leeks, white portion	2
Celery	2 pcs.
Water	6 qt.
Salt, Pepper, Sachet Bag	

Method

Blanch the bones, calves' feet, and pork skin. Rinse well in cold water. Place in a pot and add veal shank and beef. Cover with water and bring to a boil.

Skim boiling liquid, then add all the vegetables and seasonings. Cook for 5 to 6 hours on low heat. Pour stock through a strainer, cool, remove all fat. Reduce stock to 1 gallon.

CLARIFICATION FOR 1 GALLON STOCK

Ingredients

Beef, lean ground	1 lb.
Leeks, Celery, Onion, finely diced	8 oz.
Egg Whites	2
Cold Stock	1 gal.
Madeira, Port, or Sherry	1-1/2 cups

Method

Mix other ingredients well, then add one gallon of cold stock. Bring to a boil, stirring occasionally with a wooden spoon.

Simmer for 1/2 to 1 hour and strain through a cheesecloth. Add 1-1/2 cups of Madeira, port, or sherry wine. In order to know the consistency of gelatin contained in the gelee, a sample should be refrigerated. If it sets to desired consistency, the aspic jelly is ready to be used. If the jelly is to be used to make aspic molds, it is necessary to add an extra amount of unflavored gelatin that has been dissolved in water or wine.

Variations

The above recipe produces clear aspic with practically no color. A light to dark golden aspic can be obtained by using a brown stock. For this stock, brown the bones, meat, and vegetables and proceed in the same manner described for white aspic jelly.

For poultry aspic jelly, substitute chicken or other fowl bones for veal bones and shank. A game aspic jelly can be obtained by using veal bones with game bones added for special flavor.

Whatever the aspic to be produced, it is only necessary to brown the appropriate bones and then follow the recipe for white aspic jelly.

ASPIC OR MEAT JELLY (*Commercial*)

Yield: 3 qt.

Ingredients

Beef, lean, chopped	12 oz.
Celery, Onion, Leeks, finely diced	1 cup
Parsley Stems	2–3
Tarragon Sprigs (fresh or dried) (If fresh or dried chervil is available, use instead of tarragon)	2
Black Peppercorns	1 tsp.
Salt	1–2 tsp.
Egg Whites	5–6

(continued)

Aspic or Meat Jelly (*continued*)

Gelatin	3–4 oz.
Meat Stock (Chicken, Veal, or Beef)	3 qt.

How to Clarify the Aspic

1. In a large pot, put the beef and mirepoix of celery, onions, and leeks together with parsley, tarragon, peppercorns, salt, egg whites, and the gelatin. Mix well. Add meat stock and fold into the mixture.
2. Heat slowly just to the point of simmering. Agitate the pot gently, either by shaking or by stirring slowly with a wooden spoon, so that the ingredients will be thoroughly mixed with the liquid. Simmer 30–40 min.
3. Remove from heat and let rest for 5–10 min. so the raft can settle to the bottom of the pot.
4. Carefully ladle aspic through a fine sieve or a strainer lined with cheesecloth. At this time adjust the seasoning.
5. Cool in the refrigerator, remove fat, and melt aspic before using.

NOTE: If fish stock is used, use herbs and egg whites only for clarification. If a golden color is desired, add 1 cup of finely diced carrots.

How to Prepare Aspic Croutons

Pour some of the clarified, chilled liquid aspic into a sheetpan, filling it approximately 1/2 in. thick. Let it set. This aspic sheet has to be very cold and firm (hard) before it can be used.

NOTE: Make sure there are no air bubbles present in the liquid aspic. For garnitures, cut the hard aspic sheet into large squares, triangles, serrated half-moons, stars, diamonds, or plain half-moons. The aspic can also be diced (finely or coarsely) to arrange along borders of display pieces or to use to fill in bare spots on platter.

How to Make Aspic Color Sheets

For decoration, or as background for various food presentations, aspic color sheets are very effective. The recipe that follows is considered a basic formula and can, therefore, be used for all kinds of color sheets. A list of the colors that can be created follows the recipe.

ORANGE ASPIC SHEETS

Size of Sheet: 14–17 inches

Ingredients

Pimento, canned	3-1/2 oz.
Water	3/4 cup
Salt	pinch
Unflavored Gelatin	1 oz.

Method

Combine pimento and warm water in blender; puree to a fine paste. Slowly add salt and plain gelatin and mix together well. Remove from blender into a small pot and place in hot water-bath for 2 or 3 min. to remove the air bubbles. Then pour onto a slightly oiled, half-size sheet-pan and cool.

Variations

For other colors use the above recipe, substituting one of the following for the pimento.

For red aspic, use 1/2 pimento, 1/2 tomato paste.

For yellow aspic, use boiled egg yolks.

For white aspic, use boiled egg whites.

For green aspic, use blanched or frozen spinach.

For light green aspic, use fresh watercress or spinach.

For black aspic, use truffle peelings.

For brown aspic, use a mixture of half glace de viande and half aspic.

NOTE: If the mixture is too thick, add aspic jelly until desired thickness is derived. Wine can also be added.

Why True Blue Is Not Suitable

In working out color formulas for aspic sheets, one color is not used; "true blue" is not considered suitable for edible foods because:

1. Blue is not found in natural products, therefore, artificial color would have to be used. Artificial colors may run into other colors and, therefore, are avoided by professionals.

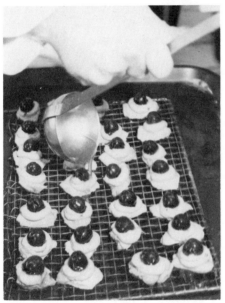

Medallion of Veal. To prepare, cut filet of veal into round slices, 1–2 in. thick and about 1 in. diameter. Season and saute. Chill. When cold, pipe a circle of turkey liver pate (see Pate) around the veal medallion; place a fresh or canned black cherry on top and cover with a coat of clear aspic. A centerpiece for the platter of medallions can be prepared to fit the theme of the buffet. For a Polynesian buffet, a tree can be made from carrots and a green pepper. Left: For best results, never touch refrigerated aspic; always use a ladle when dipping aspic out of the container it is stored in.

Aspic croutons can be cut in many shapes and they can also be diced as in dish at left or chopped into finer sizes as in dish at right.

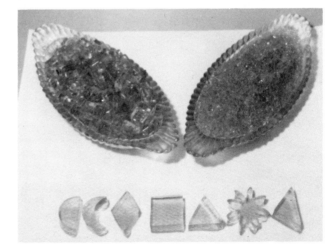

This bouquet of flowers was created from pieces of egg yolk, pimentos, radish skins, truffle-colored aspic, and leeks.

Pieces of aspic that have been colored with pimento were arranged to make this striking red lobster.

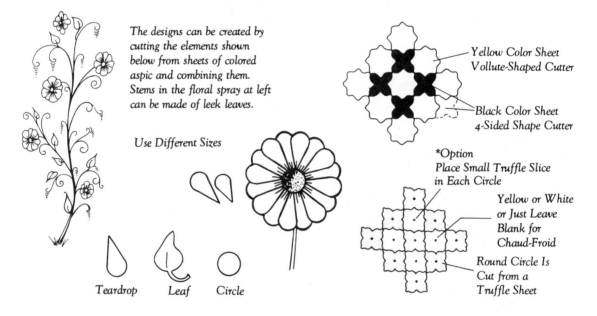

The designs can be created by cutting the elements shown below from sheets of colored aspic and combining them. Stems in the floral spray at left can be made of leek leaves.

Use Different Sizes

Teardrop   Leaf   Circle

Yellow Color Sheet
Vollute-Shaped Cutter

Black Color Sheet
4-Sided Shape Cutter

*Option
Place Small Truffle Slice
in Each Circle

Yellow or White
or Just Leave
Blank for
Chaud-Froid

Round Circle Is
Cut from a
Truffle Sheet

2. Even if blue were found in natural products, it would not be used because of its adverse psychological effect on diners. (Can you imagine eating blue potato salad or blue egg salad?)

3. The only way to get a color approximating blue is to blanch red beets or the leaves of red cabbage in water and vinegar, but when used the moisture might be absorbed by the product covered, which could ruin the effect of the decoration. Both red cabbage and beets run.

FISH ASPIC JELLY

A fish aspic jelly is obtained by first clarifying a reduced fish fumet (a reduced fish stock) and adding either white or red wine to it, the choice depending on the use to be made of the jelly.

The chaud-froid coating highlights colorful decorations made from pieces cut from sheets of colored aspic. Design on left was made from truffle sheet, egg sheet, and pimento sheet. Center: truffle sheet, skin of tomatoes, and dill. Right: truffle and egg sheets. Decorated chaud-froid items should always be given a coat of clear aspic as a finishing touch. The aspic adds sparkle to the designs.

CHAUD-FROID

A popular cold sauce used extensively in the garde manger is the chaud-froid sauce. The French word "chaud-froid" means "hot-cold," as the sauce is prepared hot, but used cold.

There are several types of chaud-froid and their usage is different:

1. Classical chaud-froid
   a. Red chaud-froid
   b. Green chaud-froid
2. Cream sauce chaud-froid
3. Mayonnaise chaud-froid
4. Brown chaud-froid

CLASSICAL CHAUD-FROID SAUCE

This chaud-froid is used to coat meat products, especially poultry, galantines, but mostly pieces of white meat. If well prepared, this chaud-froid will enhance the flavor and the presentation of the displays.

Yield: 2 qt.

Ingredients

Veal Stock*	1 qt.
Heavy Cream	1 qt.
Unflavored Gelatin	1/2–1 oz.
Salt	1/3 tsp.
Hot Pepper Sauce	3 drops
Egg Yolks	3

*VEAL STOCK

Veal Bones	6 lb.
Carrots	2
Celery	3 stalks
Parsley Stems	4
Wine	1/2 bottle
Salt	1/2–1 oz.
Peppercorns	2 tsps.
Lemon, juice of	2
Garlic Cloves	2

Method

To make veal stock for chaud-froid, cut 6 lb. of veal bones into small pieces, blanch, and wash in cold water.

Brown bones with carrots, celery, and parsley stems. Deglaze with 1/2 bottle of white wine. Add salt, peppercorns, juice of two lemons, and two cloves of garlic. Place mixture in a stock pot, and cover with water. Simmer for four hours, then strain stock through a cheesecloth.

Reduce the veal stock to 1 qt.

Add 1-1/3 pt. of heavy cream in which 1/2 to 1 oz. of gelatin powder has been diluted. Season with salt and hot pepper sauce. Simmer sauce 5–10 min.

Make liaison with the remaining cream and egg yolks. Add to the chaud-froid sauce. Strain sauce through a cheesecloth, and cool to the desired consistency.

✥✥

CHAUD-FROID NO. 2

Due to the shortage of personnel in most kitchens, and in order to save time, the following recipe is a good substitute for the Classical Chaud-Froid.

Yield: 3 qts.

Ingredients

Butter	4 oz.
Flour	4 oz.
Aspic Jelly	2 qts.
Heavy Cream	20 oz.
Salt	1/3 tsp.

Method

Prepare a roux with butter and flour. Add aspic, mix well, and stir until the sauce comes to a boil. Simmer for 15 min. on low fire.

Add cream and reduce sauce for 5 min. on low flame. Season with salt and strain through a cheesecloth.

NOTE: If this chaud-froid is used for ham, add 1/2 cup of sherry wine. When cooling the sauce, be sure to stir occasionally to prevent formation of skin.

ક્ષ ⁀ષ્ટ

CHAUD-FROID TOMATE
(Red Chaud-Froid)

Yield: 1 qt.

Ingredients

Chaud-Froid Sauce	1 qt.
Tomato Paste	2 tbsp.
Hungarian Paprika	1/2 tbsp.
Heavy Cream	1 oz.

Method

Use ready-made chaud-froid sauce to which tomato paste is added. Mix paprika with cream and add to the sauce.

ક્ષ ⁀ષ્ટ

CHAUD-FROID VERT
(Green Chaud-Froid)

Yield: 1 qt.

Ingredients

Classical Chaud-Froid Sauce	1 qt.
Fresh Spinach Leaves or Green Asparagus	7 oz.

Method

In a blender, puree spinach or asparagus with a little chaud-froid and bring to a fast boil. Strain through a cheesecloth, add to remaining chaud-froid. It is important to cool this sauce rapidly as it may lose its green color and turn greyish.

ક્ષ ⁀ષ્ટ

CREAM SAUCE CHAUD-FROID

Yield: 5 qt.

Ingredients

Flour	8 oz.
Shortening	8 oz.
Milk, boiling	1 gal.
Unflavored Gelatin	1 cup
Salt	1 to 2 oz.

Method

Make a roux with shortening and flour. Add boiling milk and mix until thick and smooth. Cool sauce for 5 min. and slowly pour in 1 cup of high-bloom unflavored gelatin powder.

NOTE: The cream sauce chaud-froid is a white sauce, generally used on nonedible displays for exhibitions and dummy show pieces for buffets. There are several methods for preparing chaud-froid for nonedible displays. Some chefs simply mix light cream with unflavored gelatin. Others use sour cream, cream cheese with water, and unflavored gelatin. These methods give excellent results as far as the whiteness of chaud-froid is concerned; however, it is better to keep the cost of this type of chaud-froid to the minimum by using the above recipe.

Mayonnaise Chaud-Froid or
Mayonnaise Collee

A mayonnaise chaud-froid is made by mixing one part of mayonnaise with one part of cold liquid aspic jelly. Do not whip, as bubbles may form. Mayonnaise chaud-froid is usually used to coat fish.

If the mayonnaise is freshly prepared, it is important to use the chaud-froid as soon as it has reached the right consistency. A mayonnaise

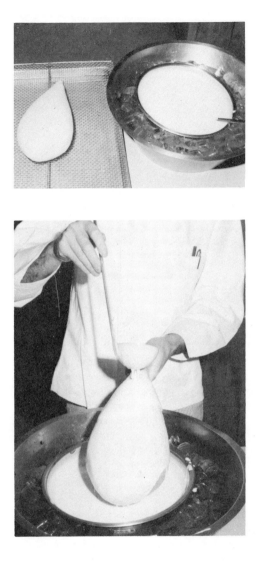

Items to be coated with chaud-froid sauce should be smooth and well chilled. Here a ham has been placed on a wire rack with a clean pan under it to catch overflow of coating. Melt chaud-froid sauce and set container in an ice-filled pan to cool. Chaud-froid must be stirred frequently while it chills to prevent lumps from forming (top left).

Using a ladle, coat object evenly and swiftly, being careful not to let ladle touch surface. Set in refrigerator to set. Repeat this step if another coat seems necessary.

When coating has chilled and set, cover with a coat of clear aspic and the surface will be ready for decorating. Note frill on ham, first step in decorating.

chaud-froid containing fresh mayonnaise is apt to break if reheated. A mayonnaise chaud-froid containing commercially made mayonnaise can be reheated safely, if necessary.

Brown Chaud-Froid
A brown chaud-froid consists of:

    1/3 Glace de Viande

    1/3 Aspic Jelly

    1/3 Tomato Sauce

Melt glace de viande with aspic jelly and combine with tomato sauce. Generally, brown chaud-froid is flavored with Madeira or sherry wine and is used to coat roast meats (beef, pork, turkey, etc.).

How do you use chaud-froid sauce?
The method of application of a chaud-froid sauce on cold foods plays an important role in the success of a finished food platter. The temperature of the chaud-froid will determine the con-

Prior to decorating a ham, it should be covered with chaud-froid sauce. The chaud-froid holds decorations on the ham and also helps preserve the flavor of the meat. After coating the ham, layer thin slices of ham around it, leaving the top of the ham as an oval of white chaud-froid.

To create designs such as this Statue of Liberty, first trace the desired design on a sheet of parchment paper with a soft lead pencil. Then press parchment against the cold chaud-froid to mark outline of design. To fill in the picture, melt down colored aspic sheets and use liquid to "paint" within the outline. A border of half moon aspic cut-outs frames the decoration. Thin slices of ham rolled around pickles are arranged to complete the display.

sistency of the sauce. A hot chaud-froid is light in consistency but when cooled becomes thicker and will congeal if kept under refrigeration or on ice. The sauce should be placed in a double boiler to melt.

When applying a chaud-froid sauce, several steps must be followed in order to be successful:

1. The food to be coated should have a smooth surface and be held in the refrigerator.
2. The item to be coated should be placed on a wire rack with a sheetpan underneath it.
3. When chaud-froid is at the right consistency, ladle it over the food item. The method of application may have to be adjusted depending on the food product. A flat smooth surface, such as turbot or sole, can easily be coated with a mayonnaise chaud-froid just by pouring the chaud-froid over the surface. Due to their shapes, ham, turkey, galantine, etc., cannot be coated as easily. To obtain the best results, it is necessary to coat the sides of the item first, then the top.
4. During the process, the chaud-froid will have to be reheated in a double boiler, then cooled on ice, to reach the right thickness.
5. The item covered with chaud-froid should be refrigerated for a few minutes to allow the coating to congeal, then a second coating can be applied.
6. A chaud-froid coating should be smooth and not too thick. Generally, two coatings, sometimes three, are sufficient. If lumpy chaud-froid has been used, remove coating and start all over.
7. The excess sauce that accumulates on the sheetpan can be used again.

There are several advantages to be gained from covering food items with chaud-froid sauce:

Pate en croute is sliced, then each slice is coated with clear aspic. Aspic preserves the appearance and flavor of cold foods.

Aspic, timbale, and barquette molds come in many shapes and sizes: 1. cornet holder for forming ham and salami rolls; 2. heart-shaped aspic mold; 3. small timbale for liver mousse; 4. large aspic mold; 5. timbales for small aspic molds, spinach, eggs, etc.; 6. large aspic mold; 7. rectangular aspic mold; 8. variety of barquette molds; 9. decorative aspic mold.

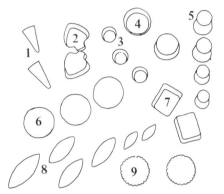

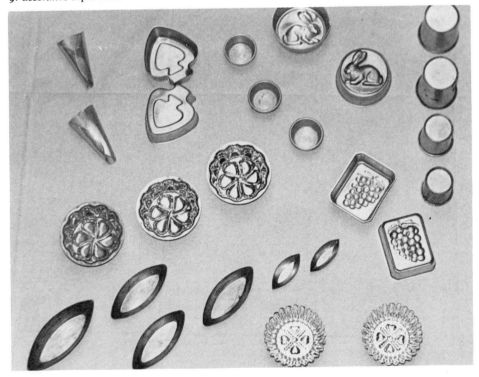

1. The sauce preserves the food for a longer period of time, providing the whole surface is covered.
2. The smoothness of the chaud-froid coating can provide the base for a large variety of decorations.
3. Nonedible products can be used inconspicuously to save the cost of food. For example, a styrofoam ham or turkey can be covered with chaud-froid and used as a background display on a buffet table.

CHAPTER FIVE

APPETIZERS-
HORS D'OEUVRE

"*Faire manger les sans appetit, faire briller l'esprit de ceux qui en out et faire trouver a ceux qui en desirent, est le supreme role des Hors d'Oeuvre.*" (To those who are not hungry...to perk up the spirit of some and to give spirit to others who are without it, this is the major task of the appetizers on a menu.)

Hors d'oeuvre is a French expression and its true definition is: a preparation served outside of the menu proper, at the beginning of a meal before the main course. Therefore, the hors d'oeuvre must be a small tidbit; it should be light, attractive, very delicate, and tasty. Hors d'oeuvre should not be spelled with a final *s*, since there is no plural form of the word in French.

There are four main types of hors d'oeuvre:

1. Cold hors d'oeuvre
2. Hot hors d'oeuvre
3. Zakuski
4. Canapes (hot and cold)

What is a cold hors d'oeuvre?
The cold hors d'oeuvre can be divided into two categories:

1. The ready to serve variety, available in today's market in every conceivable type and form (like antipasto, smoked or pickled fish, sausages, etc.).
2. Those that require culinary preparation and that, when made properly, have the advantage of being freshly prepared from fresh ingredients with maximum flavor and appeal. This is where fine cuisine can make a very important contribution to eating pleasure.

Cold hors d'oeuvre are also broken into further classifications:

1. Hors d'oeuvre frequently served at luncheons and generally known as *Hors d'Oeuvre a la Francaise*. This variety is served in small oval, oblong, or square dishes called *raviers*. The basic qualification of an Hors d'Oeuvre a la Francaise is that all of it be edible, and included are small salads made from meat, fish, vegetables, eggs, as well as various ham, sausage, or marinated fish dishes.
2. The hors d'oeuvre served before the meal.

The luncheon hors d'oeuvre is part of the meal and has its place in the proper sequence of dishes served at the meal, while the dinner hors d'oeuvre is usually served with cocktails at a time prior to the meal and is not a part of the menu served. It is of vital importance that the chef be given the proper time before service so that all the hors d'oeuvre may be prepared properly.

What are hot hors d'oeuvre?
Hot hors d'oeuvre are generally served at a cocktail party or before a dinner, but seldom if ever are served with a luncheon. Although there are some hot appetizers that could be considered classical, there are many others that are strictly prototype and serve as a basis for many different preparations. As a matter of fact, every branch of cookery, when reduced to tidbit proportions, is or could be used in the preparation of hot hors d'oeuvre.

For example, from the pastry department we can secure the Paillettes or Allumettes, the Beignets or Frittes, Bouchees, Croustades, Petits Pates, the Rissoles, the Ramequins, or the ever classic Quiche Lorraine.

From the saucier and the entremetier, we can get the Attereaux, one of the first hot hors d'oeuvre belonging to the old school of cookery. These are delicious when served in small morsels. The Beurrecks, which are of Turkish origin; the Blinis for caviar consumption; the oysters, Casino or Rockefeller; the souffles and, of course, the Cromesquis or Croquettes, and many other commercial preparations help to round out the endless list of hot hors d'oeuvre. While not essential to a meal, they are nevertheless the first contact the guests make with the culinary performance of the operation. The impression made by their preparation and presentation is the basis for the guests' expectations of the dinner.

What are Zakuski?
In the 1890s, Zakuski, or in other words, canapes a la Russe, became very popular. These cold hors d'oeuvre of the canape variety are classical, made up of certain specified ingredients; one of these is made of toast covered with smoked fish and finished with a thin gelee or aspic. Their presentation is left to the originality of the chef. Zakuski are essentially dinner hors d'oeuvre and are larger in size than the average canape.

How do you define the cold canape?
These tiny open-faced sandwiches are cut into rectangular, round or other shapes, the size and thickness depending on the nature of the ingredients used. Cold canapes are mostly made of toasted bread, crackers, or pumpernickel, covered with various butter spreads and topped with various accompaniments. As labor is the important factor in making cold canapes, this type of hors d'oeuvre should be ordered as early as possible. In costing the canape, the price of labor should also be considered. In the past years, canapes, hot or cold, have become very popular and are usually served at cocktail parties or other gatherings to foster the drinking of cocktails.

ARTICHOKE HEARTS A LA GRECQUE

Yield: 16 servings

Ingredients

Carrots	3
Shallots	8
Olive Oil	1 cup
Artichoke Hearts, raw	16
Bouquet Garni	1
White Wine	4 cups
Chicken Stock	2 cups
Salt	to taste
Black Peppercorns, crushed	1/2 to 1 tsp.
Coriander Seeds	12
Lemons	juice of 2

Method
Cut the carrots and shallots into small dice, and saute them in 4 tbsp. olive oil for 15 min. When soft, add the raw artichoke hearts, the bouquet garni, the wine and the stock; season with salt and peppercorns; add coriander and lemon juice. Cover and simmer for about 30 min.

When the artichoke hearts are tender, remove from heat; add the rest of the oil and let stand for 2 hours. Remove the artichoke hearts, carrots and shallots; place in a crock. Discard bouquet garni, strain the liquid and reduce to 1-1/2 cups; allow to cool. Pour over artichokes and serve cold.

TOMATOES STUFFED WITH MUSSELS

Yield: 4 servings

Ingredients

Ripe Tomatoes, medium	4
Salt	pinch
Black Pepper, freshly ground	1/3 tsp.
Mussels (see recipe on this page for mussel preparation; omit curry)	1-1/4 lb.
Mayonnaise	3/4 cup
Chervil and Dill, combined	1 tbsp.
Lemon, cut in wedges	1
Parsley Sprigs	4

Method

Cut tops off tomatoes; scoop out insides; sprinkle cavities with salt and pepper. Prepare mussels, remove from shells; cool them in their liquid. When mussels have cooled, drain them and mix together with mayonnaise. Use mixture to stuff tomatoes, cover with tops; sprinkle tops of stuffed tomatoes with fine chopped herbs; serve with lemon wedges and a sprig of parsley. NOTE: Tomatoes may be blanched and peeled.

MUSHROOMS A LA GRECQUE

Yield: 24 oz.

Ingredients

Use recipe for Artichoke Hearts a la Grecque. Substitute 2 lb. of whole mushrooms for artichokes and reduce cooking time by 15 min.

MUSSEL SALAD A LA BOMBAY

Yield: 3–4 servings

Ingredients

Mussels	1-1/4 lb.
Shallots, chopped	1-1/2 tbsp.
Dry White Wine	1/2 cup
Parsley Stalks	2 to 3
Black Pepper, crushed	1/2 to 1 tsp.
Mild Curry	1 oz.
Mayonnaise	3/4 cup

Method

Clean the mussels, put in large kettle together with the shallots, wine, parsley stalks, pepper and 3/4 oz. curry. Cover and cook over high heat for 5–10 min. until shells are open. Remove mussels from shells, strain the liquid, cool and store mussels in stock.

When using mussels for a la Bombay, mix mussels with mayonnaise, remaining curry and a little of the stock. Serve with croutons in a glass dish.

MUSSELS IN MUSTARD SAUCE (*Moules a la Moutarde*)

Yield: 4 portions

Ingredients

Mayonnaise	4 oz.
French Mustard	1 oz.
Celery, finely diced	4 oz.
Mussels	8 oz.
Lemon Juice	a few drops
Radish Rose	1

Method

Combine mayonnaise, mustard, celery, and mussels. Flavor with lemon juice. Serve in a shallow dish, decorated with a radish rose.

Canapes: Assembled on the tray, from left to right—croutons (first row) topped with apricot marmalade, liver pate, and truffle dot; (second row) oyster butter, slice of hard-cooked egg, smoked oyster, and a pimento strip; (third row) parsley butter, cornet of salami, and gherkins; (fourth row) mustard butter, ham, and radishes; (fifth row) cream cheese and truffle slices; (sixth row) green butter, sardine, and truffle dot.

AVOCADO SALAD, MEXICAN STYLE

Yield: 4 portions

Ingredients

Lobster, diced	1/2 cup
King Crabmeat, diced	1/2 cup
Romaine Lettuce, shredded	1 cup
Capers	4 tsp.
Mayonnaise	4 tbsp.
Lemon	juice of 1
Black Pepper, freshly ground	1/2 tsp.
Avocados, large	2
Parsley, chopped	3 tsp.
Lobster Coral	2 tsp.

Method

Mix the diced seafood with the shredded romaine and the capers. Bind salad with mayonnaise, lemon juice, and pepper. Adjust seasoning with salt as needed.

Cut the avocados in half lengthwise and remove seeds. Fill each cavity with salad, and sprinkle with parsley and lobster coral. Garnish with lobster claw. Serve on ice.

LOBSTER SALAD WITH GRAPEFRUIT

Yield: 4 portions

Ingredients

Grapefruit, cut into sections	2
Lobster Meat, diced	8 oz.
Lemon	1/2 tsp.
Worcestershire Sauce	a few drops
Tomato Catsup	1/2 cup
Chablis (white wine)	4 tbsp.
Croutons	4

Method

Line four supreme cups with grapefruit sections. Mix lobster meat with lemon and Worcestershire sauce. Portion lobster into center of supreme cups. Mix catsup with Chablis and pour over lobster pieces. Decorate with a small heart-shaped crouton dipped in parsley.

ALASKA KING CRABMEAT HORS D'OEUVRE (*King Crab Salad a la Lucullus*)

Yield: 4 portions

Ingredients

King Crabmeat, cut in 1- to 2-in. cubes	8 oz.
Sour Cream	1-1/2 oz.
Mayonnaise	1-1/2 oz.
Horseradish, freshly grated	1/2 tbsp.
Cocktail Sauce	3 tbsp.
Paprika (Hungarian)	1/3 tbsp.
Chopped Almonds	1/2 tsp.
Brandy	1/3 oz.
Dill, chopped	1/2 tsp.
Monosodium Glutamate	a pinch
Seedless Green Grapes	3 oz.

Method

Cube crabmeat and squeeze some moisture out. Mix sour cream, mayonnaise, horseradish, cocktail sauce, paprika, chopped almonds, brandy, dill, and monosodium glutamate. Add salt if necessary. Add seedless grapes to crabmeat and marinate in sour cream-mayonnaise mixture for 15–20 min. Serve on a bed of lettuce.

SHRIMP SALAD

Yield: 4 portions

Ingredients

Shrimp, medium	8 oz.
Orange Sections, fresh	4 oz.
Lemon	juice of 1/3
Black Pepper, freshly crushed	pinch
Salt	pinch
Mango Chutney	2 tsp.
Fresh Dill, chopped	1/2 tsp.
Horseradish	1-1/2 tsp.
Whipped Cream, unflavored	1/3 cup
Boston Lettuce	4 leaves
Lemon Sections, to garnish	4
Orange Sections, to garnish	4

Method

Mix shrimp and orange sections together. Add lemon juice, pepper, salt, mango chutney, dill, and horseradish; then fold whipped cream into center of shrimp-orange section mixture. Line four supreme cups with lettuce and fill with the shrimp salad. Garnish with lemon and orange sections (one of each), and a little parsley. Serve cold.

TARTELETTES A LA WALTERSPIEL

Yield: 12 portions

Ingredients

Langostinos	12 oz.
Horseradish, grated	1 to 2 oz.
Heavy Cream, whipped	1/2 cup
Salt	1/3 oz.
Sugar	1/3 oz.
Paprika (Hungarian)	2 tsp.
Lemon	1/2 tsp.
Tartelettes, small	12
Caviar	1/2 oz.

Method

Mix langostinos with horseradish, whipped cream, salt, sugar, and paprika. Season with a few drops of lemon juice. Stuff tartelettes with mixture, and garnish with a little caviar.

NOTE: Mayonnaise may be substituted for heavy cream.

CUCUMBER DANISH STYLE (*Concombre a la Danoise*)

Yield: 4 sherry glasses

Ingredients

Cucumbers, large	2
Vinaigrette Sauce	1/2 cup
Smoked Herring, pureed	8 oz.
Eggs, chopped	2
Horseradish, freshly grated	2 oz.
Ripe Olives	4

Method

Peel cucumbers, remove seeds, and cut into small dice. Blanch in salt water and cool in ice water. Marinate with a little vinaigrette sauce.

Mix pureed smoked herring with chopped eggs and horseradish. Put into a sherry glass, alternating a layer of smoked fish puree with a layer of cucumbers. Top with a ripe olive.

SEAFOOD COCKTAIL

Yield: 4 portions

Ingredients

Tomatoes, large	2
Grapefruit	2
Langostino Tails	20

(continued)

Roast Breast of Turkey Waldorf

Cucumber Danish Style

Seafood Cocktail (continued)
SAUCE

Mayonnaise	1/2 cup
Tomato Catsup	3 tbsp.
Tarragon, chopped	1/3 tsp.
White Wine	2 tsp.
Lemon Wedges, to garnish	4

Method
Cut tomatoes into wedges; section grapefruit. Mix tomatoes and grapefruit sections with langostino tails. Combine sauce ingredients. Put first mixture in grapefruit shells and top with sauce. Garnish each serving with a lemon wedge. Serve in a glass dish.

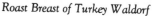

CHICKEN SALAD COCKTAIL

Yield: 4 portions
Ingredients

Grapefruit	2
Chicken, diced	8 oz.
Chopped Ginger	1 tsp.
Curry Powder	1/2 to 1 tsp.
Sour Cream	4 oz.
Tomato Catsup	4 tsp.
Mango Chutney	1 tsp.
Salt	1/2 tsp.
Pepper	1/3 tsp.
Celery, julienne	4 oz.
Vodka	4 tsp.

Method
Section grapefruit. Mix chicken and grapefruit sections together with chopped ginger, curry powder, sour cream, tomato catsup, chutney, and seasonings. Fill grapefruit shells with mixture, garnish with julienne of celery, and sprinkle with vodka. Serve olives and salted almonds separately.

STUFFED CUCUMBERS (*Concombres Farcis*)

Yield: 3 cucumbers
Ingredients

Salmon, smoked	8 oz.
Butter	8 oz.
English Mustard	1 tsp.
Lemon Juice	a few drops
Cucumbers	2 to 3

Method
Puree salmon and mix with butter, English mustard, and lemon juice. Peel cucumber and remove

Decorated pickled egg halves and tomato roses add definition to sliced galantine and pate display.

seeds and pulp from center. Fill cavity with salmon mixture. Chill. Cut filled cucumber into 1- to 2-in. slices and serve on Russian pumpernickel bread.

STUFFED LEEKS

Yield: 18 portions

Ingredients

Leeks, large	18
Rice, boiled	1-1/2 cups
Sausage Meat, cooked	1/2 lb.
White Breadcrumbs	6 oz.
Parsley, Chervil, Dill, chopped	1-1/2 tbsp.
Eggs	1-1/2
Salt	1/2 oz.
Cayenne Pepper	pinch
Grated Nutmeg	pinch
Oil	5 oz.

Method

Trim leeks by cutting off roots and green ends. Wash leeks thoroughly. Blanch in boiling salted water for 5 to 10 min. They should be firm (al dente). Drain them well.

Put rice into a bowl, add sausage meat, breadcrumbs, herbs, and eggs. Season with salt, cayenne pepper, and nutmeg. Mix well.

Core leeks with a vegetable knife and fill the opening with a little of the stuffing. Set the leeks side by side in an oiled shallow casserole dish, sprinkle more oil on top of stuffed leeks, and cover with aluminum foil. Cook at 350°F. for 35–40 min. Cool and serve.

SHRIMP A L'INDIENNE (*Tiny Shrimp Salad*)

Yield: 4 portions

Ingredients

Tiny Shrimp	8 oz.
Bananas, sliced	3 oz.
Green Peppers, julienne	2 oz.
Lemon Juice	1/2 lemon

SAUCE

Curry	1/2 tsp.
Butter	1/2 tsp.
White Wine	to moisten
Mayonnaise	1/3 cup

GARNISH

Lettuce Leaves	4
Lemon Wedges	4
Croutons, dipped in parsley	4

(continued)

Shrimp a l'Indienne (continued)
Method

Saute curry slightly in butter, deglaze with a little white wine, cool, and add mayonnaise to mixture. Mix well.

Combine shrimp, bananas, and peppers, and season with lemon juice. Mix into above sauce. Adjust seasoning.

Serve salad in a small glass shell lined with a lettuce leaf. Garnish with a lemon wedge and crouton dipped in parsley.

MARINATED TROUT

Yield: 6 portions

Ingredients

Trout, fresh or frozen	6, 8–10 oz. each
Mushrooms, sliced	8 oz.
Shallots, chopped	6
Parsley Stems	3
Dill Stems	3
Salt	1 oz.
White Wine	1/2 cup
Lemon	juice of 1
Court Bouillon	2 cups
Lemon Wedges	to garnish
Parsley	to garnish

Method

Wash trout well. Place in buttered shallow casserole. Add mushrooms, shallots, parsley, dill, and salt. Cover with wine, lemon juice, and court bouillon. Bring to a boil and simmer 5 min. per lb. of trout; remove from heat and cool trout in stock.

Filet or serve whole with part of the marinade. Garnish with lemon wedges and a sprig of parsley.

TOMATO COCKTAIL

Yield: 4 portions

Ingredients

Tomatoes, large	4
Lemon	juice of 1
Oil	4 tbsp.
Salt	1/2 tsp.
Black Pepper, crushed	1/2 tsp.
Creamed Horseradish	to garnish
Tomato Catsup	to garnish
Caviar	to garnish

Method

Peel, remove seeds, and dice tomatoes. Marinate with lemon juice, oil, salt, and pepper. Fill a supreme glass and top with a spoonful of tomato catsup and a little creamed horseradish (see cold sauces). Top portion with a sprinkling of caviar.

HORS D'OEUVRE PROVENCALE

Yield: 14 4-oz. portions

Ingredients

Fennel Bulbs, fresh	9 to 12
Peeled Tomatoes	1 lb. 2 oz.
Garlic	8 cloves
Olive Oil	2 tbsp.
Tarragon, fresh	4 sprigs
Pepper	1/3 tsp.
Salt	1 to 1-1/2 oz.

Method

Bring salted water to boil. Cut fennel in small pieces lengthwise and cook until tender. Do not overcook.

Chop tomatoes and garlic. Place tomatoes in pot, add oil, and reduce tomatoes until thick. Add garlic, tarragon, salt, and pepper. Add fennel, cook briefly to blend flavors, then pour mixture into a dish and allow to cool. Serve cold.

Massed for maximum color impact, these canapes combine flavors certain to please all tastes. Starting with wedge at upper left: Stuffed Deviled Eggs; Shrimp Canapes surrounded by stuffed green olives; Domino Canapes (Swiss cheese slices over truffles on toast triangles); Beluga Caviar Canapes topped with cream cheese; Ham Rolls stuffed with pickle slices; Stuffed Eggs Mimosa, topped with a caper; Anchovy Canapes, topped with circles of stuffed green olives and arranged with edging of red pimento strips; Salmon Mousse, with chaud-froid and truffle decorations; Fresh Smoked Trout, butter decorations; Pimento Canapes; Cherry Tomatoes filled with Tunafish Mousse; Salmon Caviar Canapes. Colorful circle of canapes in lettuce frame is arranged around mound of stuffed green olives topped with a tomato rose. Tempting triangles are separated by twisted ropes of cream cheese and circled with lettuce to frame display (see Chapter 5, page 81).

Galantine of Duck (see recipe, page 138, 139). Centerpiece: Pineapple with turnip daisies and cabbage orchid and diced blue and green grapes. Duck centerpiece: Liver mousse, oranges, grapes. Garniture: Poached apple baskets, cranberry relish, pickled beet eggs, stuffed olives.

Combination Fish and Vegetable Platter (shown below left). Center: Salmon Pate (recipe, page 130) decorated with egg whites and truffle, tomato rings, poached cucumbers. Left and right: Vegetable Pate (recipe, page 128) decorated with tea eggs and aspic cubes. Poached salmon, stuffed olives, and radish.

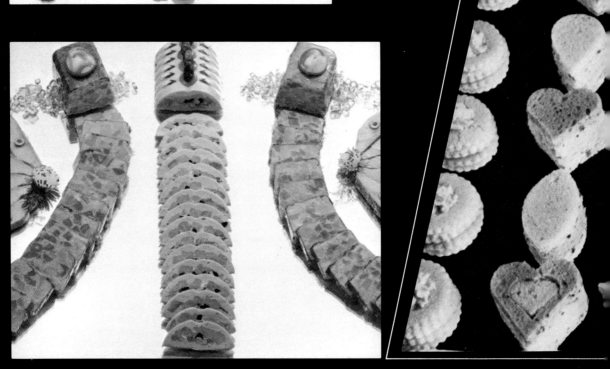

Salt Dough Sculpture. When deciding on a pattern for a display piece it is essential that it match the theme of the buffet, and, if possible, be useful for future buffets.

Fancy Sandwiches. These sandwiches are cut into rectangular, round, or other shapes, the size and thickness depending on the nature of the ingredients. Sufficient preparation time is important in order that they may provide maximum flavor and appeal (see Chapter 5, page 81).

Vegetable Flower Centerpiece. Shown at right, with a Pineapple base are: Zucchini Butterflies, Turnip Daisies, Carrot Tiger Lilies, a Cabbage Orchid, Radish Flower, and Leek Daisy (see Chapter 13, page 167).

Combination Veal Galantine (see recipe, pages 136, 137). Centerpiece: 1/3 of galantine decorated with leek, pimento, gherkins, baby corn tips. Liver mousse, mushrooms. Hatelet: Lemon slice, tomato star, mock truffle, mum radish, Boston lettuce, aspic cubes. Vegetable flowers: carrot tiger lily, cabbage orchid, radish or potato. Garniture: Zucchini stuffed with paprika cream cheese, radish. Zucchini baskets filled with marinated corn, tomato circle.

TURBAN OF RICE IN JELLY (*Turban de Riz Compose en Gelee*)

Yield: 8 3-oz. portions

Ingredients

Rice Pilaf	10 oz.
Green Olives	4 oz.
Smoked Salmon	6 oz.
Mayonnaise Collee	1 cup

Method

Prepare rice pilaf. Chop green olives and smoked salmon fine. Mix with rice pilaf.

Blend in approximately 1 cup of mayonnaise collee (see Chaud-Froid, p. 76) freshly made. Line a ring mold with aspic and pack rice mixture into center of mold. Let mold set for 2 to 3 hours.

❧ ❧

MOUSSE OF TUNA IN LEMON SHELL (*Citrons a la Creme de Thon*)

Yield: 12 lemon halves

Ingredients

Lemons	6
Tuna	1 lb. can
Butter	4 oz.
Dry Mustard	1 level tbsp.
Paprika	1/2 tsp.
Black Pepper, freshly ground	1/3 tsp.
Egg White, beaten to stiff froth	1
Pimento, thin strip	to garnish
Parsley, chopped	to garnish

Method

Cut lemons in half. Remove pulp, being careful not to damage skins. Remove all seeds and save skins. Set pulp and juice aside.

Drain tuna and grind fine in chopper or blender; add butter, mustard, paprika, and pepper. Mix well to obtain a very smooth batter. Mix in 1/3 of the lemon pulp. Add egg white to lighten the mixture. Heap mixture in lemon shells. Garnish filled shells with: thin strip of pimento, sprinkle of paprika, and chopped parsley. Refrigerate for 1 hour.

❧ ❧

PICKLED BEETS

Yield: 3-1/2 lb.

Ingredients

Fresh Beets, cooked	3 lb.
Onion, finely sliced	1
Beet Juice	1 cup
White Vinegar	1-1/2 cup
Sugar	1-1/4 cup
Cinnamon Stick	1
Thyme	1/2 tsp.
Salad Oil	1/4 cup
Ground White Pepper	1/4 tsp.
Salt	1/2 tsp.

Method

Bring all ingredients except beets to boil, turn heat down, and simmer mixture for 5 min. Cool. Add sliced beets, mix well, and refrigerate.

❧ ❧

CANAPES AND ZAKUSKI

Anchovy Canape. Butter a canape with anchovy butter; lay strips of anchovies on top, leaving a space in the center to be filled with chopped egg yolks mixed with parsley.

Shrimp Canape. Butter a canape with shrimp butter, arrange shrimp tails on top, finish with a sprinkling of fines herbes.

Caviar Canape. Butter a canape with caviar butter; place a layer of caviar on top, border with chopped yolks and whites of eggs, a sprinkling of chives on top.

Caviar Cigarettes. Spread caviar on a very thin slice of bread; roll to form a cigarette.

Canape Rigoletto. Butter a canape with cayenne butter; sprinkle with a mixture of finely chopped whites and yolks of eggs, ham, tongue, fines herbes, and truffles.

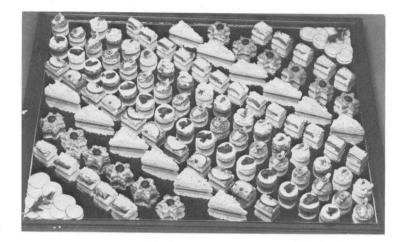

Arrangement of Canapes

Canape a la Danoise. Butter a rye canape with horseradish butter; arrange slices of smoked salmon, caviar, and filets of marinated herring on top of canape.

Canape of Langostinos. Butter a canape with langostino butter; arrange slices of langostino tails on top; decorate with langostino butter.

Canape of Tongue. Butter a canape with mustard butter; arrange slices of tongue on top and decorate with mustard butter.

Canape of Ham. Follow same procedure as for tongue (see above) replacing the tongue with ham.

Canape of Lobster. Butter a canape with lobster butter; arrange slices of lobster on top; border with chopped eggs.

Canape of Eggs. Butter a canape with mayonnaise; sprinkle top with chopped whites of eggs; border with chopped yolks.

Canape of Eggs a la Grecque. Butter a canape with mustard butter; place a hard-cooked egg half on top; cover with mayonnaise; border with chopped eggs and sprinkle fines herbes on top.

Canape of Game. Butter a canape with cayenne butter or a game cheese; arrange small mounds of chopped game meat on top; border with fines herbes and chopped capers.

Canape of Fish. Butter a canape with herring roe butter; arrange slices of cooked fish on top of butter; cover with mayonnaise and border with chopped capers and fines herbes.

Canape Cancalaise. Butter a canape with tunafish butter; top with a poached mussel; border with ravigote butter.

Canape of Smoked Salmon. Butter a canape with horseradish butter; place a slice of smoked salmon on top; border with chopped chervil and chives.

Canape of Sardine. Butter a canape with sardine butter; arrange a sardine filet on top; decorate with anchovy butter.

Canape of Lobster Eggs. Butter a canape with lobster cheese, top with a sprinkling of lobster coral; decorate with lobster butter.

Domino Canape. Butter domino-shaped canapes with truffle butter; cover with thin slices of gruyere cheese of the same shape. Cut holes in the cheese to simulate spots on dominoes and fill holes with pieces of truffle.

Canape Rejane. Butter a canape with lobster butter; top with a mound of chopped eggs and mayonnaise. Cover with a light mayonnaise and border with chopped lobster coral. (NOTE: When langouste or lobster coral cannot be obtained, substitute grated egg yolks that have been tinted during cooking.)

Canape of Goujons a la Russe. Poach some cleaned goujons in a court bouillon of white wine; cool. Place on canapes and cover with gelatin-mayonnaise and sprinkle lightly with chopped parsley.

Breast of Chicken Bombay. Slice of chicken breast is placed in tablespoon; cavity is filled with mousse of chicken with curry added, then topped with a second slice of chicken breast. The combination is covered with curried chaud-froid sauce and garnished with radish and leek flowers.

Canape of Sole a la Brasset. Butter round canapes with herring roe butter; place a small paupiette of sole on top and cover with a light mayonnaise. Decorate the sides with chopped coral and put a bit of chopped truffle on top.

Canape a la Nicoise. Butter round canapes with anchovy butter; place three small stuffed green olives on the canapes; put a fourth olive on top of the three. Fill in between olives with anchovy butter and decorate as desired.

Canape Paulette. Butter round canapes with anchovy butter; sprinkle one half of canape with chopped egg whites and the other half with chopped egg yolks; separate halves with a row of shrimp.

Small Brioche of Foie Gras. Place a small piece of truffle in the center of a ball of foie gras; wrap unsweetened brioche dough around foie gras, shaping it like a small loaf of bread. Bake and cool before serving.

Profiteroles. Bake a pate of choux into tiny round shells. These may be garnished with any kind of puree of meat, fish, or cheese.

Canape Vie Ville. Cover a canape with tarragon butter, then top with a slice of ham; decorate with tarragon leaves.

Canape a la D'Arkangel. Cover one half of a small tartlet with caviar, the remaining half with puree of smoked salmon. Separate halves with a filet of anchovy.

NOTE: Most canapes should be spread with either a butter- or cheese-flavored compound to complement the main ingredient to be placed on the canape. A large variety of canape ingredients is available on the market in cans or jars. These may be used either as hors d'oeuvre or as garnish for canapes.

FISH AND SHELLFISH

Anchovies, Moscovite. On a large circle of cooked potato, place marinated anchovies to form a crown. Place caviar in the center of the crown. Garnish top of caviar with chopped egg white.

Boutargue (Mullet Eggs). These are available salted and smoked, to be served like caviar. They are highly appetizing.

Salted Codfish a l'Indienne. Soak 2 lb. of codfish overnight; cut in scallop-size pieces; roll in flour and fry quickly in hot oil. Saute 2 tbsp. of finely chopped onions in olive oil till golden; sprinkle with curry powder and simmer for one min. Add 1 cup of dry white wine, juice of 1 lemon, 3 crushed garlic cloves and boil for 5 min. Place codfish pieces in this marinade, bring to a boil, cover and let cool. Serve cooled pieces with some of the marinade. Yield: 12 portions.

Langostine a 'Amiral. Defrost langostino carefully so the form of the shell remains intact. Bake a small barquette. Fill barquettes with a ragout made from langostino meat mixed with an anchovy mayonnaise.

Crayfish a la Moscovite. Remove the tail shell from cooked crayfish and serve tails with anchovy mayonnaise. Top with a sprinkling of chopped parsley.

Frog Legs a la Bearnaise. Saute frog legs in olive oil; add diced tomatoes, white wine, lemon juice, and herbs; use plenty of salt and pepper; simmer for 5 min. Serve with some of the liquor they were cooked in and sprinkle with fines herbes.

Goujons a la Russe. Poach some cleaned goujons in white wine and lemon juice. (Remove goujons and reduce cooking liquor by 1/2.) Arrange goujons on a small plate, top with mayonnaise thinned with some of the reduced cooking liquor. Use cucumber salad to complete the plate.

Lobster a la Boulognaise. Cut cooked lobster meat into small pieces, add an equal quantity of celery and finely chopped beets. Mix these ingredients with mayonnaise; season well with finely chopped chervil, tarragon, and cayenne. Arrange lobster mixture on lettuce leaves and sprinkle with finely chopped lobster coral.

Herring a la Dieppoise. Poach cleaned, fresh filets of herring in a marinade of white wine, vinegar, carrots, and onions a la russe, and herbs. Serve with some of the marinade.

Herring a la Livonienne. Remove filets and reserve heads and tails of 12 salted or smoked herrings. Remove skin and dice filets. Place in bowl with equal quantity of diced boiled potatoes and fresh apples. Season with the following dressing: 1/2 tsp. salt; pinch of freshly ground white pepper; 1 tsp. each, coarsely chopped parsley, chervil, fennel, and tarragon; 6 tbsp. olive oil and 3 tbsp. of red wine vinegar. Mix all ingredients well. On a service platter, mold this preparation into shapes resembling herring; place reserved heads and tails at each extremity, thus simulating the original fish; serve.

Herring a la Lucas. Salad of diced marinated herring in a Sauce Gribiche. Season highly.

Herring a la Russe. Arrange filets of smoked herring on a ravier; border with sliced cold potatoes. Season with a fennel vinaigrette.

Trout a la Saint Menehould with Champagne. Place cleaned trout in a pan; cook slowly for 6 min. in a liquor made by sauteeing sliced carrots, onions, garlic in butter seasoned with freshly ground pepper, grated nutmeg, herb mixture, and salt and then pouring a bottle of champagne over mixture. Cook for one hour, remove trout and strain liquor. Serve some liquor with fish. (Herring and salmon may be cooked in similar fashion.)

Mackerel in Marinade. Take 12 very fresh mackerel (about 1/2-lb. size); remove the filets and place them in a saute pan; season with salt, freshly ground pepper. Sprinkle finely sliced onion, pinch of thyme, three parsley sprigs, one bayleaf, and the juice of two lemons over fish. Add sufficient dry white wine to cover and bring to a boil; cover and let simmer for 5 min. Remove from heat and allow to cool; place in refrigerator until jellied.

Marinated Mackerel a la Suedoise. Small mackerel prepared like Herring a la Dieppoise.

Mullets a l'Orientale. Prepare the same as Mullets au Saffron, eliminating the saffron.

Mullets au Saffron. Cook mullets in oil, chopped onions, diced tomatoes, white wine, fish stock, herb mixture, and saffron. Serve mullets in liquor with sprinkling of chopped parsley.

Mussels. Poach and clean some mussels; mix with mayonnaise flavored with lemon juice and thinned with poaching liquor reduced by 2/3. Sprinkle fines herbes on top.

Mussels a l'Antiboise. Garnish a mussel shell with a puree of sardines; place a poached mussel on the puree, a chervil leaf over the mussel and glaze all with aspic.

Mussels a l'Indienne. Prepare mussels in a curry sauce. Arrange within a turban of boiled rice.

Oysters. All types.

Pickled Oysters. Parboil 48 oysters in their own liquor; as soon as liquor boils, drain oysters and reserve liquor. Boil 1 pt. vinegar with 1/2 tsp. cloves, whole white pepper, whole allspice and a pinch of mace for a few minutes, then add the oyster liquor, bring to a boil, strain and pour over oysters. Let oysters marinate in refrigerator for 12 hours.

Slices of Pickerel a la Georgianne. Clean and completely bone a pickerel. Stuff with a highly seasoned forcemeat; wrap as a galantine and cook in a court bouillon made with white wine. When fish is done, cool and cut into slices. On each slice, place a small portion of Russian salad, then place a small slice of lobster on top of the salad. Glaze with aspic.

Salmon, Canadian Style. Cut 2 lb. fresh salmon in large dice, fry briskly in hot oil; season with salt and paprika. Place in a saute pan; add 1 lb. of small fresh okra and the salmon with white wine and the juice of two lemons; let simmer for a few minutes, season to taste and cool covered. Sprinkle finely chopped green pepper over servings.

Horns of Salmon a l'Imperiale. Make horns of smoked salmon and garnish with caviar butter.

Barquettes of Filet of Dover Sole Caprice. Fill small barquettes with cucumber salad, seasoned with cream and lemon juice. Arrange small paupiettes of sole stuffed with a puree of truffles over salad, glaze all with aspic.

Paupiettes of Filet of Dover Sole. Stuff paupiettes (roulades) with puree of red pimentos, poach, cool, and cut into rings. Garnish dish with a salad of cucumbers; arrange rings on salad.

Tortillons of Dover Sole a la Diable. Tie slender bands of sole into a knot. Cook in a little oil; then add white wine, lemon juice, a few grains of coriander seed, garlic, and a little Worcestershire sauce, crushed thyme, and bayleaves. Cool sole; serve with liquor.

Smelts a la Caucasienne. Clean smelts; dry, flour, and brown in very hot oil. Place in vinaigrette.

Marinated Smelts (*known in French cookery as Escabeche*). Fry 48 thoroughly dried and floured smelts in hot oil. When done, place in a deep dish and set aside. In the same hot oil, fry one large onion and one carrot (cut into very thin round slices) with eight unpeeled cloves of garlic. When slightly brown, drain the oil, then moisten with 1 tbsp. vinegar, the juice of one lemon, 1 qt. dry white wine; add freshly ground white pepper, one bayleaf, a pinch of thyme, three parsley sprigs, three small pimentos, and salt to taste. Simmer for 15 min. When ready, cool and pour over smelts. Marinate for 24 hours. Serve smelts with strained marinade.

Shrimp. All forms.

Shrimp with Saffron a l'Orientale. Shrimp may be used with or without their shells in this dish. However, leaving the shell on is recommended. Parboil 48 small shrimp, then place them in a saute pan with enough dry white wine to cover; add 1 tsp. olive oil, salt to taste, three ripe tomatoes peeled and finely diced, three parsley sprigs, two fennel leaves, pinch of thyme, one bayleaf, three cloves of garlic, a few peppercorns and coriander seed, and 1 tsp. of saffron. Simmer for 12 min. and allow shrimp to cool in this liquor. Remove shrimp, arrange on a platter and strain liquor over them. Serve chilled.

Sturgeon a la Bariatinski. Cook filet of sturgeon in a highly seasoned marinade; cool in this marinade. Make an aspic with some of the liquor. Mix a little of this aspic, while still warm, over ice. Coat the bottom of a dish with this aspic. When aspic has set, arrange slices of sturgeon and smoked salmon over it.

Tunafish a l'Antiboise. Make a salad of potatoes and tunafish, garnish with slices of tomatoes, quartered eggs, and pitted olives; serve with mayonnaise dressing.

VEGETABLES

Artichoke l'Egyptienne. Prepare small artichokes leaving the stem attached, cook in combination of oil, white wine, lemon juice, coriander seed, salt, and pepper to which brunoise (carrots, celery, onions) has been added. Frozen artichoke hearts may be substituted for fresh artichokes.

Artichokes a la Parisienne. Remove center from small cooked artichokes and fill with diced vegetable salad blended with mayonnaise.

Artichoke Bottoms. Cooked artichoke bottoms may be garnished in many ways (puree of foie gras, peas, etc.).

Cardons a l'Italienne. Marinate cardons (oyster plants) and beets in vinaigrette dressing. Arrange slices of cardons with slices of beets.

Celery a la Grecque. See Artichoke Hearts a la Grecque, p. 82.

Cucumbers a la Danoise. Carve barquettes out of cucumber, blanch, and drain. Put herring filets and egg yolks through a fine sieve; add chopped chives, mustard, olive oil, and salt and pepper to taste. Fill barquettes with mixture; decorate with shredded horseradish.

Filets of Cucumber a la Savoyarde. Cut cucumbers in 1-in. lengths, slice chunks into ribbons, roll up again, and cut rolls to form long julienne strips. Season with oil, vinegar, salt, and pepper. May be seasoned with sour cream and lemon juice.

Knob Celery Ravigote. Julienne knob celery, parboil; chill and combine with a mixture of French dressing, mayonnaise, and French mustard.

Knob Celery a la Viennoise. Season blanched knob celery with oil, vinegar, salt, pepper, chervil, and tarragon and blend with a light mayonnaise. Decorate with anchovy filets and chopped egg yolks.

Marinated Carrots. Peel small carrots; cook in water, white wine, vinegar, herbs, garlic, olive oil, salt, and pepper. Serve chilled in cooking liquor.

Tomato Antiboise. Cut 1-1/2-in. diameter openings at the top of 12 medium-sized, ripe tomatoes. Using a small spoon, remove all seeds. Marinate tomatoes for 1 hour in French dressing. Remove tomatoes from marinade; dry on absorbent paper. Fill tomatoes with following mixture: 1 cup tunafish, two diced hard-cooked eggs, 1 tbsp. capers, a little finely chopped parsley, chervil, and tarragon. Blend with mayonnaise to which mashed anchovy has been added. Refrigerate for 1 hour and serve.

SALADS

The following salads may be used for hors d'oeuvre:

Tomato and Egg Salad
Tomato and Potato Salad
Potato and Chervil Salad
Potato and Filet of Herring Salad
Potato and Shrimp Salad
Shrimp and Egg Salad
Shrimp and Tomato Salad
Knob Celery Salad
Knob Celery and Truffle Salad
Knob Celery and Chervil Salad
Radish and Mint Vinegar Salad
Radish and Pickled Cherry Salad
Boiled Beef Salad
Cucumber Salad
Beet and Chopped Fennel Salad
Beet and Potato Salad
Mussels, Tomato, and Beef Salad
Oyster and Garlic Crouton Salad
Seafood Salad
Red Cabbage Salad
White Cabbage Salad
Lentil, White Bean, Kidney Bean (all dried legumes) Salads
Eggplant Salad
Eggplant, Tomato, and Pimento Salad

BARQUETTES

Barquettes are small boats made of pie crust dough. They may be featured as follows:

Bagration. Chicken puree, chicken breast, truffles, and aspic.

Beauharnais. Chicken and truffles, covered with mayonnaise mixed with puree of tarragon and gelatin and decorated with truffles and aspic.

Hard-Cooked Eggs, Spanish Style

Cancalaise. Mousse of fish and oysters in aspic.

Marivaux. Small dice of shrimp and mushrooms with mayonnaise collee; decorate with hard-cooked egg and aspic.

Normande. Filet of sole, mussels, and truffles. Coat with chaud-froid, fill with lobster or shrimp and aspic.

Various fillings can be served in barquettes:

Anchovy Salpicons	Vegetables
Smoked Eel	Mussels
Compound Butter for Hors d'Oeuvre	Olives
Caviar	Eggs
Cucumber	Sausages
Shrimp	Tuna
Lobster	Tomatoes
Foie Gras	Truffles
Herring	

The following may be used to decorate barquettes:

Capers	Parsley
Gherkins	Chervil
Chopped Aspic	Tarragon
Eggs	Lettuce

EGG DISHES FOR HORS D'OEUVRE

Hard-Cooked Eggs, Spanish Style (*Oeufs a l'Espagnole*). Make deviled stuffed eggs, place on marinated tomato slices. Refrigerate 1/2 hour before serving. Julienne celery and red peppers and marinate in salt, oil, and vinegar. Arrange tomato slices with eggs in circle on platter; top with marinated celery and red pepper strips. Garnish with stuffed green olives. Julienne of truffles may also be added.

Boiled Eggs Moscow Style (*Oeufs a la Moscovite*). Prepare light mousse of lobster. Cut into circles and top with half an egg decorated with a small slice of lobster and a small amount of caviar. Arrange these around a mountain of whipped cream mixed with caviar. Buttered toast is the perfect accompaniment.

Boiled Eggs Danish Style (*Oeufs durs a la Danoise*). Cut hard-cooked eggs lengthwise into halves. Remove egg yolks and stuff cavity with diced lobster salad blended with mayonnaise and egg yolks. Serve on lettuce leaf with parsley and radish rose.

Hard-Cooked Eggs Stuffed with Seafood (*Oeufs aux fruits de mer*). Cut hard-cooked eggs in half. Stuff with combination of finely diced

The Penguin

1. Mise en place: Hard-cooked eggs, black olives, carrots, salami slice, toothpick, round cutter.

2. Slice off a little of the egg to make egg stand up straight.

3. Stick a small stick of carrot into the black olive and stick with a toothpick into the egg.

4. Peel off the olive skin approximately 1/2 in. wide.

5. Cut out a small triangle from the peeled-off skin and place on either side of the egg.

6. Cut out circles from olive skin and place on penguin for buttons.

7. Cut two slivers of black olive and place in front of penguin for shoes.

8. Top with a salami sombrero and use for decoration.

smoked eel, anchovies, and a few tiny shrimp mixed together with mayonnaise and lemon juice. Garnish with chopped lobster coral and coat lightly with aspic.

Hard-Cooked Eggs Stuffed with Pheasant (*Oeufs durs a la Justice*). Cut hard-cooked eggs in half lengthwise. Pipe a light mousse of pheasant mixed with a small amount of diced truffles onto the egg. Refrigerate for 15–20 min., then coat with brown aspic and garnish with slice of truffle. Serve on buttered toast.

Russian Eggs (*Oeufs a la Russe*). Hard-cooked eggs, cut in half lengthwise, are topped with tartar sauce and decorated with a small amount of caviar.

Hard-Cooked Eggs, Norwegian Style (*Oeufs a la Norvegienne*). Cut hard-cooked eggs in half lengthwise. Pipe a small amount of creamed

horseradish (blend of whipped cream, grated horseradish, sugar, salt) over egg. Garnish with tiny shrimp and chopped, boiled lobster coral. Serve on lettuce leaf with radish rose and parsley.

Hard-Cooked Eggs, Vegetable Salad (*Oeufs a la Jardiniere*). Cut hard-cooked eggs in half. Remove yolks and strain through a fine sieve. Mix yolks with mayonnaise and finely diced, mixed vegetables. Fill whites with mixture. Garnish with diced chives.

Eggs Piquantes (*Oeufs Piquantes*). Cut hard-cooked eggs lengthwise. Remove yolks and puree them with anchovies, then whip in a small amount of butter. Pipe yolk mixture into whites. Decorate with slice of radish or small sour gherkins or a bit of anchovy or smoked lox.

Soft-Boiled Eggs Served in Tomatoes (*Oeufs Mollets aux Tomates*). A soft-boiled egg (4–5

The Sombrero

1. Cut salami slice halfway to the center. Hold with your thumbs.

2. Roll into a cone.

3. Turn upside down.

4. Bend cone into a sombrero.

min.) is placed in a marinated half tomato. Blanched vegetables cut into fine julienne are arranged over the top. A flower made of mixture of egg yolk, tomato catsup, and butter is piped on. A few bits of caviar represent center of flower. Serve with Sauce Tyrolienne.

Soft-Boiled Eggs, Farmer's Style (*Oeufs Mollets a la Paysanne*). Place soft-boiled eggs on an oval-shaped toasted crouton of white bread. Arrange a mound of diced turkey or chicken, cauliflower roses, sliced black olives, fennel

which has been marinated in oil, salt, pepper, and lemon juice, around eggs. Sprinkle with chopped fresh parsley.

Soft-Boiled Eggs Nicoise (*Oeufs a la Nicoise*). Blanch tomatoes 30 sec. and peel. Cut in half, remove seeds. Marinate in combination of oil, vinegar, and salt; top tomato half with soft-boiled egg and arrange on platter with asparagus and string bean salad. Just before serving, top with Sauce Vincent and garnish with a truffle slice.

Frog Egg   1. *Mise en place: Hard-cooked eggs, stuffed Spanish olives, pimentos, gherkins, toothpick, carrots.*

2. *Cut off bottom part of the egg at a 45° angle.*

3. *On top of egg, remove a small wedge.*

4. *Top egg with two ends of the stuffed Spanish olives for eyes.*

5. *Cut pimento into long triangle for tongue.*

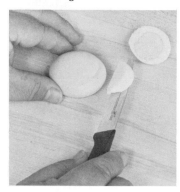

Soft Eggs on Croutons (*Oeufs sur Crouton*). Cut egg-size croutons from white bread and toast. Set soft egg on top of crouton and arrange croutons with eggs around a salad of mussels. Dredge mussels in flour, saute in oil, then marinate for 24 hours in oil and vinegar. Add to marinated mussels tiny shrimp, small cauliflower roses, chopped chives, parsley, dill, and mustard. Let stand for 1 hour.

Poached Eggs, Sicilian Style (*Oeufs Poches a la Sicilienne*). Blanch medium-sized tomatoes, remove skin, cut in half, remove seeds. Marinate with unflavored vinegar, salt, pepper, and oil. Shortly before serving, strain tomatoes and stuff with a poached egg. Top egg with braised julienne of carrots, celery, mushrooms (button),

and truffles (optional), coat with aspic and serve on a glass platter with watercress and mayonnaise.

Poached Eggs, Washington (*Oeufs Poches a la Washington*). Place poached egg in cornets made of ham. Decorate as desired with truffles and tarragon leaves. Cover lightly with aspic and arrange on platter or plate with timbales of ham mousse.

Poached Eggs, Gourmet Style (*Oeufs Poches a la Lucullus*). Fill small tartlets with lobster mousse; top with poached eggs. Coat with Sauce Chantilly and garnish with truffle bits.

Eggs in Cocottes
With the hurried pace set for today's kitchen brigade and the shortage of labor, this method of

6. *Stick pimento triangle into frog mouth. Cut gherkins into fans for feet.*

7. *Carve carrot with a paring knife into a hat and stick with a toothpick into egg.*

8. *Cut a green pepper into a flower and set frog eggs next to it. They will be a highlight of your buffet.*

preparing egg dishes is very welcome since it is not only fast but produces an item that is easy to serve. The appetizer can be made up ahead of time in any quantity. It is especially desirable for fast turnover restaurants.

In most cases, we fill the cocotte (small china mold) with any one of several different mousses, then top the filled cocotte with either a boiled or a poached egg. It can be decorated with truffles, olives, tongue, tarragon leaves or leeks, then the whole coated with aspic. If salad is used as an underlining for cocottes, the eggs should be coated with mayonnaise. To serve, arrange on a doily on a covered platter.

Eggs Hungarian Style (*Oeufs a la Hongroise*). Mix cooked calves' brains, finely pureed, with a little sour cream, prepared mustard, chopped herbs (chervil, parsley, tarragon), salt, and paprika to make thick sauce. Insert hard-cooked egg in cocotte and top with sauce.

Eggs Spatini. Mix French cut green beans, cooked al dente, with spicy mayonnaise. Place in china ramekins and top with a poached egg that has been coated with mayonnaise and pistachio nuts.

Eggs German Style. Puree filet of smoked herring with butter; pipe into small ramekins. Top each with a poached egg and coat with lobster sauce.

Eggs Margaret. Make a tasty salad from raw, sliced button mushrooms and truffles, marinated in oil, lemon, and salt. Fill cocotte with salad and top with poached egg. Top with mayonnaise and a sprinkling of chopped herbs (dill and basil) and a slice of truffle.

Eggs with Asparagus Tips. Put poached egg in a cocotte; coat with Sauce Andalouse and garnish with tips of asparagus.

Tea Eggs. Boil eggs for 5–6 min., then cool and crush each shell lightly but do not remove shells. Immerse eggs in a strong tea solution, flavored with ginger and anise. Marinate for 1–2 hours, remove shells from eggs and serve.

PICKLED EGGS

Yield: 10 portions

Ingredients

Dry Mustard	1-1/2 tsp.
Cornstarch	1-1/2 tsp.
White Vinegar	1 pt.
Sugar	1-1/2–2 tsp.
Turmeric	1/2 tsp.
Hard-Cooked Eggs	10

Method

Dilute dry mustard and cornstarch in a little water. Add vinegar and spices. Boil 10 min. Add shelled eggs and refrigerate.

CHAPTER SIX

FOIE GRAS-
TRUFFLES-CAVIAR

FOIE GRAS

Nothing is new under the sun—Egyptian maps show slaves force-feeding geese. In 52 B.C., Metellus Pius Scipio, Pompey's father-in-law, used to cram geese with figs to obtain fat livers which were used in various recipes. Romans also knew of foie gras which they used to eat hot with raisins.

Nowadays, it is chiefly the cities of Strasbourg and Toulouse that are known for their foie gras. French geese from the regions of Alsace and the southwest of France, after intensive force-feeding that generally continues for about four weeks during the winter, become plump and their livers enlarge considerably. The livers, soft pink in color, weigh between 1 and 3 lb. A plain goose liver thus becomes a foie gras, or fat liver. The birds are fed to the limit of their capacities, but their health is watched and treatment is temporarily suspended if they exhibit signs of illness.

The first pate de foie gras was made in France, in Perigueux by a pastry chef whose name was Courtois. In 1780, a French chef by the name of Clause was the first to commercialize foie gras in Strasbourg. The pates of foie gras were prepared in various ways—in terrines, en croutes—and the taste varied considerably.

At the time, truffles or "black diamonds" (described in detail on p. 103) were unknown in the region of Alsace. Francois Doyen, the chef for the Magistrate of Bordeaux, introduced truffles to Clause in 1789. As a result, the foie gras of Strasbourg reached the peak of perfection in gastronomy. All foie gras was then sold under the name "Pate de Foie Gras de Strasbourg aux Truffes du Perigord."

Since that time the manufacturing of foie gras has grown to such an extent that several factories in Strasbourg and in the southwestern region of France are now exporting their delicacies all over the world.

How is foie gras prepared?
The fattened goose livers are sorted in the factories by color, size, and consistency. Ten years of experience are required before a sorter can predict the quality of the finished product. A cooked foie gras may turn into a fatty, tough piece of liver with no interest for connoisseurs.

Therefore, professionals are essential to ensure that the best livers are selected.

The livers are cleaned by removing all sinews. They are seasoned with a special spice mixture, stuffed with truffles, then poached in Madeira or cognac. Some livers are baked in the oven. Every manufacturer has a particular method of preparation and cooking, although the results do not differ noticeably from one method to another.

Varieties of Foie Gras

Foie gras is sold fresh, in cans, or in terrines. Fresh foie gras, called *Foie Gras au Naturel*, will keep well or can be preserved for two to four weeks, depending upon the product, under refrigeration. Fresh foie gras has a noticeable flavor advantage over canned foie gras. The cooking method for fresh foie gras assures maximum flavor which, when combined with the flavor of truffles, produces a unique delicacy.

Livers from carefully fattened geese are used in the preparation of foie gras. After liver is removed, it is cleaned and all sinews are removed before it is seasoned, stuffed with truffles and poached or baked. Fresh foie gras is weighed and packed; it will keep from two to four weeks when properly refrigerated. Terrine (below right) is an attractive serving dish that can be refilled with contents of can.

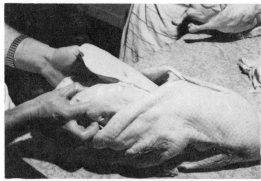

Manufacturers sell fresh foie gras under various names: Foie Gras Frais; Bloc de Foie Gras Truffe; Supreme de Foie Gras en Gelee; Melons de Foie Gras; Aspics de Foie Gras. Legally, all of these foie gras must contain a minimum of 75% goose liver unmixed with other ingredients, and a minimum of 5% truffles.

It should be clearly understood that the product described as a "pate de foie" should not be confused with foie gras. Indeed, any French pate de foie contains 80% to 90% of pork liver with less than 1% truffles and a small amount of goose fat.

Foie Gras in Cans or in Terrines

Canned foie gras or terrines of foie gras may be preserved for a much longer period than the fresh foie gras. The terrines of foie gras truffe come in various sizes holding from 2 oz. to over 1 lb. of foie gras with truffles.

The earthenware jars are elaborately decorated. A good foie gras when freshly opened should be covered with a thin layer of yellowish fat. This is rendered from the liver during cooking and should have an appetizing odor.

Canned foie gras is known by several names, which are determined by the size and shape of the can: Parfait Bloc de Foie Gras Truffe; Baby Bloc de Foie Gras Truffe; Bloc de Foie Gras Truffe; Terrine de Foie Gras Truffe. Canned foie gras should meet the same standards as fresh foie gras.

Canned foie gras products are also manufactured using trimmings and cut pieces of goose livers, mixed with goose fat and pork meat. These are called puree, mousse, or creme de foie gras and should contain a minimum of 50% foie gras mixed with the other ingredients.

Uses of Foie Gras

Foie gras is served as an hors d'oeuvre to begin a meal in chilled slices, decorated with a Madeira aspic and accompanied by toast. It may also be served after the main course, before the cheeses or desserts; in this case, a red Bordeaux, a Burgundy or a champagne brut would be most ap-

propriate as wines to serve with it. If foie gras is to be served as an hors d'oeuvre, a dry white wine such as an Alsace is acceptable.

Foie gras also finds its uses in hot cuisine, especially in sauces, and in various culinary preparations, such as Tournedos Rossini, Beef Wellington, etc.

Perhaps it has best been described by C. Gerard who said, "The goose is a kind of living hothouse in which grows the supreme fruit of gastronomy."

TRUFFLES

The black bits found in various food preparations, although called Black Diamonds or Children of the Gods by some knowledgeable professionals, are generally known as truffles. The truffle is a fungus fruit that matures underground; however, not all underground fungi are truffles.

In the days of the Roman Empire, truffles were gathered with much effort and eaten with much pleasure in western Europe, southern portions of the British Isles, all around the Mediterranean and through the Middle East.

Pythagoras, Theophrastus, Pliny, and Orelius recorded their appreciation of truffles which they considered vegetables. Large quantities were brought to Rome from Libya and Spain. This historical fact illustrates the limitation of the scientific knowledge of that age for the far superior black truffles, now known to be abundant in Italy and France, seem not to have been much used.

Classical cooking, after providing hundreds of years of good eating, disappeared with the rest of Greek and Roman civilization; truffles also disappeared, at least from literature, and were reintroduced in Spain in the fourteenth century. Since then, they have rarely been neglected.

From 1729 to 1851, the Tulasne brothers of Paris, and two Italians, Pietro Micheli and Vittorio Pico, produced magnificent studies that have been the foundation of all later scientific works on truffles.

Black truffles, native to Perigord, France, are dark brown or black. Here they are being inspected before processing.

This machine brushes the dirt from the truffles gently as the first step in their preparation.

Before 1729 the nature of truffles was unknown; they were considered to be products of the earth, since they were found under decayed leaves, branches of trees and bushes. Even through the nineteenth century, truffles remained an enigma.

The real story of the growth of truffles is a strange one. The truffle, as commonly observed, is the fruit of a widely spreading system of colorless, microscopic branching threads that penetrate the soil for distances measurable in yards. These threads, known as hyphae, touch the furthest tips of the roots of trees or shrubs.

From the interaction of root and hyphae there is formed a compound structure, part plant and part fungus. However, this fungus cannot further develop without nutrient or vitamins.

When the hyphae have absorbed enough raw material from the soil and the plant they are attached to, they proceed to develop fruit, just as does an apple tree or a grape vine. The fruit that develops from a knot of hyphae is the truffle.

Before men gathered truffles, foxes, pigs, squirrels, and deer were very fond of the fungi. Nowadays, two animals are trained to assist the gathering of truffles. In France, hogs locate the truffle by scent; Italians have trained dogs.

What do truffles look like?
Truffles vary in color from a smooth white surface to a dark chestnut brown or black. The rind is usually a compact, resistant layer composed of thick-walled tissue. They are usually round, although some species resemble fresh ginger in shape. The interior of the truffle has elaborate folds or chambers.

The flavor of truffles also varies considerably. One highly prized variety has a touch of garlic in its flavor; those best known to cooks and generally available seem to combine in one rich particle the savor of a filbert and a properly matured cheese. The odor of this is indescribable, at least in prose.

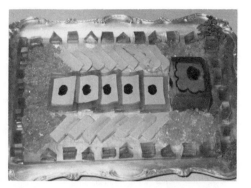

Truffles add sharp black accent to platter of pate arranged on aspic slices; chopped and cubed aspic completes arrangement of Pate Facon du Chef.

Some truffles are sold fresh in France but most of the crop is canned.

Many kinds of truffles are known: over 30 species are found on the European continent and 58 species in North America. Many of these specimens are so rare that they are preserved in museums.

In France, the region of Perigord, situated less than 50 miles from the Bordeaux region, is well known for its crop of truffles. Perigueux is the capital of the Perigord. In culinary art, Sauce Perigueux naturally contains truffles. The heart of Italy, especially the region of Umbria, produces practically the entire output of Italian black and white truffles. White truffles are not very much in demand in Europe for they are of a lesser quality than black truffles.

Geographically, the truffle regions are relatively close to wine regions. A good year for wines will probably result in a poor year for truffles and vice versa. The year 1968 is a perfect example. A rainy summer gave excellent crops of truffles but the quality of the 1968 wine vintage is considered to be fair to poor.

The value of the truffle has always been in its ineffable odor and flavor. The consumption of truffles in the United States today is negligible. However, the U.S. Dept. of Agriculture is carrying out some experiments on black truffles and they may one day be commercially grown on American soil.

From a dietetic point of view, truffles are comparable to oysters. The composition of a truffle is: 72% water, 8 to 10% protein, 4% fat, 13 to 15% carbohydrate, and 2 to 5% mineral substances.

As described in Chapter Five, truffles and truffle sheets are used for decorating a large variety of cold dishes.

CAVIAR

Though the word "caviar" brings the Cossack, and therefore Russia, to mind, it does not appear in the Russian language; there it is known as *"Ikra."*

Caviar is derived from the Turkish word *"Khavyah."* The precious roe was brought to Italy by the knights of the Holy Army. In Italy

Caviar even when served simply requires these accompaniments: lemon; butter; chopped, hard-cooked egg white; and toast points. Here to provide the elegance caviar deserves, butter balls are specially shaped, lemon halves are cut with jagged edges and garnished with parsley, and chopped egg is served in wine glass.

it was named "*Caviala*," and became quite famous in the court of Pope Julius II, in 1300 A.D.

From Italy, caviar was introduced to all European countries. Shakespeare mentioned it in "Hamlet," saying "T'was Caviare to the General!" Savarin's Dictionaire de Commerce, written around 1711, makes clear that it was not despised at the highest tables of France.

What is caviar?

What is this novelty that has such irresistible appeal to gourmets all over the world? It is the salted roe of a species of fish called sturgeon. Caviar can also be roe of salmon or other species. Sturgeon are caught in the Caspian or Black Sea as well as in some other locations.

Until industry and pollution came along, the sturgeon was found in rivers running into the Atlantic and Baltic, in the Rhine, and in North American lakes. Today all caviar comes from Russia, Iran, and Rumania.

Most fish containing roe are caught at breeding time. When they leave the deep ocean waters, like salmon they seek shallow riverbeds in order to spawn. The roe at this time is unsuitable for

consumption because it is oily and unpalatable. When caught during this period, fish are placed in submerged floating cages and, unable to find food, use up the reserve of fat that is stored in the roe, thus making the roe less oily. When roe is right for salting, the fish will be killed.

Of the varieties of sturgeon producing caviar, the Beluga is the largest, sometimes reaching 2500 pounds and producing up to 130 lb. of roe. The next size is the Ocictrova or Osetra, weighing around 400 lb., producing 40 lb. of roe. The smallest of the sturgeon family is the Sevruga which weighs 60 lb. and from which only 8 lb. of roe can be harvested.

The size of the roe, even from the same species, does not denote quality. The roe is taken from the fish, carefully sieved, all tissues and membranes are removed, and it is then steeped in a salt solution. The strength of the solution is carefully controlled as the extent of salting determines the quality of the caviar.

The amount of salt used depends on the grade of the sturgeon roe to be prepared, the weather, the condition of the roe, and the market for which it is destined. Only after the salt has

An ice carving provides an attention-getting base for a caviar set-up. Chopped onion, chopped egg white, toast points, lemon wedges, and chopped egg yolks are suggested accompaniments for caviar.

been added to the sturgeon roe does it become caviar, therefore, there is no such thing as unsalted caviar. For the U.S. market, only salt is used as a preservative; in European countries, salt and borax may be used. Caviar prepared with salt and borax tastes sweeter.

First quality caviar is known as Malosol. This word does not denote a type of caviar, as it means "little salt," and it is used in conjunction with the word Beluga, Osetra, or Sevruga.

The best caviar is prepared from sturgeon caught between March and April, when the water is cool and the fish roe are firm and fresh. Fall fishing does not produce such fine quality caviar because the weather is hotter and this causes the roe to lose its firmness.

Caviar prepared in Russia or Iran and qualifying for the Malosol grade is packed in puds weighing 41 lb. and sent to the consumer in refrigerated containers. Nonrefrigerated caviar, i.e. processed caviar, has a shelf life of about 3 months and usually comes vacuum-packed in 1 oz. to 5 oz. glass jars. After 3 months, white specks may appear; the spots are fat and crystallized salt and are absolutely harmless although not always eye-appealing.

Caviar made by one special process is known as Paiusnaya, or "pressed" caviar. After eggs (roe) have been cleaned in the usual way, caviar is packed in linen bags and hung to drain like cottage cheese. This destroys the natural shape of the roe, as they are pressed together. The caviar is then packed in puds holding 50–100 lb.

It has a much saltier taste than Malosol caviar and it looks very much like a solid mass. It is a great favorite in Russia and among connoisseurs is greatly prized.

The color of all caviar ranges between grey and black. Color is no indication of quality, although some eggs are more eye-appealing than others. There are other products sold under the label of caviar: Keta (Red Caviar), made from salmon roe and labelled as such, and the Lumpfish caviar, or whitefish caviar, which looks like caviar, but in fact is not. Lumpfish caviar is prepared, not from sturgeon, but from a fish producing yellow or green roe that is later dyed with charcoal.

All fresh caviar keeps best at a temperature between 28°F. and 32°F. Caviar should never be frozen or held below 28°F. as it will change into a soupy substance.

Caviar that has been exposed to the air should be eaten within a few days, as air will cause it to deteriorate rapidly. Any container that has been opened should be covered and kept under refrigeration.

Malosol caviar should always be served with toast and unsalted butter. A lesser quality can be served with lemon, toast and butter. Salty caviar should be served with a garnish of finely chopped white onion, chopped egg white, chopped egg yolk, lemon, toast and butter. Sometimes, caviar can be served with "blinis" (little pancakes made of fermented batter of buckwheat) and topped with sour cream. A mixture of whipped cream and caviar can also be made to be served in conjunction with blinis. Caviar should always be served on ice, as room temperature can alter its taste very rapidly.

THERE IS NO SUBSTITUTE FOR GENUINE CAVIAR!!!!!!

(Some of the above information was supplied through the courtesy of the Romanoff Caviar Company.)

CHAPTER SEVEN

FORCEMEAT

A basic element in the preparation of many specialties, farce or forcemeat, made of various seasoned ground foods, is widely used in garde manger preparation. Forcemeat, or farce, is the base for the preparation of pates, terrines, galantines, and ballotines. Farces are also used to stuff or garnish meat, eggs, fish, poultry, game, and vegetables. They are utilized in the preparation of French specialties such as quenelles and mousses.

Fish farces used in cooking are usually combined with panadas. The amount of panada added to a farce is equal to one-half of the weight of the farce. Most farces prepared with meat, poultry, or game are bound together with eggs or egg whites. Farces used for pates and galantines are seasoned with a special spice mixture described in Chapter Seven.

PANADAS

A panada is a binding agent made of flour, bread, or other starch products. Fish quenelle forcemeats contain panadas, and other fine forcemeats, especially chicken or veal, contain a panada as a substitute for eggs. In some cases, both a panada and eggs may be called for. Several versions of panadas are used.

FRANGIPAN PANADA FOR FISH AND POULTRY FORCEMEATS

Yield: 2 lb.

1. Ingredients

Flour	8 oz.
Egg Yolks	7
Melted Butter	6 oz.
Milk	1 pt.
Salt, White Pepper, Nutmeg	touch

Method

Mix the egg yolk and the flour well. Fold the melted butter under and slowly whip in the boiling milk. Season with salt, pepper, and nutmeg. Simmer for 4–5 min., constantly stirring. Fill into a clean dish. Cover with a buttered parchment paper and chill.

2. Ingredients

Water	1 pt.
Salt	1/3 tsp.
Butter	3 oz.
Flour	10 oz.

Method

Bring water, salt, and butter to a boil. Add flour at once and work as for Pate a Choux, stirring until it loosens from the pot. Fill into a clean bowl. Cover with buttered parchment paper and chill.

BREAD PANADA

Yield: 1 lb.

Ingredients

White Bread, cubed, no crust	7 oz.
Milk	1/2 pt.

Method

Combine cubed white bread and milk. Stirring constantly, bring to boil. Cook until thick. Fill into a dish. Cover with greased parchment paper and chill.

PATE A CHOUX

Yield: 3-1/2–4 lb.

Ingredients

Water	1 lb.
Butter	1/2 lb.
Flour	1 lb.
Eggs	12–16

Method

Bring water and butter to a boil. When butter has melted, add flour. Stir until it forms a ball. Cook 2–3 min., constantly stirring. Remove from heat, cool 2–3 min. Stir in eggs, one at a time. Refrigerate, covering with parchment paper to prevent forming of skin.

FORCEMEAT FOR STUFFING QUENELLES AND MOUSSES

Yield: 3-1/2 lb.

Ingredients

Turkey Breast, raw	35 oz.
White Bread, cubed, no crust	7 oz.
Egg Whites	2
Heavy Cream	1 pt.
Shaved Ice	1–2 oz.
Salt, White Pepper, Nutmeg	to taste

Method

Cube turkey meat, chill. Cube white bread, soak with egg whites and a little heavy cream. Chill.

Salt turkey meat and puree in a food processor with some shaved ice. Add some shaved ice and panada and puree well. Add pepper and nutmeg. Add heavy cream slowly while machine is working. Make dumpling test to check consistency and taste.

NOTE: If too tough, add more heavy cream. If it does not hold, add more egg whites (one egg white per pound). Raw fish, veal, or chicken may be used.

FORCEMEATS FOR FISH PATE

Yield: 2 lb.

1. Ingredients

Salmon, Striped Bass, Turbot, Halibut, Trout, or Pike	16 oz.
Cream Sauce, thick, cold	8–10 oz.
Eggs, whole	2
Egg Yolks	4
Salt, White Pepper	to taste

Method

Dice fish and chill; puree in a food processor. Add cold cream sauce and whip into mixture. Add eggs one at a time, work in well. Add the egg yolks. Season with salt and pepper.

2. Ingredients

Salmon, Trout, or Halibut	16 oz.
Pate a Choux (see recipe, this page)	8 oz.

Method
Dice fish, chill, and puree in a food processor. Incorporate pate a choux and season.

3. Ingredients

Salmon, Trout, or Halibut	16 oz.
Butter	6 oz.
Flour Panada	8 oz.
Egg Yolks	3
Egg, whole	1
Salt, Pepper	to taste

Method
Dice fish and chill. Season with salt and puree in a food processor. Add melted butter and panada and mix well. Add the egg yolks one at a time and finally add the whole egg and pepper. Mix well and cook a dumpling to check consistency and correctness.

FORCEMEATS FOR FISH MOUSSE
(Hot or Cold)

Yield: 26 oz. (1); 3 lb. (2)

1. Ingredients

Trout, Sole, Salmon, Halibut	16 oz.
Fresh Ground Pepper, Salt	to taste
Egg Whites, from large eggs	2
Heavy Cream	1/2 pt.

Method
Cube fish and season with salt and pepper. Puree in a food processor. Add egg whites and mix well. Chill for 1 hour and incorporate heavy cream slowly. Form dumplings or fill into fish filets for paupiettes.

2. Ingredients

Trout, Sole, Salmon, Halibut	16 oz.
Bread Panada	8 oz.
Butter	6 oz.
Eggs	4
Heavy Cream	1-1/2 pt.
Salt, Pepper	to taste

Method
Cube fish and season with salt. Puree in a food processor. Add bread panada, melted butter, and pepper mixture. Add eggs one at a time and mix well. Add heavy cream slowly. Adjust seasoning.

BASIC FORCEMEAT

Yield: 3-1/2 to 4 lb.

Ingredients

Turkey or Veal	35 oz.
Salt	to taste
White Bread, cubed, no crust	7 oz.
Egg Whites	2
Heavy Cream	1/2–1 pt.
Shaved Ice	2 oz.

Method
Cube turkey breast or veal. Salt lightly. Cube white bread. Soak with egg whites and a little heavy cream. Grind turkey and bread; chill. Puree in a food processor with shaved ice and slowly add heavy cream. Adjust seasoning.

GRATIN FORCEMEAT

Yield: 16 oz.

Ingredients

Fatback (pork), cubed	4 oz.
Pork Lard	1/2 oz.
Turkey, cubed	4 oz.
Poultry Livers, sliced	4 oz.
Mushrooms, sliced	1 oz.
Shallots	1/2–3/4 oz.
Thyme	1/3 tsp.
Bayleaf	1/4 small
Salt	1/3 oz.
Pepper	1/3 oz.
Madeira	2-1/2 oz.
Butter	2 oz.
Egg Yolks	2
Glace de Viande	1 tbsp.

Method
Saute cubed fat in pork lard and remove. Brown cubed turkey and remove. Stiff sliced livers in the hot fat. Add fat and turkey, shallots and mush-

Chicken Galantine slices are fanned out from a decorated endpiece as are slices of liver pate. Tomato roses provide color contrast for the chaud-froid coated endpieces bordered with designs cut from truffle sheets. The pumpkin shell filled with vegetable flowers is a focal point for the display. Tomato roses on vegetable pedestals and decorated hard-cooked egg halves complete the tray.

rooms, bayleaf and thyme. Season with salt and pepper and mix well. Add Madeira. Cover and braise for 6–7 min. Pour over sieve to remove fat. Reserve fat. Remove bayleaf, and puree in a food processor. Add butter, egg yolk, glace de viande, and the reserved fat. Mix well. Adjust seasoning. Store in a clean dish. Cover with buttered parchment paper.

NOTE: To get a very fine product, force through a sieve. For various flavors, exchange turkey and livers for pheasant or duck.

CHICKEN LIVER PASTE FOR TERRINES, CANAPES, AND BARQUETTES

Yield: 14 covers

Ingredients

Chicken Livers	38 oz.
Fatback, diced	10 oz.
Heavy Cream	4 tbsp.

CHICKEN LIVER MARINADE

Port Wine	8 oz.
Bayleaves, small	2
Thyme	1/2 tsp.
Salt, Black Pepper	to taste

Method

Combine wine, bayleaves, thyme, salt, and pepper. Add cleaned and washed chicken livers and diced fatback and marinate for 12 hours. Remove livers and fatback and dry. Heat some oil and saute fat and livers. (Liver should be pink.) Remove from saute pan and chill.

Deglaze pan with marinade and reduce by 2/3. Cool and blend in a food processor with all of the chilled livers and fat. Add the heavy cream and season with salt and pepper. Fill in an aspic-coated mold or timbales and chill.

NOTE: Can be used for piping canapes, barquettes.

CHICKEN LIVER PARFAIT WITH MANDARINS AND STRAWBERRIES

Method

Pour chicken liver mousse (recipe, p. 145) 1/2-inch thick on a sheet pan lined with parchment paper and chill. Cut chilled parfait into small medallions with a round cutter, and coat lightly with Madeira jelly. Top with a mandarin orange and strawberries.

NOTE: You may use apricots and truffles or grapes as garniture.

✣✣

MOUSSELINE FORCEMEAT (FARCE)

Yield: 3 lb.

Ingredients

Lean Veal or Raw Turkey Breast	2 lb.
Egg Whites	2 to 3
Salt	1/2 to 1 oz.
Pepper	1/3 tsp.
Heavy Cream	3/4 pt.

Method

Grind thoroughly chilled meat. Combine in food chopper with egg whites and seasonings. Add cream.

NOTE: Keep cold at all times.

✣✣

CHAPTER EIGHT

PATES-TERRINES

To many devotees of fine food, the pate sets the standard for foods to come. As defined by the French, a pate is prepared by enclosing a filling of meat, fish, vegetables, or fruit in a pastry case that has a bottom and a top. However, basically, the word "pate" should apply only to meat or fish preparations enclosed in a dough and baked in the oven. In addition, the term is also used to describe any preparation put into an earthenware dish that has been lined with thin layers of fresh pork fat and is then baked in the oven. The correct name for this type of dish is terrine, although common usage has applied the term "pate" to these preparations which are always served cold.

PATES

A large variety of ingredients and garnishes are used in pates; the most common are liver, truffles, various forcemeats, and seasonings. The use of goose liver brings a particular flavor to pates. Chicken livers may be substituted and should be soaked in milk for 24 hours. (For more details on the use of goose liver, see Chapter Six on Foie Gras.)

Europe has not only the advantage of having fresh goose liver, but also fresh aromatic truffles which play a major part in preparing pates and terrines. However, canned truffles can be used when fresh truffles are not available.

How to Work with Livers
It is essential to handle livers with care. Remove gall bladder, all veins, blood clots, if any, and surrounding skin. Then wash livers in cold water and soak in milk for 24 hours, after which they should be thoroughly drained, seasoned, and kept refrigerated.

How to Work with Truffles
Whether fresh or canned, truffles should be thoroughly washed and stored in lightly salted water. Before using, peel and slice, dice or cut into julienne, then marinate in sherry or port wine.

How to Prepare Forcemeat, or Farce, for Pates and Terrines
Forcemeat, or farce, is a ground meat mixture that can be seasoned either highly or subtly. Gen-

erally forcemeat is composed of the following combination:

> 2 parts dominant meat
> 1 part lean pork
> 2 parts pork fat

Seasonings and garnishes vary according to the recipe. The forcemeat is prepared by grinding all above-mentioned ingredients separately through the fine-to-medium plate of a meat grinder. Then chill. Season meat with salt and run through food chopper or food processor. When proper consistency, add fat and combine, then add spices. It should be mixed well and ingredients should be kept cold at all times (35–40°F.).

How to Blend the Seasonings. Before adding the seasonings to the forcemeat, the herbs and spices should be combined in a blender until pulverized, then put through a wire sieve and kept in a tightly covered container to preserve the aroma. Only dried spices and herbs should be used.

Here are four spice and herb combinations that can be blended into a forcemeat:

Seasonings for Forcemeat
1. As listed by master chef August Escoffier:

Bayleaf	1-1/4 oz.
Thyme	3/4 oz.
Coriander	3/4 oz.
Cinnamon	1 oz.
Nutmeg	1-1/2 oz.
Cloves	1 oz.
Ginger	3/4 oz.
Mace	3/4 oz.
Black Pepper	1-1/4 oz.
Cayenne Pepper	1/4 oz.
White Pepper	1-1/4 oz.

2. As listed by the authors:

Cloves	1/2 oz.
Ginger	1/2 oz.
Nutmeg	1/2 oz.
Paprika	1/2 oz.
Basil	1/3 oz.
Black Pepper	1/3 oz.
White Pepper	1/3 oz.
Bayleaf	1/6 oz.
Thyme	1/2 oz.
Marjoram	1/6 oz.

NOTE: 1/6 oz. of pate spice is used per pound of forcemeat.

Spices
1. For Fine Forcemeat

White Pepper	1-1/2 oz.
Coriander	3/4 oz.
Thyme	1-3/4 oz.
Basil	1-3/4 oz.
Cloves	3/4 oz.
Nutmeg	1-1/2 oz.
Bayleaf	1/2 oz.
Piment	3/4 oz.
Mace	3/4 oz.
Dried Cepes	1 oz.

2. For Special or Game Pates

White Pepper	3/4 oz.
Black Pepper	3/4 oz.
Hungarian Paprika	3/4 oz.
Marjoram	1/3 oz.
Thyme	3/4 oz.
Basil	3/4 oz.
Nutmeg	3/4 oz.
Mace	3/4 oz.
Bayleaf	3/4 oz.
Cloves	3/4 oz.
Ginger	3/4 oz.
Juniper Berries	1-3/4 oz.
Dried Wild Mushrooms (Mousseron)	3-1/2 oz.

NOTE: For seasoning pate forcemeats, mix 1/2–1-1/2 oz. of pate spice mixture with 16 oz. of salt and keep well covered. To season forcemeats we recommend using 1/2–3/4 oz. spice salt for 2 lbs. of mixture, or to taste.

PATE DOUGH

Yield: 4 lb.

Ingredients

Butter	12 oz.
Flour	35 oz.
Eggs	3
Water, lukewarm	10–14 oz.
Salt	3/4 oz.

Method

Flake butter into flour. Add egg, water, and salt and mix lightly. Let rest for 2 hours in refrigerator.

Preparation of Pate en Croute

1. Select a hinged mold, either round, oval, or rectangular (the type of mold will depend on the nature of the pate); oil or butter mold carefully.
2. Take 3/4 of the dough and roll it out with a rolling pin to about 1/8 in. in thickness.
3. Cut dough into four pieces. (See illustration, p. 118). Use 1-1/2 lb. of dough per mold.
4. Press dough all around the walls and into the bottom of the mold. The dough should overlap the edge of the mold about 1/2 in., and this overlapping dough will later be used to seal the lid.
5. Line the bottom and walls of the mold with thin slices of fatback or slices of bacon (optional), then cover evenly with a thin layer of an appropriate forcemeat.
6. Place the ingredients in the mold as indicated in the recipe. The ingredients put in the center are usually an arrangement of various meats (veal, pork, poultry, etc.) and truffles that have been marinated in brandy and will provide a decorative center for the finished pate. The decorative center or garnish should be placed in the center of the mold and sealed with a small quantity of forcemeat. Fill the mold with the remaining forcemeat and cover with a thin slice of fresh pork fat (optional).
7. Roll out remaining dough and cut into the same shape as the top of the mold. Moisten the edge of the dough with an eggwash and

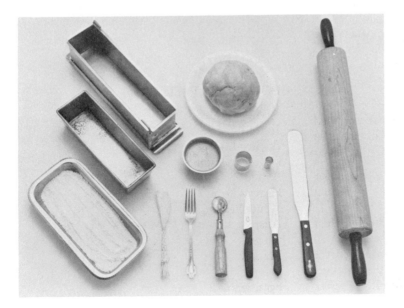

How to Prepare a Pate en Croute
1. *Mise en place: a. Hinged pate mold or loaf mold, b. pate dough, c. rolling pin, d. large and small pallette knife, e. paring knife, f. dough cutter, g. table fork, h. feather brush, i. flour to dust, j. eggwash, k. round cutters.*

(continued)

2. Roll pate dough approximately 1/8 in. thick. Cut into four pieces as shown.

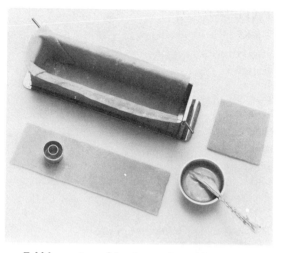

3. Fold large piece of dough into the mold, letting it overlap by 1/2 in. Brush corners with eggwash and fold smaller dough pieces over the end of the mold. Press overlapping dough corners or layers together to seal.

seal onto the top of the mold. Trim neatly with a knife.

8. Decorate the top of the mold with fancy shapes cut from the dough trimmings. Brush with eggwash. In the center of the mold, make a circular hole called a chimney, to allow steam to escape while the pate is baking. A piece of parchment paper rolled into a tube may be placed in the chimney.

How to Bake a Pate
The baking method, unless otherwise indicated in a specific recipe, is the same for all pates. To bake a pate:

1. Preheat oven to 400°-425°F. Bake pate for 10 to 15 min., or until dough is golden brown.
2. Reduce temperature to 325°-350°F., then bake pate until well done.
3. To test the doneness of the pate, insert a tester through the chimney all the way into the pate; leave it there briefly. If the tester comes out dry and evenly warm, the pate is ready. Or use a thermometer reading 160°F. internal temperature.

4. Take pate out of the oven and allow to cool for 1 hour; fill the cavity of the pate with aspic gelee; then place in refrigerator and chill.

❧ ❧

POULTRY LIVER PATE
Yield: 12 portions

Ingredients

Poultry Livers	2 lb.
Onion, medium	1/2
Butter	1 to 2 oz.
Heavy Cream	7 oz.
White Pepper	1 tsp.
Allspice	1/2 tsp.
Ginger	1/2 tsp.
Brandy	1 oz.
Salt	1/2 to 1 oz.
Eggs, whole	3

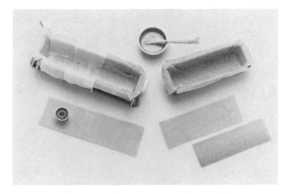

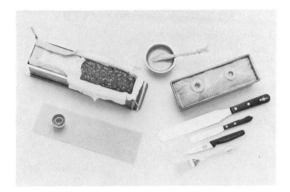

4. Outline dough-lined mold with thinly sliced fatback or turkey, ham, etc. (optional).
NOTE: If loaf mold is used, outline bottom of mold with a well-buttered parchment paper.

5. Fill mold with forcemeat and garnish. Fold lining and dough over and brush with eggwash.
NOTE: Forcemeat must be pressed well to avoid air pockets.

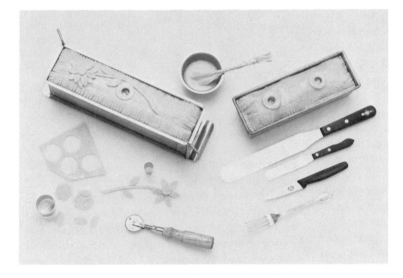

6. Top pate with rest of dough. Press down with a dinner fork on all sides to seal. Cut holes (chimneys) into the dough cover to permit steam to escape. For garnish, cut out dough as shown. Brush dough well with eggwash and decorate. Bake as described by recipe.

Flour	4 oz.
Fresh Fatback	8 oz., to line mold

Method

Prepare the livers as directed in the section "How to Work with Livers," p. 115.

Dice onion fine and saute in butter. Combine livers with onions, heavy cream, spices, brandy, and salt. Mix to a fine paste in an electric blender. Add eggs and flour and mix all ingredients.

Pour liquid forcemeat into a mold lined with slices of fresh fatback. Cover with thin slices of fresh fatback and then with aluminum foil. Puncture a hole in foil and bake pate in a waterbath for one hour at 350°F.

PATE OF CHICKEN AND LIVERS

Yield: 14 portions

Ingredients

Chicken	2-1/2 lb.
Chicken Livers, soaked in milk	9 oz.
Truffles	1 oz.
Brandy	1 oz.
Raw Chicken Leg Meat	12 oz.
Fatback, thinly sliced or	
Pig's Caul	8 oz.
Shaved Ice	1–2 oz.
Salt	1 oz.
White Pepper, Mace	to taste
Pate Dough	2 lb.
Madeira Aspic Jelly	1-1/2 pt.
Pork Fat	20 oz.

Method

Bone and skin the chicken. Save chicken breast, remove all meat from bones. Cut chicken breast in 1/2-in. strips. Clean, wash, and dry livers. Cut truffles into small cubes. Marinate chicken breast, liver, and truffles for 2 hours or overnight in brandy.

Cube the chicken leg meat except chicken breast and chill. Cube additional leg meat and chill. Cube fatback and chill. Grind or puree in food processor together with 1 oz. of chicken liver and 1–2 oz. shaved ice. Season with salt, pepper, mace, and brandy. Remove from machine.

Fold truffles into forcemeat. Line pate mold with dough and brush with eggwash. Line with forcemeat. Fill, alternating with chicken breast strips, blanched livers, and forcemeat. Top with forcemeat.

Close with pate dough, cut chimneys. Brush with eggwash and bake for 60 min. in a 350°F. oven or to 160°F. internal temperature. Let rest for 1 hour and fill cavity with Madeira aspic. Chill for 12 hours.

NOTES: You may use thinly sliced smoked dried beef, corned beef, or chicken to line pate mold instead of eggwash. Blanch marinated liver for 1 min. in boiling salt water and shock in ice water. Drain and dry.

꙳꙳

PATE OF TURKEY EN CROUTE

Yield: 14–16 portions

Ingredients

Chicken	16 oz.
Raw Turkey Meat	1-1/2 lb.
Turkey Livers, soaked in milk	6 oz.
Truffle	1–2 oz.
Salt, Pepper	to taste
Smoked Beef Tongue, small	
cubes	4 oz.

MARINADE

Carrot, diced	1
Shallots, diced	3
Parsley Stems, diced	3
Peppercorns (sachet)	10
Butter	3 tbsp.
Madeira	5 oz.
Chicken Broth or Stock	1 pt.
Fatback, thinly sliced	12 oz.

Method

Prepare marinade; saute carrot, shallots, and parsley stems in butter. Add peppercorns. Add Madeira and chicken stock. Bring to boil and chill. Bone chicken, remove skin and sinews, and cube the meat. Bone turkey, remove skin and sinews, and cube meat. Combine chicken and turkey meat, salt, and pepper, and chill. Pour marinade over meat and marinate 2 hours or overnight.

Prepare pate dough (see recipe, p. 117). Remove turkey livers from milk, dry and chop livers coarsely and mix with diced truffle. Remove meat and carrot from marinade. Line pate mold with dough. Line with fatback. Fill half with meat, carrots, and small-cubed beef tongue. Top with coarsely chopped liver and truffles. Fill in rest of meat, tongue, and carrot

How to Slice a Pate en Croute

1. To slice pate en croute, arrange a mise en place, using a pan of water and a carving knife.

2. To start slicing, slide knife forward as shown.

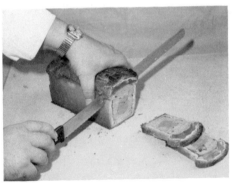

3. Continue slicing, bringing end of knife nearest you down slightly.

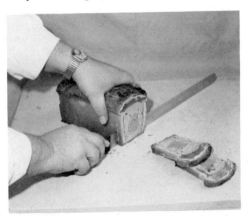

4. Cut straight down the rest of the way through the loaf, sawing gently back and forth to complete slices.

5. Place slices on rack to be arranged later. Decorate an unsliced piece of pate en croute as focal point of presentation.

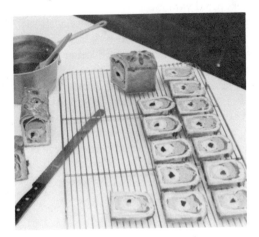

mixture. Enclose with fatback and dough. Cut chimney and decorate.

Bake pate at 325°–350°F. for 1-1/2 hours or to 160°F. internal temperature. Fill pate with aspic gelee. Chill pate overnight.

NOTES: This pate can be served hot. Instead of fatback lining, use thinly sliced dried smoked beef, corned beef, or turkey. To give better bind, liver and meat could be mixed with breadcrumbs or egg albumen.

SAUSAGE PATE

Yield: 3 lb.

Ingredients

Fatback, thinly sliced	8 oz., to line mold
Garlic Sausage, cubed	8 oz.
Red Pepper, diced	1/2
Green Pepper, diced	1/2
Lemon	juice of 1
Basic forcemeat (see recipe)	17 oz.
Lemon, grated	zest of 1
Green Peppercorn	1 tsp.
Bologna, cubed	8 oz.
Ham, cubed	8 oz.
Cervelate Salami, cubed	8 oz.

Method

Line pate loaf mold with fatback. Cube sausage, dice red and green peppers, and sprinkle well with lemon juice. Prepare basic forcemeat. Add lemon zest and green peppercorns. Fold all other ingredients into it and mix well.

Fill into fatback-lined loaf mold. Cover top with fatback. Cover with aluminum foil and bake in a waterbath for 1 hour at 300 to 350°F. or until 160°F. internal temperature. Remove from heat and weigh down with a wood board. Serve with a cold herb mayonnaise.

NOTE: 6 oz. of canned mushroom bottoms could be added.

PATE OF LAMB, SHEEPHERDER STYLE

Yield: 12–14 portions

Ingredients

Lean Lamb, diced	10-1/2 oz.
Lean Pork, diced	9 oz.
Pork Fat, diced	10-1/2 oz.
Pate Spice	2 tsp.
Basil	1 tsp.
Oregano	1/2 tsp.
Juniper Berries, crushed	5
Garlic Clove, crushed	1
Orange, grated zest	1/2
Salt	to taste

GARNISH

Lamb Filets	2–3
Salt/Pepper	to taste
Butter	1 oz.
Green Peppercorns	1 tbsp.
Ham, diced	3 oz.
Pate Dough	2 lbs.
Egg	1
Aspic Gelee	2 pts.

Method

Grind lamb and pork. Season with salt; chill. Grind pork fat—do not season; chill. Puree pork and lamb in a food processor, fine. Remove 2/3 from machine. Add pork fat and puree fine.

Add removed 2/3 of ground meat and all spices. Mix well. Make a test dumpling, simmer, and taste. Adjust seasoning.

Trim filet, season with salt and pepper. Sear in clarified butter; chill.

Fold peppercorns and ham under forcemeat. Roll out dough and line pate mold. Fill half with forcemeat, set lamb filet in center; fill with forcemeat.

Close with dough cover and wash with egg-wash. Bake in a 350°F. oven for 1-1/2 hours or until 160°F. internal temperature. Remove, let rest for 1 hour, and fill with aspic gelee; chill.

NOTE: You may want to line the pate dough with prosciutto ham.

Three-dimensional diamond designs made of egg, tomato, and truffle-colored aspic sheets highlight slices of turkey liver pate. Apple circles poached in white wine and topped with a black cherry and an almond slice offer color and flavor contrast.

well. Add Madeira and brandy marinade and mix well. Chill forcemeat for 30 min.

Roll out pate dough 1/3 in. and outline pate mold. Outline dough-lined mold with thin fatback. Line mold with forcemeat. Fill cavity with blanched, drained, and well-dried livers. Cover with fatback and forcemeat. Enclose with dough, cut chimneys and brush with eggwash, then decorate.

Bake in a 350°F. oven 60–70 min. or until 160°F. internal temperature. Remove and chill for 1–2 hours. Fill with Madeira aspic and chill. Unmold and serve.

NOTES: 1–2 oz. shaved ice may be added to turkey meat when pureeing. Fill aspic gelee into pate while still warm. To give better bind to chicken liver, add some breadcrumbs, flour, or egg albumen.

PENNSYLVANIA LIVER PATE

Yield: 5 lb.

Ingredients

Poultry Livers, soaked in milk	1-1/2 lb.
Truffles	1 oz.
Thyme, Pate Spice	to taste
Salt, Pepper	to taste
Bayleaf	1
Brandy	1-1/2 oz.
Madeira	1-1/2 oz.
Turkey Meat	14 oz.
Fatback	10 oz.
Flour	1 tbsp.
Pate Dough	1-1/2 lb.
Egg	1
Madeira Aspic	1 pt.

Method

Trim livers and soak overnight in milk. Remove, wash, and drain. Mix livers with truffle and marinate with pate spice, salt, pepper, bayleaf, and brandy and Madeira for 2 hours or overnight. Puree cubed chilled turkey and fatback in a food processor. Add salt and pepper and 2 oz. of the liver. Add one tablespoon of flour. Mix

ROOSTER A LA GABRIELLE KRIENS
(The Recipe of a Country Lady)

Yield: 12–14 portions

Ingredients

Rooster	2-1/2 lb.
Salt, Pepper, Sage	to taste
Madeira	1 oz.
Chicken Liver, soaked in milk	8 oz.
Morrels, dried	1/2 oz.
Frozen Peas	1 oz.
Pig's Caul, soaked in salt water	1
Basic Forcemeat (see recipe, page 111)	1 lb.
Pate Dough	2-2-1/2 lb.
Eggwash	1 egg

Method

Butterfly rooster (see galantine, page 135). Sprinkle with salt, pepper, sage, and a few drops of Madeira and refrigerate. Marinate chicken liver 2 hours in Madeira. Drain, blanch, shock in ice water and dry.

Mix liver, dried morrels, and frozen peas with basic forcemeat. Spread pig's caul on a cheesecloth. Top with butterflied rooster. Top with

Pate of Pheasant, sliced and covered with clear aspic for extra sparkle, is arranged with whole pears poached in white wine and garnished with mint leaves. Skewer on portion of uncut Pate adds height.

forcemeat. Roll like galantine and enclose with pig's caul and refrigerate.

Roll out pate dough 1/3 in. thick. Wash with eggwash and enclose rooster roll. Cut chimney into dough and decorate. Wash with eggwash. Let rest for 30 min., then bake in a 325°–350°F. oven for 1-1/2–2 hours or to 160°F. internal temperature. Cool and fill with Madeira aspic. Chill overnight. Garnish with orange, apples, and grapes.

ॐ ॐ

PATE OF PHEASANT

Yield: 3 to 4 lb.

Ingredients

Pheasants (bone and reserve for garnish)	2

FOND

Bones	
Oil	3 tbsp.
Carrot } mirepoix	1
Onion, small }	1
Water	3-1/2 pt. (or more)

BOUQUET GARNI

White Leek	1
Celery Stick	1
Parsnip	1/2
Bayleaf	1
Salt (optional)	1 tsp.
Juniper Berries	8
Garlic	1 clove
White Peppercorns	6

GARNISH

Breast of Pheasant	4
Pate Salt, White Pepper	sprinkle
Butter	1 oz.
Shallots, diced	2
Brandy	1 oz.
Juniper Berries, crushed	5
Garlic	1/2 clove
Orange, grated zest	1/4
Lemon, grated zest	1/4
Poultry or Pheasant Liver, marinated (optional)	5 oz.
Port Aspic Gelee	1-1-1/2 pt.
Pistachio Nuts	1-3/4 oz.
Diced Tongue	1 oz.
Truffle	1
Pate Dough	24 oz.
Eggwash	1 egg

FORCEMEAT

Pheasant Meat, cubed	8–9 oz.
Lean Pork, cubed	4 oz.
Fresh Pork Fat, cubed	9 oz.
Pate Salt	1/3 oz. or to taste

Juniper Berries, crushed	8
White Pepper	1/2 tsp.
Orange, grated zest	1/4

Method

Bone birds, remove skin, sinews, save breast, trim off meat (8–9 oz.).

FOND

Brown bones, skins in oil (400°F. oven). After 10 min. add mirepoix and brown, add water, simmer 2–3 hours (30 min. before add bouquet). Strain, reduce.

GARNISH

Season breast with pate salt and pepper, sear in oil. Remove breast and chill. Remove oil. Add butter to pan, saute shallots golden. Add brandy, 18 oz. fond, juniper berries, garlic, and orange and lemon zests. Reduce by 2/3, pour over breast, and chill.

Blanch liver, chill and cube. Peel pistachio nuts, dice truffle, dice tongue; chill.

FORCEMEAT

Grind twice through fine blade or puree in a food processor the pheasant meat, pork, and fat; add all spices and seasoning. Fold in garnish.

Outline pate mold with dough, outline dough with 1/3 forcemeat, alternate breasts and forcemeat, brush each layer with fond. Close with dough. Brush with eggwash. Bake at 350°F. 50 min. or until 160°F. internal temperature. Fill with port aspic gelee and chill.

ᴄᵛ ᴋ

PARFAIT OF PHEASANT

Yield: 14 portions

Ingredients

Pheasants (2 lbs. each)	3
Onions, sliced thin	3 oz.
Bayleaves, small	2
Juniper Berries	10
Cream	2 pts.
White Bread, cubed	11 oz.

Slab Bacon, cubed	7 oz.
Nutmeg, Paprika, Salt	to taste
Currants	1-1/2 oz.
Fatback, thinly sliced	8 oz.
Madeira Aspic	1 pt.

Method

Bone pheasants and remove breast and save. Simmer bones, skin, neck, heart, and giblet with onions, bayleaves, and juniper berries in 2-1/2 pt. chicken stock for 1 hour. Strain and reduce to 1 pt. Add cream and reduce to 1-1/2 pts. and cool.

Soak bread in boiling water, squeeze, and cool. Cube bacon and render. Strain and chill fat. Cube pheasant breast and chill. Season with salt and puree in a food processor. Add white bread and blend. Add chilled bacon fat and mix well. Add paprika and nutmeg. Add reduced cream slowly. Fold in currants.

Outline pate mold with fatback. Outline mold with 2/3 of forcemeat. Puree pheasant liver and mix into the rest of the forcemeat. Fill into center of pate mold. Enclose with regular forcemeat. Cover with fatback. Top with buttered parchment paper.

Cover with aluminum foil and poach in a waterbath (light heat) 40–50 min. or to 160°F. internal temperature. Chill and unmold. Decorate and coat with Madeira aspic. Serve with Cumberland sauce.

ᴄᵛ ᴋ

COLD SEAFOOD PATE SURF AND TURF

Yield: 6 lb.

Ingredients

Fresh Striped Bass or Sole	28 oz.
Bread Panada	9 oz.
Brandy	1/2 oz.
Pepper	1/2 tsp.
Egg Whites	9
Turkey Breast or Chicken Breast	14 oz.

(continued)

Cold Seafood Pate Surf and Turf
(continued)

Shrimps	14 oz.
Dry Vermouth	2 oz.
Heavy Cream	1-1/2 pt.
Chicken-lobster, cooked for garnish	1
Lobster Tails, cooked	2
Pistachio Nuts, peeled, or Green Peas	2-1/2 oz.
Truffle	1 oz.
Fresh Mushrooms	6 oz.

GARNITURE

Mushroom Buttons	4 oz.
Asparagus Tips	15
Tomatoes, blanched	4
Cucumbers	2
Fresh Dill, Lemon Wedges	as needed
Hatelet	

Method
FIRST FORCEMEAT
Cube filet of striped bass and chill. Season with salt. Puree in a food processor with 1–2 oz. of shaved ice and 6 oz. bread panada (see recipe). Add cold brandy, pepper, and 6 egg whites and blend well. Add up to 1 pt. of heavy cream slowly while machine is working. Mix well and chill forcemeat.

SECOND FORCEMEAT
Cube turkey breast and shrimps. Season with salt and chill. Puree in a food processor with 2 oz. shaved ice. Add 3 oz. panada, pepper, and vermouth, and mix well. Add 3 egg whites, blend well. Add 1/2 pt. of heavy cream slowly and blend well. Make a test dumpling and poach.

Remove tailmeat from chicken-lobster. Dice all lobster tails roughly. Peel pistachio nuts. Dice truffle and 2–3 oz. of the mushrooms. Fold diced lobster meat, pistachio nuts, truffle, and mushrooms into turkey-shrimp forcemeat and chill.

SEAFOOD PATE
Grease 2 3-lb. loaf molds with butter and dust with flour. Line molds evenly with 1/2 of the first forcemeat and chill. Fill with second forcemeat and cover top with first forcemeat. Cover with aluminum foil. Poach in a waterbath in a 200°–225°F. oven until 160°F. internal temperature.

Remove from waterbath, let rest for 30 min. Lightly weight down. Remove from mold and chill. Coat with fish aspic.

FOR GARNITURE
Form rest of first forcemeat into oval fish dumplings and poach in a fish fumet. Chill.

Blanch 4 oz. of mushroom buttons. Poach asparagus tips. Blanch tomatoes and peel and cut into wedges. Cut cucumbers into olivettes and blanch. Prepare lobster carcass for garnish. Prepare marinade of 1/2 cup vinegar, 3/4 cup water, 1 tsp. salt, and 1 tsp. sugar and marinate vegetables.

Slice 3/4 of pate and brush with aspic. Top large piece at will with fish dumpling and vegetables and dill sprigs. Let fall over to the side like a cornucopia. Set lobster carcass onto the pate for effect. Prepare hatelet and set into place. Arrange cut slices of pate like a fan around centerpiece. Cut lemon into wedges and incorporate into the set-up. Serve with Tyrolliene sauce.

⚜

VENISON PATE EN CROUTE
Yield: 2 lb.
Ingredients

Venison Meat, possibly from leg	5 oz.
Lean Pork	5 oz.
Pork Fat	5-1/2 oz.
Pate Salt	1/3 oz.
Juniper Berries, crushed	5
Orange, Lemon, grated zest	1/4 each

Method

Cut venison, pork, and pork fat into cubes, chill, and grind twice fine or puree in food processor together with juniper berries and zests. From bones prepare a fond.

GARNISH

Ingredients

Venison, cut like a filet from the leg meat, or use loin	2, 9 oz. each
Pate Salt	1/2–1 tsp.
Oil	2 tbsp.
Butter	1 tbsp.
Shallots	1 oz.
Brandy	3/4 oz.
Game Fond	16 oz.
Juniper Berries, crushed	4
Orange, Lemon, zest	1/4 each
Pistachio Nuts, peeled, coarsely chopped	1 oz.
Ham, diced	1-1/2 oz.
Tongue, diced	2 oz.
Truffle	3/4 oz.

Method

Heat oil and sear venison filet; remove oil and filet; add butter; add shallots, brandy, juniper berries, and zest; add fond; reduce by 2/3, and pour over filet and chill.

Ingredients

Pate Dough	21–24 oz.
Eggwash	1 egg
Mold	2 lb.

Method

Prepare pate as designated on page 117, bake for 40 min. in a 350°F. oven or to 160°F. internal temperature.

❧ ❧

PATE OF RABBIT

Yield: 3–4 lb.

Ingredients

Rabbit	5 lb.(approx.)
Rabbit Trimmings	14 oz.
Lean Pork (loin)	14 oz.
Fat	14 oz.
Salt	2 tsp.
Green Pepper, dried	1/2 tsp.
Mace	1/2 tsp.
Thyme	1 tsp.
Rosemary	1/3 tsp.
Eggs	2

GARNISH

Butter	1 oz.
Rabbit or Chicken Liver	1
Brandy	3/4 oz.
Garlic Clove	1
Shallots	2
White Peppercorns	10
Cardamom	1/3 tsp.
Mushrooms, cubed	3-1/2 oz.
Ham, diced	5 oz.
Prosciutto, thinly sliced	16 oz.
Pate Dough	2 lb.

FOND

Rabbit Bones	All
Veal Bones	16 oz.
Oil	3 tbsp.
Onion	1
Carrots	3-1/2 oz.
Celery	3-1/2 oz.
Bayleaf	1
White Peppercorns	5

Method

Bone rabbit and save loins for garnish. Trim the leftover meat (14 oz.) and cube. Cube pork, and combine and add salt and spices and chill. Cube fat and chill.

FOND

Take bone trimmings of rabbit and veal bones, cut small and brown in oil. Add onions, carrots, celery, bayleaf, peppercorns, and water. Simmer 1–2 hours, strain, and reduce to 1/4.

GARNISH

Heat butter, sear loins and liver, add brandy and flame. Remove loins and liver. Add shallots, garlic, peppercorns, cardamom, and fond. Reduce to 1/2 cup. Strain and cool.

FORCEMEAT
Grind or puree rabbit, pork, and fat. Fold in eggs and fond (combine egg and fond first). Add green pepper, mace, thyme, and rosemary. Fold in diced liver, mushroom, and ham.

MOLD
Outline pate mold with dough and prosciutto or ham. Fill half with forcemeat and top with loin. Finish with forcemeat and press well. Enclose with prosciutto or ham and dough. Brush with eggwash. Bake in a 350°F. oven until 160°F. internal temperature. Rest for 1 hour, fill with port aspic.

VEGETABLE SAUSAGE PATE
Yield: 3 to 3-1/2 lb.
Ingredients
Oil	to grease the mold
Boston Lettuce or Romaine Lettuce	
Onion, diced finely	1
Savoy Cabbage, shredded	1
Beef Broth	1-1/2 pt.
Bayleaf	1
Pepper, Salt, Thyme, Basil	to taste
Plain Gelatin	1 oz.
Heavy Cream, whipped	1/2 pt.

GARNISH
Bologna, cut in julienne	16 oz.
Ham, cut in julienne	16 oz.

Method
Oil pate mold. Blanch lettuce in boiling salt water. Cool and drain well. Outline mold with 2–3 layers of lettuce; let lettuce overlap by 2 in.

Dice onions and saute in butter. Add shredded cabbage. Add 1-1/2 pt. beef or chicken stock. Add bayleaf and simmer until cooked.

Remove bayleaf and puree in blender. Season with salt, basil, pepper, and thyme. Add enough hot beef stock to make 1 pt. of mixture. Add gelatin. Whip heavy cream and fold into cabbage mixture. Fold the julienne bologna and ham into the mixture.

Fill into lettuce-lined mold. Cover with overlapping lettuce leaves. Chill well. Unmold and cover with aspic.

NOTE: Instead of sausages you can use 8 oz. cubed, blanched carrots; cubed, blanched rutabaga; cubed, blanched turnips; or cubed, blanched cucumbers. Instead of ham and bologna, you can use cooked turkey meat and salami, 16 oz. of each.

PATE OF SALMON MORNING GLOW
Yield: 14 covers
Ingredients
Milk	2 oz.
Flour	3 oz.
Egg Yolks	3
Salt, Pepper, Nutmeg	to taste
Fresh Butter	1-1/2 oz.
Striped Bass or Fresh Sole or Halibut	10 oz.
Egg White (whole)	1
White Wine	1 oz.
Brandy	1 oz.
Fresh Salmon	21 oz.
Pistachio Nuts or Peas	1-1/2 oz.
Truffles	1 oz.

Method
Prepare panada by mixing cold milk with flour, egg yolks, salt, pepper, and nutmeg. Stir constantly, bring it to a boil. Stir until thick. Remove from heat and fold in butter. Put back on heat and stir for 2–3 min. Chill for 30 min. or until cold.

Cube striped bass and chill. Puree in a food processor. Add panada and blend well. Add egg white, white wine, and brandy. Blend well. Cut salmon into 1/2-in. cubes. Season with salt and pepper, and chill.

Grease a loaf mold with butter and dust with flour. Fill, alternating forcemeat, salmon cubes, pistachio nuts, and truffles. Cover with parchment paper and aluminum foil (pierce aluminum foil). Bake in a waterbath in a 325°–350°F. oven for 1-1/2 hours or until 160°F. internal temperature. Let rest for 1 hour. Lightly press down and cool. Remove from pate mold and chill. Coat with aspic and decorate.

꙳ ꙳

VEAL AND HAM PATE

Yield: 12 covers

Ingredients

Pate Dough	1 lb.
Beef Jerky or Bacon, thinly sliced	10 oz.
Lean Veal	21 oz.
Onions, finely diced	3 oz.
Parsley, chopped	3 tbsp.
Salt and Pepper	to taste
Ham	21 oz.
Eggs, hard-cooked	4 oz.
Veal Aspic, strong	1/2–1 pt. (approx.)

Method

Line quiche pie mold or cake mold with dough. Line with thinly sliced beef jerky or bacon.

Cover bottom of pie with thinly sliced and sauteed veal. Sprinkle with onions, parsley, salt, and pepper. Top with sliced ham. Sprinkle with onions, parsley. Top with sliced eggs.

Repeat steps in preceding paragraph. Fold beef jerky over the eggs; fold dough over. Wash with eggwash.

Top with pate dough. Seal sides. Cut chimney and decorate. Brush with eggwash and bake in a 450°F. oven for 15–20 min. Remove and cool. Fill with aspic and chill. Serve with mustard vegetables.

꙳ ꙳

STUFFED SOUTH PACIFIC HALIBUT

Yield: 30 covers

Ingredients

Striped Bass or Sole	10 oz.
Frangipan Panada	11 oz.
Salt, Cayenne Pepper, Nutmeg	to taste
Shaved Ice	1–2 oz.
Eggs, whole	2
Egg Yolks	2
Truffles	2–3 oz.
Langostinos	3 oz.
Red Peppers, peeled, deseeded	7
Green Pepper, peeled, deseeded	1
Halibut (one)	5–6 lbs.
Fish Fumet, enforced with gelatin (2–3 oz. gelatin for each gallon of fumet)	1–2 gal.

Method

Cube striped bass and chill. Prepare frangipan panada and chill.

Season fish with salt, pepper, and nutmeg. Puree in a food processor. Add ice and panada and blend well. Add whole eggs and egg yolks. Mix well and remove from machine. Fold in the diced truffle, langostinos, and blanched, roughly cut red and green peppers. Refrigerate.

Butterfly halibut filets on the dark side. Remove fins. Remove the bone. Season with salt and pepper. Fill lightly with forcemeat and roll into plastic wrap. Set with the dark side down on a wire rack and set into a poacher. Cover with hot fish fumet (with gelatin) and simmer at 170°F. for 1-1/2 hours or to 150°F. internal temperature.

Press lightly while cooling. Remove from fish jelly. Remove plastic wrap and all remaining bones. Coat with aspic. Decorate head and tail. Cut into portions and arrange.

NOTE: For garnish use per portion: (1) stuffed egg garnished with asparagus, black olives, and pimento strips, or (2) oval zucchini slices topped with tomato mousse and baby corn.

꙳ ꙳

RIVER SALMON PATE

Yield: 12 portions

Ingredients

PANADA

Flour	4 oz.
Butter	3 oz.
Egg Yolks	4
Milk	1/2 pt.
Salt, Pepper	to taste

FORCEMEAT

White Mushrooms	7 oz.
Butter	3 tbsp.
Salmon	28 oz.
Shallots, finely diced	3 tbsp.
Parsley, chopped	1 tbsp.
White Wine	3 oz.
Salt, Pepper	to taste
Egg Whites	4
Heavy Cream	1 pt.

Method

Mix flour, butter, egg yolks, salt, and pepper. Add boiling milk and stir until thick and it loosens from the pot. Chill. Julienne mushrooms and saute in butter. Chill. Cube 7 oz. salmon and saute over high heat quickly. Chill. Saute shallots and parsley in butter. Add white wine. Reduce by half and pour over salmon pieces. Chill.

Cube 21 oz. salmon; add salt and pepper. Chill. Blend in food processor into a fine paste. Add panada and blend well. Add egg whites and blend for 3–4 min. Add heavy cream slowly and blend well. Remove from machine and make the dumpling test (cook a dumpling in water). Fold prepared salmon and mushrooms into the forcemeat.

Butter a loaf mold; line with buttered parchment paper. Fill with forcemeat. Cover with parchment paper and aluminum foil. Poach in waterbath in a 200°–225°F. oven 1-1/2 hours or until 160°F. internal temperature.

NOTE: If served cold, add 1 oz. diced truffles to forcemeat. If hot, serve with white wine sauce; if cold, serve with an herb mayonnaise.

STRIPED BASS PATE, GULF OF MEXICO

Yield: 3-1/2 lb.

Ingredients

Fresh Striped Bass, without bones or skin	16 oz.
Veal Suet, watered	16 oz.
Salt, Pepper, Nutmeg, Pate Spice	to taste
Flour Panada	16 oz.
Egg Whites	3–4
Heavy Cream	1/2 pt.
Fatback, thinly sliced	10 oz.
Truffle, diced	1 oz.
Pistachio Nuts, peeled	2 oz.
Striped Bass, cubed and salted	3 oz.
Shrimps, cubed	3 oz.

Method

Grind striped bass and veal fat. Chill well and season with salt and spices. Blend in a food processor. Add panada; blend well. Add egg white; blend well. Add heavy cream slowly. Make test quenelle.

Line a long loaf mold with thinly sliced fatback. Fold diced truffle and peeled pistachio nuts, shrimps, and striped bass cubes into the forcemeat. Fill mold with mixed forcemeat. Enclose with fatback. Top with a board and tie with string. Poach in a waterbath in a 200°F. oven for 2 hours or until 160°F. internal temperature.

Cool for 1 hour. Remove from mold and chill. Decorate. Serve with dill mayonnaise.

NOTE: Salmon cubes could be used instead of striped bass and shrimps.

TERRINES

Terrines contain the same ingredients as pates. The only difference is that they are cooked in a fireproof earthenware or china dish also called a terrine and are always served cold. Pictured on

First put layer of forcemeat around inside of terrine.

How to Prepare a Terrine

All of the items needed to prepare a terrine are assembled in this mise en place. Shown from top to bottom, left to right: dish for terrine, liver, forcemeat, fresh pork fat, spices, Madeira, salt, water for rinsing spatula.

Then cover chicken livers with forcemeat, mounding it in center.

(continued next page)

Next, place chicken livers in center of forcemeat.

---

page 133 are some of the dishes most frequently used in preparing terrines. Both the dish and the contents are called terrines. (See terrine ready for service.)

How do you prepare a terrine?

The same kinds of ground meats are used as in liver pate. Directions for preparing one kind of terrine follow; there are other varieties.

1. Line terrine evenly with forcemeat.

2. Arrange prepared chicken livers in center of mold and dot with truffles.
3. Shape remaining forcemeat into a dome and cover with slices of bacon or thinly sliced fresh pork fat.
4. Cover terrine with lid and bake in a water-bath. A terrine containing 2 lb. of forcemeat will take 1 to 1-1/2 hours to bake at 300°F.
5. When the terrine is cooked, allow to cool for 10 min. Then fill with a mixture of 1/2 chicken fat and 1/2 pork fat. Refrigerate. A

How to Prepare a Terrine (continued)

Arrange slices of fresh pork fat to cover all of forcemeat.   Terrine is now ready to bake.

When terrine has chilled, take out of dish and remove all fat; put back in dish and cover with thin layer of aspic.

Family Style Terrine is ready for service when garnished with aspic, hard-cooked egg slices, and bits of truffle.

---

terrine prepared in this manner may be stored up to 5 weeks. If desired, butter can be substituted for chicken fat and lard.

6. When terrine is ready to be served, take out of the dish. Remove all fat; put back into the dish and cover with a thin layer of gelee or aspic. Serve in terrine.

FAMILY STYLE TERRINE

(These terrines may be made of veal, chicken, rabbit, or game.)

Yield: 8-9 portions

Ingredients

Chicken Meat, diced	12 oz.
Lean Veal, diced	12 oz.
Fresh Pork Fat, diced	10 oz.
Salt and Pepper	1/2 oz.
Pate Spices	pinch
Onion, finely chopped	1
Parsley	1 oz.
Chervil	1 oz.
Madeira or White Wine	1 oz.

Method

Saute meat and fat until browned but do not cook completely. Combine meat with spices, herbs, and seasonings.

Pour into terrine, add wine. Cover and allow to rest 2–3 hours. Bake terrine in waterbath for 1–1-1/2 hours. When cold, cover with aspic.

RILLETTES

(This is a French regional specialty from Tours.)

Yield: 4 lb.

Ingredients

Pork Shoulder	5 lb.
Pate Spices	1 tsp.
Salt	1 tsp.
Black Pepper, ground	1/2 tsp.
Bayleaves	2

Method

Bone pork shoulder and separate fat from meat. Cut the fat and meat into large julienne. Season with spice blend, salt, pepper, and bayleaf.

Dishes that hold terrines are also called terrines and come in a variety of shapes.

Cook in heavy pot over very low heat for 4 hours or until meat falls apart. Strain fat and reserve. Crush meat into coarse fibers with fork. Press into an earthenware dish and pour strained fat over the meat. Let cool.

When cold, cover with foil. This dish may be kept for several months.

༈ ༈

CALVES' LIVER TERRINE

Yield: 2-1/2 lb.

Ingredients

Calves' Liver	12.3 oz.
Oil	2 tbsp.
Hungarian Paprika	2 tbsp.
Pork, lean	10-1/2 oz.
Shallots	2 oz.
Butter	1 oz.
Brandy	1/3 oz.
Port	7 oz.
White Bread, no crust	1-2 oz.
Egg White	1
Salt	1-1/2 tsp.
Garlic, mashed	1/2 clove
Green peppercorns	1/2 tsp.
Basil	1/2 tsp.
Pate Spice, delicate	1/2-1 tsp.
Fatback	9 oz.
Ham	3-1/2 oz.
Truffle	1-1/2 oz.
Fatback, thinly sliced	8 oz. to outline mold
Loaf Mold	3 lb.
Terrine	

Method

Remove skin and sinews from calves' liver; cube. Heat oil, stirring constantly; sear liver. Sprinkle paprika over the liver and reserve 1/3 for garnish. Cut pork meat into strips or bars and combine with calves' liver.

Saute diced shallots in butter till golden. Add port wine and brandy and reduce by 1/2. Chill.

Slice or dice whole bread and add to liver mixture. Add the egg white, salt, and spices. Add cold reduction, marinate well. Cube fatback and add to mixture, grind twice through fine blade or puree in food processor. Fold in liver cubes, diced ham, diced truffle, and peppercorns.

Outline mold with thinly sliced fatback. Fill with forcemeat. Close with fatback and cover with a lid or aluminum foil. Bake in waterbath for 15 min. at 375°F.; then turn to 300°F. and bake until 160°F. internal temperature.

❧❦

TERRINE WITH CHICKEN LIVERS

Yield: 14 covers

Ingredients

Lean Turkey Breast	16 oz.
Pork Butt	16 oz.
Poultry Livers	7 oz.
Chicken Livers	16 oz.
Eggs, whole	2
Flour	1 tbsp.
Marinade	3 tbsp.
Bayleaf	1/2
Salt, Pepper, Nutmeg	to taste
Fatback, sliced, to outline terrine	4-5 oz.
Bayleaf	1/2
Peppercorns, Thyme	to taste

MARINADE

Dry White Wine	3 oz.
Madeira	1 oz.
Brandy	1 oz.
Salt, Pepper, Dry Tarragon	to taste
Garlic	2 cloves
Onions, sliced	2 oz.

Method

Cube turkey, pork, and 7 oz. liver and marinate in marinade. Soak rest of liver overnight in milk, then for 30 min. in Madeira and pepper. Remove turkey, pork, and liver from marinade; grind through medium-sized plate. Combine ground meat with 12 oz. coarsely chopped chicken livers, the eggs, flour, 3 tbsp. of marinade, salt, pepper, and nutmeg, and mix well.

Line an oval or round terrine with thinly sliced fatback or pig's caul. Fill terrine half with forcemeat. Remove rest of chicken livers from marinade and dry; salt lightly and top with forcemeat. Cover with the rest of forcemeat. Enclose with fatback or pig's caul. Top with a bayleaf, some peppercorns, and some thyme.

Cover with a lid; seal lid with aluminum foil. Bake in a waterbath in a 325°F. oven for 2 hours or until 160°F. internal temperature. Chill overnight and coat with a thin coat of aspic and decorate.

❧❦

CHAPTER NINE

GALANTINES

Galantines, which are always served cold either as an entree or an a la carte item or attractively displayed on buffet tables, are made of boneless poultry or meat and stuffed with forcemeat, then shaped symmetrically and cooked in a rich stock.

The word "galantine" comes from the old French word "galine," meaning chicken. There was a time when galantines were made only of poultry; today, galantines are prepared using a variety of meats or fish, such as salmon, eel, suckling pig, etc.

How Does a Ballotine Differ from a Galantine?
In a list of French culinary terms, the word "ballotine" might possibly be confused with "galantine," since a ballotine is prepared mostly from boneless legs stuffed with forcemeat or, in the case of fish, is stuffed, rolled, and shaped like a cone. However, most ballotines are baked or braised and served as hot entrees; for example, Ballotine of Chicken, Ballotine of Veal or Lamb. What distinguishes the Ballotine from the Galantine is the method of cooking and the shape of the item.

GALANTINE DE VOLAILLE

Yield: 7 lb. 3 oz.

Ingredients

Capon	4–5 lb.
Brandy	3 tbsp.
Fresh Lean Pork	4 oz.
Fresh Lean Veal	4 oz.
Fresh Pork Fat	8 oz.
Eggs	2
Salt, per lb. of forcemeat	1 to 2 oz.
Pate Spice, per lb. of forcemeat	1/4 tsp.

GARNISH

Ham, finely diced	4 oz.
Beef Tongue, cooked, finely diced	4 oz.
Truffles, finely diced (optional)	5 oz.
Pistachio Nuts	1 oz.

Method
Cut wings of capon at first joint and chop knuckles off drumsticks. Slit skin along backbone. Carefully bone capon. Remove all meat

The central motif of this display is a chaud-froid rectangle, decorated with a border of truffle sheet or ripe olive bits. In the center of the rectangle, place a whole piece of galantine with a row of aspic croutons on either side. Honeydew melon cut to serve as a container for sugar-frosted grapes adds dramatic height.

from carcass, making sure meat is free of sinews and fat. Marinate in brandy.

Combine veal, pork, and pork fat. Put through the fine plate of the grinder three times. Add whole eggs, salt, and pate spice. Combine forcemeat with garnishes and mix well.

Prepare a rich chicken stock using bones of the carcass, strain. Place skin side down on a linen cloth. Spread the forcemeat, to which the brandy used for marinating has been added, all over the capon.

Shape the skin by rolling into a large sausage. Wrap tightly in cheesecloth and tie both ends. Also tie roll loosely with string three times through the middle to hold in shape.

Simmer the galantine in the strained chicken stock for 1-1/2 hours. When cooked, remove stock from heat and cool completely and decorate as desired.

GALANTINE OF PHEASANT

Yield: 12–14 portions

Ingredients

Pheasant	1
Fresh Pork Fat	7 oz.
Lean Pork	7 oz.
Pheasant Meat, lean	5-1/2 oz.
Pheasant Livers	6-1/2 oz.
Eggs	2
Heavy Cream	7 oz.
Flour	1 oz.
Pate Spices	1/3 tsp.
Salt	1/2 to 1 oz.

GARNISH

Veal Tongue, diced	1
Small Gherkins, diced	3
Truffles, diced	2 oz.
Mushrooms, whole and sauteed	3-1/2 oz.

Method

Prepare pheasant the same as capon in preceding recipe for Galantine de Volaille.

Cube pork, pheasant, and livers; put through a food chopper to make into a fine paste. Combine forcemeat with the eggs, heavy cream, flour, and seasonings; mix well. Add garnish to the prepared forcemeat.

Prepare galantine as described in preceding recipe.

Serve galantine with a Cumberland Sauce containing fresh seedless grapes.

COMBINATION VEAL GALANTINE

Yield: 14 covers

Ingredients

Veal Breasts, boned	3 lb.
Lean Pork	7 oz.
Turkey Breast	7 oz.

Poached Turbot Facon du Chef uses boned turbot filets that have been made into a galantine. A whole poached turbot is opened and filled with vegetable salad, then slices of turbot galantine are arranged over the salad. A fluted mushroom topped with a ripe olive triangle is centered on each slice. Shrimp and mussels ravigotte frame turbot.

Pork Fat	7 oz.
Shaved Ice	2–3 oz.
Heavy Cream	4 oz.
Pork Filets	2
Fatback, thinly sliced	3 oz.
Pork Tongue, pickled	10 oz.
Truffle	1 oz.
Aspic	1-1/2 pt.

Method

Bone veal breast and butterfly. Cube the pork, turkey, and pork fat and season with salt. Puree with ice in a food processor or food chopper. Add heavy cream and blend well, chill.

Salt pork filet and brown on all sides, chill well. Roll into thin fatback slices. Cube the tips of tongue coarsely, trim the rest of the tongue. Dice the truffles. Fold diced and cubed tongue and truffles into forcemeat.

Set veal breast skinside down on an oiled cheesecloth. Fill 1 in. high with forcemeat. Set pork filet on one side and pork tongue on the other side. Top with rest of the forcemeat. Roll one side over pork filet and the other side over the tongue. Roll into cheesecloth and tie with string.

Cube carrots, onions, and celery, and set in pan. Top with galantine and roast in a 350°F. oven until 160°F. internal temperature. Remove. Set into a clean pan and press lightly and chill. Add 2 tsp. tomato paste or 4 tbsp. tomato catsup to the vegetables and brown. Add two large ladles of aspic, puree in a blender, and strain through a fine mesh strainer. Brush cold galantine with this mixture and chill. Slice 2/3 and decorate centerpiece with vegetables.

NOTE: Garnish with zucchini baskets filled with kernel corn or with tomato mousse medallions and asparagus.

✿ ✿

GALANTINE OF SCALLOPS (Gardners Bay)

Yield: 2-1/2 lb.

Ingredients

Fresh Scallops	20 oz.
Filet of Sole (fresh) or Striped Bass	10 oz.
Salt, Pepper	to taste
Bread Panada	7 oz.
Egg Whites	4
Heavy Cream	5–6 oz.
Brandy	1/2–1 oz.
Dill, chopped	2 tbsp.
Fish Fumet, Fish Aspic	1 gal.

Method

Blend dry scallops and fish filet in a food processor. Add salt and pepper and panada; blend well. Add egg whites; blend well. Add heavy cream slowly. Season with brandy and chill for one hour.

Mix half of the forcemeat with 2 tbsp. chopped dill. Spread dill forcemeat on plastic wrap. Refrigerate 10 min. Top with plain forcemeat and roll. Tie into a roll and poach in fish

1.

2.

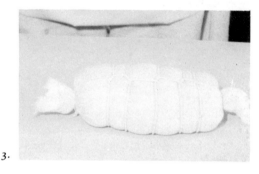

3.

These are the preparation steps required for
Galantine of Chicken:

1. *Remove skin from chicken carefully. Place rectangle of skin on cheesecloth; cover skin with forcemeat.*
2. *Fold skin over filling, then use cheesecloth to roll tightly into an oblong shape.*
3. *Use string to tie roll at both ends and in middle to hold it in shape during cooking. Poach in a strong chicken stock (made from bones of the carcass) about 20 min. per lb. Cool in stock. When cold, remove galantine from cloth and decorate.*

For presentation, slice galantine and arrange slices as shown later in chapter. Along one side of slices, place

stuffed tomatoes on circles of liver pate. Use carved pickled mushrooms and a coconut carved into a face with a piece of decorated galantine to complete tray.

fumet strengthened with some gelatin powder at 150°F. temperature for 30 min. Cool in stock.

Unmold and slice; glaze with fish aspic. Decorate with sliced Spanish stuffed olives. Serve with Pittsburgh sauce.

NOTES: For Pittsburgh sauce use 2 parts mayonnaise, 1 part tomato catsup, some white wine, and some chopped chervil. Also, for poaching liquid, use 2 oz. powdered gelatin to 1 gal. of fumet.

✴ ✴

GALANTINE OF DUCK

Yield: 16 portions

Ingredients

Duck (one)	3 lb.
Turkey Breast, raw	16 oz.
Salt	to taste
Shaved Ice	up to 12 oz.
Duck Livers (Poultry Livers), soaked in milk	10 oz.
Eggs, whole	2
Pate Spice, Curry, Cayenne Pepper	to taste
Large Pig's Caul, soaked in cold salt water	1
Truffle	1–2 oz.

Method

Butterfly duck starting on the backbone. Remove all bones. Remove all meat from skin. Set skin on a tray into refrigerator and chill. Cube duck and turkey meat; season with salt and chill.

Puree duck, duck fat and turkey meat together with shaved ice in a food processor. Add 4 oz. poultry liver and blend well. Add eggs and 1/2 tsp. curry, 1/2 tsp. pate spice, and a touch of

Galantine of Breast of Veal (recipe, this page) is fanned out in carefully placed half slices and garnished with tomatoes styled three ways: cherry tomatoes and whole tomatoes stuffed with tomato mousse; plus a cluster of tomato roses to crown the portion of unsliced galantine; note wedges cut from whole stuffed tomatoes placed in a circle around galantine.

cayenne; blend well. Chill. Marinate 4 oz. of poultry liver in 3 tbsp. brandy.

Set duck skin on a moist cheesecloth. Top skin with pig's caul and spread the forcemeat over it. Set marinated and blanched chicken livers into the center of forcemeat and line each side with trufflesticks. Cover garnish with the rest of the forcemeat.

Roll into a galantine. Make sure all meat is covered by caul and duck skin. Tie with string to keep shape. Poach in a strong stock at 180°F. until 160°F. internal temperature. Press lightly and chill in stock.

Remove and slice for service. Serve with duck aspic croutons and poached apple baskets filled with cranberry relish.

NOTE: Galantine may be coated with chaud-froid or glace de viande.

⚜ ⚜

STUFFED BREAST OF VEAL (Galantine of Veal)

Yield: 14 covers

Ingredients

Ingredient	Amount
Veal Breast, boned	4 lb.
Sweetbread, well watered	1
Lean Veal	5 oz.
Lean Pork	5 oz.
Butter	2 oz.
Onions, diced	2 oz.
Garlic, mashed with salt	1 clove
Heavy Cream	1-1/2 oz.
White Wine	1-1/2 oz.
Breadcrumbs	4 oz.
Beef Tongue, smoked	3 oz.
Frozen Peas	3 oz.
Eggs	9
Salt, Pepper, Nutmeg, Marjoram	to taste
Lemon	little zest

Method

Remove all bones from veal breast. Butterfly veal breast. Boil 5 eggs and peel. Heat butter and saute onions and garlic golden; cool.

Cube veal and pork and grind through fine plate. Fold into the meat the onions, heavy cream, white wine, breadcrumbs, salt, pepper, nutmeg, marjoram, lemon zest, and 4 raw eggs. Mix well. Fold diced beef tongue and frozen peas into the mixture and let rest for 1 hour. Refrigerate.

Spread forcemeat over veal breast and place hard-boiled egg into the center. Roll into oiled cheesecloth. Roast on a bed of vegetables (carrots, celery, onions) in a 350°F. oven until 160°F. internal temperature. Cool pressed between two boards. Remove cheesecloth and slice into portions. Glaze with aspic.

Galantine of Veal in Aspic

NOTE: Frozen gourmet egg may be used instead of hard-boiled egg.

✤✤

BALLOTINE SHRIMPS

Yield: 10 covers
Ingredients

Chicken or Turkey Breast, raw	7 oz.
Shrimps, raw	4 oz.
Salt and Pepper	to taste
Egg Whites	3
Brandy	1/2 oz.
Heavy Cream	1/2 pt.
Truffle	1 small
Mushrooms	3 oz.
Pistachio Nuts or Frozen Peas	1 oz.
Tomatoes, firm	10 large

Method

Cube chicken meat and 3 oz. shrimps and chill. Puree in a food processor. Add salt and pepper. Add egg whites and brandy and mix well. Add heavy cream slowly.

Dice 1 oz. shrimps, truffle, and mushrooms. Peel pistachio nuts and mix into forcemeat. Hollow tomatoes carefully, starting by stem core, and fill with forcemeat. Cover tightly with plastic wrap and aluminum foil. Set on a wire rack over some water. Put on cover and steam at 175°–180°F. for 25 min.

Remove plastic wrap and aluminum foil; remove tomato skin and chill. Glaze with lemon aspic gelee. Garnish with tourned marinated cucumbers and New Orleans sauce.

NEW ORLEANS SAUCE
Ingredients

Mayonnaise	1-1/2 pt.
Curry (Madras)	1 tbsp.
Lemon	juice of 1
Tomato Catsup	7 oz.
Sour Cream or Yogurt	4 oz.

Method
Mix well.

✤✤

Chicken Galantine a la Rosenthal

GALANTINE OF SALMON

Yield: 20 portions

Ingredients

Salmon	5–6 lb.
White Bread, crusts removed	10 slices
Egg Whites	8
Heavy Cream	2 cups
Salt	3 tbsp.
White Pepper	1 tbsp.
Nutmeg	to taste

GARNISH

Combine 1-1/2 oz. pistachio nuts; 14 oz. red pepper blanched, peeled, and cut in large dice; and white truffle paste (adds very delicate flavor to galantines). Prepare strips of salmon marinated in white wine or strips of smoked salmon.

Method

Remove head and tail of salmon. Bone out salmon without damaging skin. Remove meat, keeping meat and skin intact. Chill meat thoroughly. Prepare stock from fish bones.

Mince meat very fine, put through a wire sieve to remove muscles and bones. Return to refrigerator. Soak bread in heavy cream and egg whites, mix well.

Combine fish, bread, salt, pepper, nutmeg and rest of heavy cream. Place in chopper. Mix until forcemeat is smooth. Remove forcemeat from chopper and add pepper and pistachio nuts. It is very important that the mixture be kept cold at all times.

Poach a teaspoonful of mixture in boiling water; taste it and adjust the seasoning if necessary.

Spread moist cheesecloth on table and place the salmon skin on top. Spread fish mixture over half the skin. Stuff slices of smoked salmon with some forcemeat and roll up to resemble roulades. Arrange them down the center of the galantine lengthwise. Place remaining fish mixture on top. Fold the skin around the forcemeat. Roll it up in cheesecloth, tie both ends, and tie loosely 3 or 4 times between the ends.

Poach in fish stock at 170°F. for 15–20 min. per pound or to 150°F. internal temperature. Remove and chill in fish stock.

CHICKEN GALANTINE

Yield: 10–12 portions

Ingredients

Chicken (one)	2–3 lb.

FORCEMEAT

All leg meat and additional chicken meat or veal to make	12 oz.
Fresh Pork Fat	10 oz.
Chicken Livers, marinated in milk	1–2 oz.
Shallots, sauteed	3 oz.
Salt	to taste
Pate Spice	1/4 oz.
Port	2 oz.
Whole Egg	1

GARNISH

All Marinated Chicken Breast Meat	
Smoked Tongue, cubed	3 oz.
Ham, cubed	3 oz.
Fatback, diced (optional)	1 oz.
Truffles, diced	1–2
Frozen Peas	2 oz.
Pimento, cubed, canned	2 oz.

Method

Butterfly chicken. Remove bones and meat. Cube chicken breast and marinate in port.

Set chicken skin on a tray into the refrigerator. Cube leg meat and additional meat and chill. Cube pork fat. Chill.

Grind or puree chicken meat and pork fat in a food processor or food chopper. Add 1–2 oz. shaved ice and chicken liver and mix well. Add sauteed shallots, salt, and pate spice. Add 1 oz. port and egg and mix well. Remove from machine. Fold in the tongue, ham, fatback, truffles, peas, pimento, and diced chicken breast.

Set chicken skin on a moist cheesecloth. Fill with forcemeat and roll into cheesecloth and tie with a string. Poach in a chicken stock for 1-1/2 hours or to 160°F. internal temperature. Cool in the stock. Unmold and slice.

NOTES: Instead of egg, 1/2 oz. clear gelatin can be used. Instead of peas, pistachio nuts could be used. If artificial truffles are used, soak in port.

CHAPTER TEN

MOUSSE

The cold mousse is a delicacy that is sure to delight the eye and the palate of patrons. In the garde manger department, the definition of a mousse is: a mixture of cooked ingredients, pureed and held together with unflavored gelatin, veloute sauce or aspic jelly, then mixed with cream and flavored with wine. As a garde manger preparation, the mousse is always served cold, attractively molded.

Other preparations are also called mousses but they are served hot. A fish quenelle forcemeat (see Chapter Seven, Forcemeat) can be baked in a mold and served hot with a fish sauce and is called a mousse. Some other hot fish mousses are Mousse of Dover Sole Joinville, Mousse of Salmon Americaine. Other delicacies also listed as mousse are served as desserts. Examples of these are Chocolate Mousse, Peach Mousse, and Strawberry Mousse.

Whether served cold, hot, or as a dessert, the mousse is a light and delicate preparation containing heavy cream. In this chapter, the preparation of the cold mousse will be explained since this preparation is part of the work of the garde manger.

How is a cold mousse prepared?

In the garde manger department, a mousse is made with cooked meat, fish, or poultry. The method of preparation is similar for all recipes: the ingredients are pureed, mixed with a binding agent containing gelatin, then heavy cream and seasonings are blended in. If well prepared, any mousse can be an impressive dish, either for service on a luncheon menu or on a cold buffet table.

The following recipes are for various mousse preparations, using either freshly cooked ingredients or leftovers.

HAM MOUSSE, STRASBOURG STYLE
(Mousse de Jambon Strasbourgeoise)

Yield: 2-1/2 lb.

Ingredients

Pullman Ham, or Leftover Baked Ham	1 lb.
Liver Pate	4 oz.
Unflavored Gelatin	1 oz.
Water	1/2 cup
Veloute Sauce	1-1/2 cup

(continued)

143

Molds for mousse come in a variety of shapes that fit many patterns of food presentation.

Ham Mousse, Strasbourg Style
(continued)

Mayonnaise	1/2 cup
Heavy Cream	1/2 cup
Salt	1 tsp.
White Pepper	1/4 tsp.

Method

Grind ham and liver pate through fine blade. Combine gelatin with water and add to ham mixture. Mix in veloute sauce with mayonnaise. Whip heavy cream and carefully fold in ham mixture. Add a touch of beet juice to intensify pink ham color. Season with salt and pepper and pour into a mold.

❧ ❦

MOUSSE OF SMOKED SALMON AND TROUT WITH CAVIAR

Yield: 2 lb.

Ingredients

Salmon, lightly smoked or Gravelox (page 163)	5 oz.
Fish Veloute (no salt)	3-1/2 oz.
Gelatin	1/3 oz.
Fish Stock	5 tbsp.
White Pepper, Salt	to taste
Heavy Cream, whipped	4 oz.
Trout Filet, smoked	5 oz.
Fish Veloute or Mayonnaise	3-1/2 oz.
Gelatin	1/3 oz.
Fish Stock or Chicken Stock	5 tbsp.
Pepper, Salt	to taste
Whipped Cream	4 oz.
Molds, outlined with aspic gellee and decorated with truffles	2

GARNITURE

Caviar	3 oz.

Method

Outline mold with aspic gelee and decorate. Cut smoked salmon into pieces, puree with veloute (warm), dissolve gelatin in stock, add to mixture while machine is working, fold in whipped cream, adjust seasoning, and fill into mold. Mold should be half filled with smoked salmon mousse. Place a row of caviar down the middle.

Prepare trout mousse, place on top of salmon mousse and caviar, and chill. Unmold and serve.

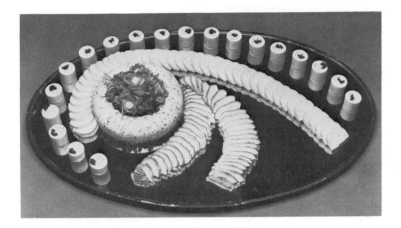

Combination Poultry Platter.
*Sliced Breast of Roasted Capon.
Mousse of Capon (see Chapter 10).
Ring of Vegetable salad, carrot
flower decor, page 170.
Stuffed gourmet eggs, fried parsley
decor.*

NOTE: Trout Caviar or salmon caviar can be substituted for Beluga caviar.

MOUSSE OF CAPON ROTHSCHILD

Yield: 5 lbs.

Ingredients for Base

Chicken Breast Meat, cooked	2 lbs.
Chicken Aspic Gelee	2 pts.
Heavy Cream, whipped	2–3 cups

FOR LAYERS

Lobster Claw, cooked	1, 2 oz.
Lobster Coral, cooked	2 tbsp.
Tomato Catsup	1–2 tbsp.
Madeira and Brandy	a touch
Medium-sized Green Peppers, blanched, peeled, and dissected	2–3
Truffle, chopped	1–2 tbsp.
Almonds, whole, soaked in hot water	2–3 oz.
Applesauce, flavored with applejack	2–3 oz.

Method

Puree meat and warm aspic gelee to a very fine consistency. Press through a sieve and separate into equal portions. Puree one portion at a time with above items, except truffle, which should be chopped and folded in.

Fold in each part equal parts of whipped cream and pour in layers into a glass bowl. Let each layer chill before topping with next layer. Suggestion is to pour apple mousse first, then pepper, truffle, almond, and lobster, in that order. Chill and top with a layer of light chaud-froid sauce. Decorate with lobster claw, capon slice, truffle, green pepper wedges, and whole almonds.

CHICKEN LIVER MOUSSE

Yield: 58 oz.

Ingredients

Chicken Livers	2 lb.
Onion	12 oz.
Celery	3 oz.
Bacon	3 oz.
Bayleaf, small	1
Brandy	3 oz.
Hard-Cooked Eggs	3
Heavy Cream	1/2 cup
Worcestershire Sauce	dash
Ripe Olives, diced	1 oz.
Butter or Chicken Fat	6 oz.
Salt	1 tbsp.

Method

Clean livers; devein. Peel onion and celery and dice fine. Cut bacon into small strips and saute in

Platter of Poached Salmon: Filet salmon and poach, chill, and cut into portions; place one spear of white asparagus on each slice. To complete arrangement, angle strips of pimento over asparagus. Alternate salmon slices with blanched cucumber ovals filled with salmon mousse (use recipe for fish mousse). Top with strips of truffle. Fill center with a colorful decoration made from parsley sprigs and radish roses.

saute pan. Combine onion and celery and cook until transparent. Add livers and bayleaf and cook for a few minutes until dry. Pour in brandy and mix well. Reduce. Remove bayleaf. Put mixture through a meat grinder, then into chopper. Transfer to a bowl. Add chopped hard-cooked eggs, heavy cream, Worcestershire sauce, ripe olives, and butter or chicken fat. Season with salt.

BROCCOLI MOUSSE

Yield: 10 portions

Ingredients

Sherry Aspic Gelee	to line molds
Beef Loin, roasted, pink (or leftover roast beef)	8–9 oz.
Carrots	2 discs
Truffle	2 discs
Broccoli, cleaned	12 oz.
Salt	1/2 tsp.
Gelatin	1/3–1/2 oz.
White Pepper	to taste
Nutmeg	a touch
Thyme and Basil	to taste
Heavy Cream, whipped	9 oz.
Puff Paste	32 oz.
Egg Yolk, to wash	1
Brown Fond	6 tbsp.

Method

Line two round molds with sherry aspic gelee. Arrange chilled roast beef slices on a circle of carrots and truffle. Cook broccoli in salt water till soft, drain, and chill; puree in a blender with salt, add prepared gelatin, adjust seasoning, and add (fold) in whipped cream. Fill into aspic mold and chill for 12 hours.

Roll out puff paste 1/3 in. thick and cut larger than mold, possibly in star shape. Brush with egg yolk, pierce, and bake for 10–12 min. in 400°F. oven.

NOTES: Let puff paste rest for 15 min. before baking. To serve, unmold mousse onto baked puff paste circle. Dissolve gelatin in brown fond before adding to mixture.

FISH MOUSSE

Yield: 2 lb.

Ingredients

Salmon, Sole, Halibut, Pike, or similar fish, cooked	1 lb.
Unflavored Gelatin	1-1/2 tbsp.
Liquid Fish Aspic	1/2 cup

Saddle of Venison, Florida: Prepare saddle as directed on p. 156. Remove filet and brush remainder of saddle with glace de viande. Top saddle with orange wedges that have been flavored in port wine. Pipe liver mousse into center of saddle and top with row of alternating pineapple chunks and grapes. Arrange filet slices as shown. Arrange apple medallions filled with pineapple and walnuts, whole brandied peaches and blue grapes to fill tray.

Salt	1 tsp.
Pepper	1 pinch
Worcestershire Sauce	1 dash
Dill, chopped	1 tsp.
Mayonnaise	1/2 cup
Dry White Wine	1/4 cup
Heavy Cream, whipped	1/2 cup

Method

Carefully remove all bones and skin from fish. Dissolve gelatin in aspic. Put fish into chopper, adding the aspic gradually. Add seasonings and blend the mixture to a paste consistency.

Transfer the fish mixture to a stainless steel bowl. Add mayonnaise and wine. Mix well with a wooden spoon, then cool on ice. When mixture has partially congealed, fold in whipped cream.

Fish mousse can be poured into aspic molds and served on buffets. The mousse can also be used as a filling to stuff various items used to accompany the mousse, such as barquettes, vol au vent, cucumbers, tomatoes, mushroom caps, and artichoke bottoms.

An interesting variation can be prepared by mixing several kinds of fish mousse in combinations, as follows:

1/2 trout mousse and 1/2 sole mousse.

1/3 salmon mousse, 1/3 sole mousse, and 1/3 crabmeat mousse.

MOUSSE OF CHICKEN

Yield: 2-3/4 lb.

Ingredients

Shallots, minced	3 tbsp.
Butter	1 tbsp.
Strong Chicken Stock	2 cups
Gelatin, softened in 1/4 cup white wine	2 tbsp.
Cooked Chicken Meat	2 cups
Liver Pate	1/2 cup
Brandy	3 tbsp.
Salt	1 tbsp.
Pepper	1/2 tsp.
Whipped Cream	3/4 cup

Method

Lightly saute shallots in butter. Add chicken stock and gelatin mixture and simmer for 1 min.

Combine poultry meat and liver pate. Place in chopper or blender, then add the above liquid ingredients and the brandy. Season with salt and pepper.

Remove mixture from chopper or blender. Place on ice and when the mixture starts to gel, gently incorporate the whipped cream. The same recipe can be used substituting ham or other poultry or game for the chicken meat.

Chicken mousse or other similar meat mousses can be molded in small ramekins or small aspic molds and used as a garnish on a meat platter. The mousse can also be used as stuffing for ham, salami, or bologna roulades.

A mousse can also be displayed as a piece montee. For that kind of service, the mousse is portioned into a larger mold and decorated. Sometimes, large molds of various sizes are used and built up in tiers. In addition, mousse can also be used to fill cavities in whole hams, poultry, and

Stuffed Ham Gabriele: To prepare, shape ham mousse to resemble whole ham. Coat with chaud-froid sauce. Use black and brown aspic sheets to create design on ham. Circle ham with thin slices of cooked ham. Coat all with clear aspic jelly. Use decorated, stuffed, whole tomatoes on aspic crouton bases. Accompanying Pate en Croute slices are edged with chopped aspic and flower-topped cherry tomatoes. Note effective use of apple birds.

fish and to level and smooth uneven areas on ham, poultry, etc.

CHAPTER ELEVEN

MARINADES

A marinade—a seasoned liquid either cooked or uncooked—is used to season the food steeped in it and thus to improve its flavor. A marinade can also soften the fibers of certain meats as well as make it possible to hold fish and meat for a longer period of time.

How long can meat be kept in a marinade?
The length of time foodstuffs should be left in a marinade depends on their size and texture and on the temperature of the marinade. In winter, large cuts of meat or game like deer (venison) should be left in a marinade up to six days. In the summer, however, they should be marinated only 24–28 hours; only very large pieces can be left in the marinade for longer periods of time and it is important to watch the marinating product closely in hot weather because of its tendency to sour. Marinades may be cooked or uncooked or a brine may be used if the ingredient placed in it is to last a longer period of time.

COOKED MARINADE
Yield: 2 pt.
Ingredients

Carrots	3
Onions	2
Shallots	3
Black Pepper, ground	1/2 tsp.
Cloves	2 to 3
Juniper Berries	1/2 tsp.
Parsley Stalks	4
Thyme	pinch
Bayleaf	1
Water	1-1-1/2 qt.
White Wine	1-1/2 pt.
Vinegar	1/2 pt.
Salad Oil	1/4 cup

Method
Combine all ingredients and boil for 1 hour. Cool. Do not pour the marinade over the meat until the liquid is completely cold. If the meat (or game) is fresh, it will take less time for it to marinate. Large pieces will require 24 hours, smaller pieces, 4–5 hours. For game marinade add juniper berries and coriander.

UNCOOKED MARINADE FOR BEEF, LAMB, OR VENISON

Yield: 4 pt.

Ingredients

Red Wine	6 cups
Vinegar	1-1/2 cups
Oil	1/2 cup
Bayleaves	10
Salt	1/2 tbsp.
Black Pepper, ground	1/2 tsp.
Monosodium Glutamate	1/2 tsp.

Method

Combine all ingredients and pour over the meat. Marinate 2–3 days.

UNCOOKED MARINADE FOR PORK

Yield: Enough to marinate a 3–4 lb. piece of pork.

Ingredients

Salt	2 tsp.
Black Peppercorns, ground	2/3 tsp.
Thyme or Sage	large pinch
Bayleaf	1
Allspice	large pinch
Garlic, crushed	1 clove

Method

Mix all ingredients and rub mixture into the surface of the pork. Place in a covered plastic or stainless steel bowl. Marinate 6–24 hours. It is helpful to turn the meat once in a while. Before cooking, scrape the marinade off and dry the meat well.

MARINADE FOR COOKED BEEF

Yield: Enough for 2–3 lb. of sliced beef.

Ingredients

Vinegar	4 tbsp.
Oil	14 tbsp.
Tomato Puree	4 tbsp.
Onion, chopped	2 tbsp.
Worcestershire Sauce	1 tbsp.
Salt, Pepper	to taste

Method

Carve the cooked roast into thin slices and put in a dish. Pour marinade over the sliced meat and marinate for 2–3 hours. Garnish with chopped eggs, capers, and pickles.

MARINADES FOR BEEF, LAMB, OR GAME

BEER MARINADE
Yield: 2 pt.

Ingredients

Ale or Dark Beer	1-3/4 pt.
White Vinegar	1/4 pt.
Sugar	7 tbsp.
Onion, medium, sliced	1
Bayleaf	2
Cloves	5
Black Pepper, ground	1/3 tsp.
Juniper Berries, crushed	2-1/2 pt.
Allspice, crushed	1/3 tsp.

Method

Mix ingredients in a crock. Put meat in it and hold it down with a weight. Meat should be well covered with liquid. Keep in a cool place. Marinating time: 1 week.

WINE MARINADE
Yield: 2-1/2 pt.

Ingredients

Red Wine	1 qt.
Vinegar	1/4 pt. (5 oz.)
Oil	7 tbsp.
Salt	2 tsp.
Onion, medium, sliced	1
Sugar	1 tsp.
Thyme	1 tsp.
Ginger, fresh	1 piece
Bayleaves	1

| Cloves | 2 |
| Black Peppercorns | 10 |

Method

Mix ingredients, then put meat in marinade; set weight on top of meat to hold it down. Marinating time: 1–2 weeks.

MARINADE FOR SMALL CUTS OF GAME, MEDALLIONS, NOISETTES, OR CUTLETS

Yield: 1/2 pt.

Ingredients

Vinegar	4 oz.
Red or White Wine	4 oz.
Oil	1 oz.
Juniper Berries, crushed	1/2 tsp.
Thyme	pinch

Method

Place the small cuts of game in a china dish. Pour the liquid over the meat and marinate 24 hours. Turn meat once or twice.

What is a brine?

This is a solution of coarse sea salt to which sugar, saltpeter, and spices are added. Its purpose is to preserve foodstuffs for a longer period of time.

LIQUID BRINE FOR RAW HAMS (2 to 3)

Yield: 10 qt.

Ingredients

Fresh Ham, medium-size	2 to 3 whole hams
Salt	5 lb.
Saltpeter or dry curing mixture	1 oz.
Sugar	1 oz.

BRINE

Salt	5 lb.
Saltpeter or curing mixture	1 oz.
Sugar	1 oz.
Ice Water	17-1/2 pt.

SACHET BAG

| Pickling Spices | 2 oz. |
| Juniper Berries | 1 oz. |

Method

Rub mixture of salt, saltpeter, and sugar all over the hams, then pack tightly into a large crock or wooden barrel, putting more of mixture between hams as you pack them in. Put a board over the container and secure with a weight. Marinate for 14 days at about 38° to 42°F. Remove hams and rotate them from bottom to top.

On returning hams to crock, put more curing mixture between layers. Mix ingredients together to make a brine. Cover the hams with brine and marinate 2 weeks longer. Ham can be served either cooked or raw.

MARINATED HAM

Ingredients

Ham, boned	5 lb. weight
Coarse Salt	1 lb.
Saltpeter	1 oz.
Granulated Sugar	8 oz.

Method

Mix salt, sugar, and saltpeter and rub boned ham with it. Special care should be taken to cover the parts without skin. Let meat remain in the mixture. The next day, repeat the procedure. Repeat for 2 more days. This will make a total of four periods of rubbing and curing. After this process is completed, scrape off any salt clinging to the ham and put meat into the prepared brine (recipe, below).

BRINE FOR HAM, POULTRY, AND FISH
(mild in flavor)

Yield: 7 qt.; enough for Marinated Ham recipe above.

Ingredients

| Water | 6 qt. |
| Coarse Salt | 12 oz. |

(continued)

Brine for Ham, Poultry, and Fish
(continued)

Brown Sugar	12 oz.
Saltpeter	1 tbsp.

SACHET BAG

Juniper Berries	1 tsp.
Nutmeg	a piece
Thyme Sprigs, fresh	3
Pepper, ground	1 tsp.
Cloves	4

Method

Combine all ingredients in a large pot and bring to a boil. Stir occasionally. Remove brine and strain. Add sachet bag and cool the liquid. Marinate ham in brine for 6–7 days. Remove ham and squeeze dry. Roll ham tightly in a cheesecloth. Tie and hang in a dry place at 50°–60°F. for 10–15 days. If you are not sure that ham will dry properly, hang the ham for 3 days only.

Cook 20–30 min. per pound. Set ham in cold water and bring to a boil. Simmer, taste liquid, and change it if it is too salty.

To finish, leave ham in liquid to cool for 1–2 hours. Then remove and press into an oval-shaped mold, holding in place with a board and weight. Hold ham in a cool place for 12 hours before serving.

The best way to serve a ham as a hot dish is to glaze it. To glaze, first peel the skin off, then coat ham with brown sugar, prepared mustard and a little brandy, and bake.

CORNED DUCK

Yield: 8–10 portions

Ingredients

Ducks	2
Lemon	1/2
Salt	10 oz.
Sugar	3-1/2 oz.
Saltpeter	1 oz.

BRINE

Salt	10-1/2 oz.
Sugar	2-1/2 oz.
Liquid	6 qt.

Method

Rub duck with dry ingredients. Chill 12 hours. Rinse the duck.

Bring brine to a boil and cool. Place duck in brine. Marinate for 48 hours.

For cooking, prepare court bouillon of carrots, onion, peppercorns, 1/2 bayleaf, and parsley. Truss duck and boil for 1–1-1/2 hours. Serve hot or cold. Duck can also be smoked. Follow method described in Chapter Twelve for smoking of fish. Use 3 cups of hickory sawdust and smoke for 30–35 min. Chicken can also be smoked for 20–25 min.

Shown at right is an arrangement of open-face sandwiches. When carefully prepared from fresh ingredients, they make an important contribution to eating pleasure (see Chapter 5, page 81).

Mousse of Ham and Ham Rolls (see Chapter 10, page 143). Centerpiece: Ham mousse coated with tomato chaud-froid and decorated with cornets of ham, tomato mushroom; ham rolls filled with cantaloupe mousse; blanched tomatoes filled with cucumber salad; zucchini stuffed with horseradish cream cheese and decorated with radish slices.

Arrangement of Tiny Sandwiches Decorated with Tomato Roses (see Chapter 5, page 81). Shown below are olive rolls; whole wheat, cream cheese, white bread checkerboards; ham closed sandwiches; paprika, pimento cream cheese strips; triangle sandwiches with cream cheese and olives.

Pate en Croute de Jambon (top of facing page). Mousse of ham and liver; mousse of cheese, cranberry; stuffed cherry tomato with capers; butter sculpture centerpiece (see Chapter 8, page 115).

Pate of Chicken and Livers (facing page, bottom right). Centerpiece: Pate decorated with ring of watercress and circle of tomato color sheet; hatelet with tomato star, mock truffle; Boston lettuce, radish; carrot tiger lily. Garniture: Pears poached in red wine, filled with red currant jelly and orange slices, topped with Waldorf pear

brandy. Salad timbale and blue grape; orange wedge star (see recipe, page 120).

Salt Dough Sculpture. To successfully execute a display piece it is essential to have a photograph or model in order to keep the correct proportions. A solid structure and base are important, especially if the piece must be transported.

Fruit and vegetable decorations heighten the impact of food presentation. Shown at right is an apple bird perched on a pineapple pedestal with carrot and leek flowers (see Chapter 13, page 167).

Pate of Striped Bass, Gulf of Mexico (see recipe, page 130). Pate centerpiece topped with tomato mousse, truffle, and pistachio nuts; cabbage orchids; aspic croutons; poached salmon-stuffed olives; poached zucchini baskets; marinated vegetable; stuffed eggs; tomato and watercress color sheet; tea eggs (page 100) and mum radish.

CHAPTER TWELVE

ESSENTIAL INGREDIENTS

Meat, poultry, game, fish, and shellfish are basic ingredients of the principal dishes prepared in the garde manger. The reputation of the garde manger department depends on proper selection and handling of these basic items. *The Professional Chef* presents detailed information about the selection and preparation of these ingredients.

This chapter only briefly summarizes areas of importance in garde manger work. Techniques that assure proper preparation of these important ingredients are also illustrated and explained in this chapter.

MEAT

An average foodservice operation spends 25% of its food dollar for meat. This investment certainly makes meat an item of importance. Preparation of all meat items should be planned for maximum effectiveness because this is where the chefs can use their talents to create excellent dishes not only from the expensive prime cuts but also from the cheaper cuts. Chefs in the garde manger (or cold kitchen) department use

their skills to transform these inexpensive cuts of meat into the full-flavored, attractive food items that are most appealing to the general public.

Beef

The quality of beef varies considerably and is revealed in the marbling, smoothness, and fineness in the grain of the meat and the color of the bones, which should be white. The finer the muscle fibers, the more tender the meat will be.

The following beef cuts are the most suitable for buffet and a la carte items: tenderloin, sirloin, butt, strip loin, and rib. They are the prime cuts of beef and are found to be very effective when presented on buffets.

Beef cuts of lesser quality can also be used but are usually most satisfactory when cooked slowly and combined with sauces, marinated, or used as salads. (See Chapter Sixteen for meat salads.)

Veal

Veal is the flesh of milk-fed calves from 10 to 12 weeks old. Veal has less fat and more moisture than beef and will dry out if cooked too long or at too high a temperature. If the veal is reddish in

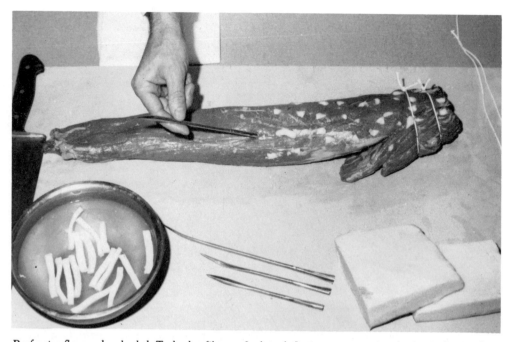

Beef gains flavor when larded. To lard a filet cut fresh pork fat into narrow strips about 2 in. long and insert into meat with larding needle. Tie filet to hold shape while broiling.

color, the animal has not been milk fed and is of lower quality.

Quality veal cuts are usually used in garde manger to make forcemeats. They are also used in pates, terrines, etc. Calves' feet and bones are used to prepare aspic and enrich stocks. The cuts used most often on buffets and as a la carte items are the veal saddle, breast, and rack. Calves' liver, feet, and bones also find many uses in the garde manger department.

Pork

Pork is usually tender since hogs are bred solely for their meat and are marketed at an early age. The best cuts of pork have a coating of fat and the meat is white.

Many different methods of cookery are used in the preparation of pork in the garde manger department and many lesser quality cuts are used. The fresh pork fat is used in pates, galan-tines, etc. Pork caul is used in special recipes. The liver goes into pates and forcemeats. The shoulder, fresh ham, or loin can be smoked, cured, or eaten fresh.

Smoked hams are specialties in many countries and in individual regions of the same country. A great variety of sausages are derived from pork and there are countless other recipes, such as rillettes (see p. 132), head cheese, pate de campagne, and blood sausage that are made from pork.

GAME

During the hunting season, which is usually in late fall, fresh game is available. During the rest of the year the game that is supplied is frozen. Game meat is usually dark in color and is very lean with a strong, wild odor. Since the flesh of most game is dry and contains almost no fat, the

Stuffed Smoked Ham, Maison Style: Shape ham mousse to resemble whole ham; cover with ham slices. Decorate with colorful figure and surround with ham slices rolled around additional ham mousse.

Ham provides eye-catching element in food display when covered with white chaud-froid, then decorated with sprays of leek leaves attached to small ears of pickled corn. Border on ham is made of black aspic ovals on larger sliced ham ovals. Stuffed tomatoes are topped with egg white daisies with ripe olive centers. Ham rolls between tomatoes are stuffed with mushroom salad (at left).

meat is best if it is larded when it is to be used for cold entrees.

The parts of game generally used in garde manger are the rump, saddle, filet (for medallions), rack, and, in the case of elk, the tongue. For buffet and a la carte dishes, the most suitable prime cuts of red deer are leg, saddle, rack, and filet. Hare is used whole for pates, galantines, and terrines.

Feathered birds such as pheasant, quail, snipe, partridge, etc. are prepared in a variety of ways for buffet displays.

POULTRY

From the culinary standpoint, poultry is divided into these two classifications:

1. Domestic Birds—chicken, fowl, duck, turkey, goose, cornish hen, etc.
2. Game Birds—pheasant, grouse, partridge, woodcock, mallard duck, wild goose, or turkey.

Domestic Birds are sold fresh or frozen throughout the year. They are usually plucked

To lard Saddle of Venison use larding needle to run narrow strips of fresh pork fat about 2 in. long through saddle. Tie saddle as shown to retain shape while roasting.

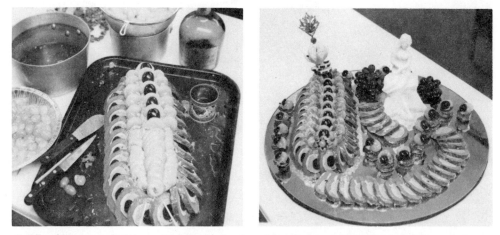

Saddle of Venison a la Diane: Venison that has been butterflied is stuffed with chicken livers and truffles, then roasted. After cooling, slices are carved out and brandy-flavored liver mousse is mounded over roasted saddle carcass.

and drawn; some are sold New York–dressed, which means not eviscerated. Frozen poultry is always sold plucked and eviscerated. The giblets (neck, liver, heart, and gizzard) are wrapped separately. For commercial use, chickens are also cut into breast, legs, or wings and sold separately.

Game Birds are available mostly during the fall hunting season which extends through part of winter. Fresh game birds are only available at this time. However, frozen birds are sold all year long.

Freshly shot game birds should be aged, or, as it is usually described, hung for a period of time to ensure tenderness. If water birds, like mallard ducks, are used, only young birds should be used, as old birds have a strong fishy odor.

Preparation of the Poultry

Today, with modern facilities and processing systems, poultry preparation has been considerably simplified. In some cases, no further preparation of raw poultry is required after it

Trussing Poultry Method 1

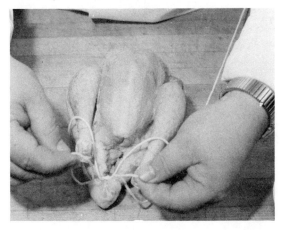

1. *Positioning bird on its back, run butcher's twine twice around tail, leaving enough twine to complete trussing.*

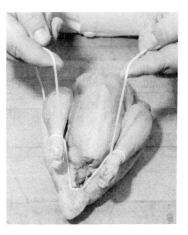

2. *Wind twine around lower ends of thigh bones and pull them tight against side of bird.*

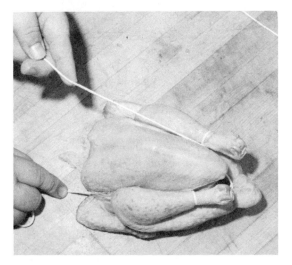

3. *Pull twine toward you, positioning it between thighs and back of bird.*

4. *Tighten twine and wind it around bird's neck; pull it tight and knot it.*

arrives in the kitchen. Both fresh and frozen poultry can be obtained "oven ready" or cut into portions.

Before roasting, braising, or boiling, domestic or game birds should be thoroughly washed or rinsed and then tied. Domestic birds are often rubbed inside and outside with lemon juice so the meat becomes whiter and fresher in flavor.

Some lean birds, like pheasant, are larded with rashers of bacon or fresh pork fat. Another method of preparation requires trussing the bird, especially for poultry specialties produced in the

Trussing Poultry Method 2

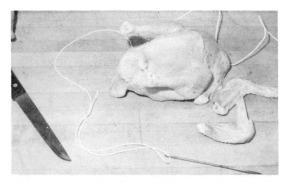

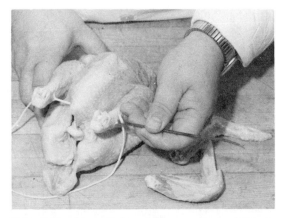

When sewing poultry, first remove wings and then put bird on its back. Have a trussing needle and thin butcher's twine at hand.

Bring thighs close to body and insert needle through both thighs to hold in place.

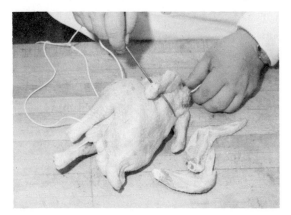

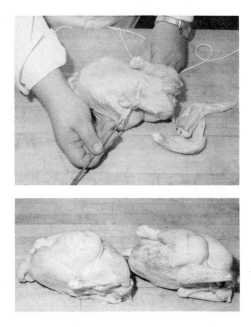

Next, insert needle through one wing, push needle on through neck skin which has been folded back and then on through other wing.

Pull needle all the way through, then pull string tight to hold wings in position. Tie string tightly to keep bird neatly trussed.

garde manger or kitchen. Poultry requires boning and cutting if it is to be used to make pates or galantines. Frozen birds should be thawed before cooking; thawing preferably should be done at room temperature.

How to Cook Poultry

Poultry is prepared in various ways. It can be roasted, grilled, or boiled or, in the garde manger department, made into forcemeats for use in aspic molds or to be coated with chaud-froid. Birds that are roasted or grilled should be young and of good quality. Old fowls should be boiled or used for forcemeats, although young fowls or plump chickens, while usually roasted, are also good for boiling.

Cold domestic birds or game birds in aspic are always decorative. This specialty can be pre-

How to Carve a Roast Chicken for Display

After whole roast chicken has been cut into portions to meet service needs, pieces can be neatly arranged for display and service as shown here. Carrot flower makes an attractive, attention-getting decoration for the arrangement of crisp-skinned chicken portions.

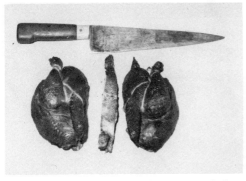

Depending on the number of portions desired, there are several ways to carve a roast chicken for maximum eye appeal. The first step will be to cut chicken in half by removing backbone.

Then cut chicken into four pieces, two breasts and legs, as shown.

For smaller sections, cut breasts and legs with backbone into 12 pieces.

If smaller pieces are needed, cut as shown to provide 16 pieces.

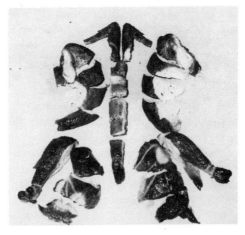

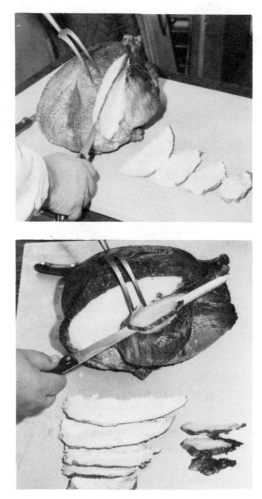

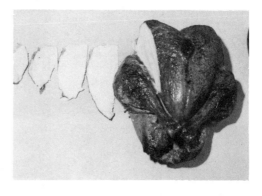

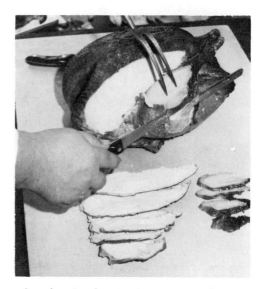

How to Carve a Turkey for Buffet Service
To carve turkey for buffet service, holding knife and fork as shown top left, first carve thin breast slices. Slices should be about 1/4 in. thick, leaving skin on slices, top right.

To cut slices from leg, first slice horizontally, as shown above left, then vertically, positioning carving knife and fork as shown above right.

pared in advance without any loss in flavor. The aspic (see p. 71) should be flavored with care, then brushed over the birds and decorated with truffles or other designs.

Another variation in poultry presentation is to coat the slices or pieces of meat from the bird or the whole bird with chaud-froid, then garnish, decorate, and coat with aspic.

Jellied poultry molds are usually made from boiled chicken. This is a good way to use leftovers which can be enhanced in flavor with the use of tomatoes, cucumbers, or hard-cooked eggs.

The Carving of Poultry
The method of cutting or carving a bird depends on its size and how it is to be served.

Roast Turkey Chaud-Froid
After removing breast from roast turkey, stuff cavity with potato salad; cover salad with mayonnaise colle. Use cut-outs from colored aspic sheet for design on turkey. Turkey slices and whole pears poached in wine and apple juice circle turkey. Birds made of fresh apples flank display and carrot flowers and radish rose centers top it off.

1. Small birds are cut in half or divided into four parts.
2. Large birds can be carved in various ways, depending on whether the slices are to be portioned on a dish or returned to the carcass.

When serving large birds with slices taken from breasts and rearranged on the carcass, it is advisable to cut off the under part of the carcass so that the bird will be flat on the dish, making the presentation neater and more decorative. Carving is usually done in the kitchen, but can also be done on the buffet. When carving is to be done on the buffet, large birds are required.

FISH AND SHELLFISH

Many kinds of fish can be used in garde manger work. The fish may be purchased whole or cut into steaks or filets. After it is cleaned, the fish is usually poached, unless the final preparation requires some other style of cooking. Fish for garde manger use can also be purchased frozen (in cans), marinated, or smoked.

How can you tell that fish is fresh?
When buying fresh fish, be sure to check for these important points:

1. Skin should be bright in color.
2. Scales should adhere tightly.
3. Eyes should be bright and transparent.
4. Gills should be light in color.
5. Flesh should be firm and stiff.

Because of its strong penetrating odor, never store fish with other food. A separate refrigerator or a separate section of the refrigerator should be set aside for fish storage. If fish is to be stored for several days, it should be covered with crushed ice and placed in a 34°–36°F. refrigerator.

Do not expose fresh fish to the air unnecessarily, as oxidation will alter the flavor. Keep shellfish, especially clams and oysters, cold but do not pack in ice.

How should frozen fish be handled?
Do not thaw frozen fish until you are ready to use it. If it has been defrosted, do not freeze it again. There is some difference of opinion as to the best method of thawing. Formerly, the accepted method was to soak fresh fish in water. This

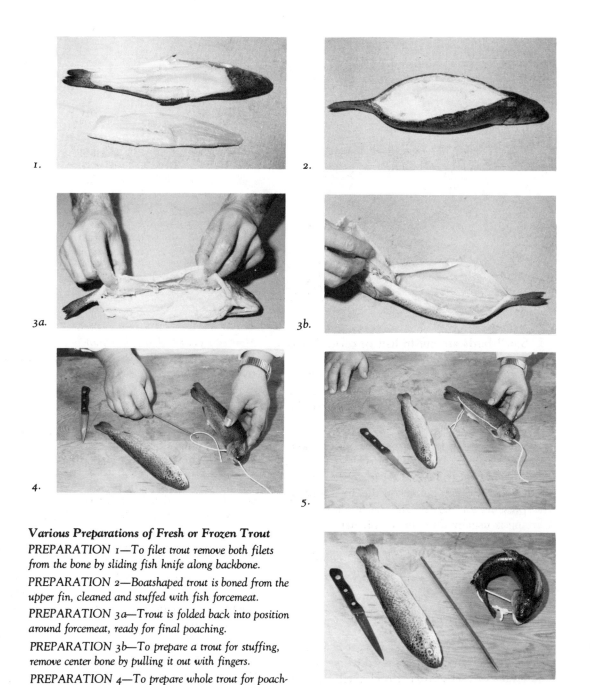

1.

2.

3a.

3b.

4.

5.

Various Preparations of Fresh or Frozen Trout

PREPARATION 1—To filet trout remove both filets from the bone by sliding fish knife along backbone.

PREPARATION 2—Boatshaped trout is boned from the upper fin, cleaned and stuffed with fish forcemeat.

PREPARATION 3a—Trout is folded back into position around forcemeat, ready for final poaching.

PREPARATION 3b—To prepare a trout for stuffing, remove center bone by pulling it out with fingers.

PREPARATION 4—To prepare whole trout for poaching, first pull 2 ft. piece of twine through mouth and gills.

PREPARATION 5—Next run other end of twine through bone above tail. Pull twine tight until the trout is shaped as shown, then tie it in position.

Trout tied as shown is ready to be poached in court bouillon. Poach for 5 min. per lb. at 170° to 175°F.

method speeds thawing, but if the fish is eviscerated or fileted, the water leaches much of the flavor and nutrition out of the fish during the thawing period. Consequently, slow thawing in unopened packages at room temperature is more frequently recommended. Many processors advise that fish filets be cooked without thawing as they then retain maximum flavor.

Fish Most Often Used in Garde Manger

Fresh Fish

Bluefish—Available all year, but abundant from May to October.

Brook Trout or Rainbow Trout—Can be obtained all year round, although the best season is from May to October.

Dover Sole (the Genuine Sole)—Dover sole is caught all year round in the English Channel. Lemon or gray sole may be used as a substitute for Dover sole in preparing fish forcemeats. Dover sole is a very delicate fish and is widely used in cooking.

Herring—Caught all year round. Herring can be smoked, marinated, or pickled.

Pike—Freshwater fish. Best season is June. It is a lean fish, with a firm, flaky flesh and is excellent for use in fish forcemeat.

Salmon—Caught all year round. There are several varieties of salmon: chinook, sockeye, cohoe, steelhead, etc. The pink color and the rich flavor of some species of salmon give them great versatility for garde manger preparations.

Turbot—Caught all year round. The turbot has a white, delicate, firm flesh and can be adapted to various cold dishes very successfully.

Canned Fish

Many kinds of canned fish are available for use in cold dishes. The most common canned fish used are:

Tunafish—There are four varieties:

1. Albacore. This is the only one that can be described as white meat.
2. Yellow fin
3. Blue fin — These must all be labeled
4. Skipjack — light meat.

Caviar—For more details see pp. 105–108.

Herring—Comes in cans, marinated, or smoked. Different varieties can be found: Holland, bismarck, matjes, etc. The most popular of all herring is that packed in sour cream. As an appetizer, it is highly regarded by most patrons.

Salmon—Different grades of salmon are available canned. The best grade is the chinook or king salmon from the Columbia River. The second grade is the sockeye red or blueback; the third is the medium red silver or cohoe. Humpback or keta, labeled pink salmon, is the lowest priced. Tall cans are filled with the tail pieces; flat cans hold center cuts. Smoked salmon is also available in cans.

More and more, fish and shellfish are canned in various ways. Sardines are packed in olive oil, tomato sauce, or mustard sauce. Clams, oysters, and mussels are canned in their own cooking liquor.

Lobster, crabmeat, and shrimp are pasteurized in cans and generally they should be kept under refrigeration to preserve maximum flavor.

GRAVELAX OR MARINATED SALMON

Yield: 4–5 lbs.

Ingredients

Sides of a 10–11 lb. Salmon	2
Lemons	juice of 2
Oil	3/4 oz.
Brandy	3/4 oz.
Sugar	8 oz.
Fine Salt	7 oz.
White Peppercorns, crushed	7 oz.
Fresh Dill, chopped	1 lb. or 2 bunches

Method

Filet salmon; remove bones. Do not remove skin. Brush fish with mixture of lemon juice, oil, and brandy.

Mix sugar, salt, peppercorns, and dill, and pack around salmon filets. Roll into plastic wrap. Set into stainless steel tray or plastic tray. Weight down and marinate for 4–5 days.

SPICED HERRING

Yield: 4 lb.

Ingredients

Herring	4 lb.
Water	3-1/2 pt.
Vinegar	4 oz.
Allspice, crushed	4 tbsp.
Black Pepper, ground	4 tbsp.
Salt	4 oz.
Sugar	2 lb.
Bayleaves	15

Method

Clean the herring, remove the heads and wash. Mix the vinegar and water and steep the herring in the solution for 24 hours. Take out and drain.

Mix the salt, sugar, and spices and put the herring and the mixture in alternate layers in a crock. Cover the crock and let stand in a cool place for 72 hours.

HERRING IN SHERRY PICKLE

Yield: 20 portions

Ingredients

Schmaltz Herring	10
Sherry	1 pt.
Water	10 oz.
White Vinegar	10 tbsp.
Sugar	20 oz.
Allspice, crushed	1 tbsp.

Method

Clean the herring and soak in water for 12 hours.

Skin and filet the fish; wash and drain the filets. Mix the remaining ingredients; steep herring in mixture for 24 hours. Serve with dill and sliced onions.

The Preparation of Smoked Fish

The chief reason for smoking fish is to increase its keeping qualities. However, in the process, the fish acquires aromatic flavor. Most smoked fish is sold commercially. However, fresh fish, such as trout, mackerel, bluefish, or sturgeon, can be freshly smoked by using the method commonly used by sportsmen.

To smoke fish using this method, the following equipment is needed.

1. Large, heavy-duty double roasting pan with a cover.
2. Wire rack, the size of the pan.
3. Four metal risers.
4. Hickory sawdust.

Sprinkle 2 cups sawdust lightly over the entire surface of the pan. Set the risers in place and place roasting pan holding wire rack on top of them. Wash fish thoroughly. Set in a salt brine 30 min. for each pound of fish. Remove, dry well, and oil, place on wire rack, and cover roasting pan.

Preheat stove to highest temperature. Place roasting pan holding fish on top of the stove for 15–20 min., depending on the size of the fish.

Remove the pan from the heat and set aside, letting it stand for 5 min. uncovered, then remove fish. Fish smoked by this method can be served cold with creamed horseradish.

For the brine, combine salt, water, and spices. Use the egg test to determine if the proper amount of salt has been added. Set a raw whole egg into the water. If it rises to the top, there is too much salt. If it sinks to the bottom, there is not enough salt. If it stays in the center of the water, there is the proper amount of salt. Spices added could be juniper berries, garlic, bayleaf, or cloves.

NOTE: This method of smoking can be used for poultry and small meat or fish. For chicken (2 lb.) soak in brine for 4 hours. Then follow trout method. Smoke for 35–40 min. For duck (3-1/2 lb.) smoke for 35–40 min., then remove from smoking pan and finish roasting in the oven.

Shellfish

What kinds of shellfish are there?
Shellfish have long been regarded as a luxury, but this attitude is now rapidly disappearing. Some kinds of shellfish can certainly be economical when the supply is plentiful. Shellfish can also be obtained frozen, potted, and canned. The term shellfish includes lobsters, shrimp, crabs, Maryland crabs, crayfish, oysters, clams, mussels, and snails.

Clams—There are several species of clams. Soft clams are found mainly north of Cape Cod. The hard clams are suitable for eating on the half shell; they are small quahogs called cherrystones. Most clams are marketed alive in the shell, although they are also canned. The peak season is from June to September, however, fresh clams can be bought all during the year.

Crabs—There are several varieties of crabs. The most common are blue crabs, dungeness crabs, king crabs, and rock crabs. Crabs can be bought alive or ready cooked. Live crabs are greyish brown, but, on boiling, turn to a brownish red. They should be well filled, heavy, firm, and should not gurgle when gently shaken. The tails of live or cooked crabs should be firmly closed under the body. Crabs are canned in Alaska, Maryland and in Norway, Russia, and Japan.

Crayfish—A freshwater crustacean, the freshwater crayfish has firm flesh, but it is subtly and delicately flavored. In this country, crayfish are rare in the East but are easily obtainable in the West and Midwest.

Lobsters—There are two types of lobster commonly used: one found in European waters, another in most American waters. Most of the lobsters found on the eastern coast of North America are caught in New England. According to the U.S. Fish and Wildlife Dept., a five-year-old lobster measures about 10-1/2 in. and has moulted 25 times. Lobster is marketed live, boiled, or canned. Almost all of the lobster available in the United States is sold live.

Mussels—These are edible mollusks found in oceans all over the world but they are especially plentiful in the cold regions. The species most often used is called the common mussel. It has a long shell with a very slight roughness along the back. Mussels are very often used for seafood salads or cold canapes.

Oysters—Oysters are a bivalve mollusk, often eaten raw. Oysters on the Atlantic Coast are in season from September until May and are sold fresh. Oysters coming from a certain bed have come to be esteemed as most desirable and have acquired trade names such as Blue Point, Lynnhaven, Sea Tags, etc. Pacific Coast oysters are sold all year round. If oysters are to be used for hot appetizers, buy them in gallons, frozen.

Shrimp—Shrimp vary from the large size found off the southern coast that average one dozen to a pound, to the tiny shrimp, averaging 40 to a pound. The titi shrimp are caught in Alaska and northern New England. These shrimp are less popular, but have better flavor and are excellent for salads or canapes.

Storage and Handling of Shellfish
Shellfish should be kept for as short a time as possible and should always be stored in a cool place. Shellfish, if not fresh when eaten, can cause serious food poisoning. Fresh shellfish should be alive when purchased. Whether alive or canned, shellfish should have a fresh smell and a clean appearance.

Live shellfish must be rinsed with cold water before using. The shells of clams or oysters should be brushed and rinsed before opening.

Cooking of Shellfish

All shellfish, with the exception of clams and oysters, must be cooked. When they are to be used for cold dishes, lobster, crabs, or crayfish should be boiled in salted water with dill and a mirepoix of vegetables. Do not overcook as they will become tough and lose flavor. Shellfish should also be allowed to cool in the liquid they were cooked in.

Cooked lobsters and crabs must always be opened before serving. Mussels, however, should be cooked unopened either in a court bouillon or in their own juices. If they are to be used for cold salads, mussels should be allowed to cool in their own juice.

How to Cut Apart a Boiled Lobster for Service

To cut apart a boiled lobster for service, first remove claws and legs. Then using a French knife, split the tail in half.

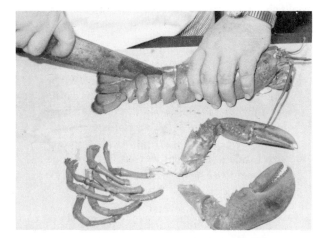

As the final step, split the body as shown. All pieces can now be easily handled.

Here, pieces of boiled lobster are arranged for service.

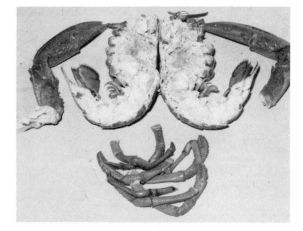

CHAPTER THIRTEEN

FOOD DECORATION

Food decoration is the art of shaping and arranging raw or cooked food in pleasing designs, created by putting proper emphasis on the combination of patterns, color, and texture of the design elements in relation to the kind and size of food to be decorated. These decorations should preferably be made up of foodstuffs. Only when a color cannot be found in natural food products is it permissible to resort to artificial food coloring, with one exception. *Blue* is not considered conducive to tantalizing appetites and, therefore, is not recommended.

Patterns and designs often serve to identify the type of dish that may seem "buried" under a thick coating of chaud-froid sauce. For example, a piece of fish filet, after being coated, may be decorated with an outline design of the fish from which the filet was cut. Or the true nature of the coated piece may be indicated by a simple fish figure made of assorted ingredients and put in place with various decorating tools.

When the shape of the food to be decorated is readily recognizable to viewers, as in the case of a whole ham, then the pattern or design used might be geometrical, or the "artist" may choose

a subject such as an animal or human figure. When a theme has been set for an occasion, the food may be decorated with a design appropriate to the theme. If a ham were intended to be displayed on a Dutch or International Buffet Table, for example, the top of a whole ham might be decorated with a pair of wooden shoes carved from turnips.

How many ways are there to decorate food?
Although there are countless ways to decorate food and food platters, the following two major approaches should be understood before considering the types of materials available to the "Garde Manger," or the cook or chef in charge of preparing, decorating, arranging, and displaying cold dishes. These are:

1. The Classical Approach
2. The Commercial Approach

The Classical Approach—Marie-Antoine Careme, called Antonin Careme (1784-1833), was responsible for what is known today as the Classical Cuisine and its application to food decoration. Too poor to finance his education toward a career in architecture, he instead chose to apply architectural principles to food decoration. In his day, food decoration and the general appearance of food platters on buffet tables were often gaudy. In fact, these displays often exhibited atrocious taste, as the heavy use of nonedible materials took away from the artistry in the "piece-montees."

Careme felt that the food decoration should be appropriate to the recipe involved and that design elements should be assembled with simplicity and taste. Later, Master Chef Auguste Escoffier (1847–1935) supported Careme's approach by his emphasis on exclusive use of edibles in food decoration. This approach has been abandoned today, except in a few exclusive eating establishments, because labor costs and food costs have become prohibitive, because the taste of today's diners is less sophisticated, and because they are not willing to pay the high prices engendered by this type of food preparation.

The Commercial Approach—There continues to be a great challenge to today's chefs to find feasible methods to decorate food and food platters, as well as entire buffet tables, and to train others to follow in their steps. The methods stem from the past, but must be adapted toward economic feasibility to meet today's marketing conditions.

The methods described and pictured in this book meet modern economic requirements although, on occasion, they will be reminiscent of the methods used by the great Careme and Escoffier. The return to the methods of earlier days only occurs in those situations where old-time results cannot be achieved by new technological means.

What are the edible ingredients used in food decoration?
There are 12 *basic* ingredients that can be used efficiently and economically in food decoration:

Fresh raw vegetables
Fresh cooked vegetables
Canned or marinated vegetables
Fresh raw fruits
Canned fruits
Candied fruits
Fresh herbs
Aspic sheets
Hard-boiled eggs
Fish roe
Baked goods
Dairy products

How are fresh raw vegetables used in food decoration?
The following are the vegetables chiefly used in food or food platter decoration; however, others not listed here can also be used at the garde manger's discretion, based on experience and imagination:

Carrots	Leeks	Turnips
Radishes	Tomatoes	Celery
Cucumbers	Red Cabbage	Potatoes

These vegetables can be used in three *basic* ways:

1. Slicing
2. Carving, for instance into "flowers"
3. Arranging in "bouquet"

Fresh raw vegetables that are to be sliced should be *blanched* and *marinated* first. However, those that are to be used for carving do not have to be either blanched or marinated.

NOTE: Blanching ensures adherence of the slices to other foodstuffs, especially aspic or other coatings, such as chaud-froid sauces.

Slicing—Fresh raw vegetables can either be peeled or left unpeeled before slicing, depending on the effect desired. However, fresh vegetables should always be *thoroughly washed*.

Carving—Beginners who want to learn how to carve vegetables can start developing their skills by carving flowers, since they are relatively simple and do not require much time to create.

Depending on the artistic talent of the preparer, the time element, and the way the selected vegetables hold up through the final stages of carving, designs of all kinds can be fashioned.

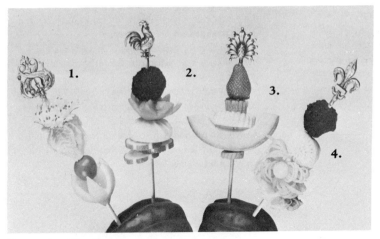

Decoration Hatelet

To beautify various foods we suggest using hatelets
(decorative silver skewers). These silver skewers can also
be used to identify food products like fish, lobster,
chicken, etc.

1. Mum Radish, Boston Lettuce (small heart), Cherry
   Tomato, Lemon Crown.
2. Mock Truffle (see recipe on this page), Star Tomato,
   Fluted Mushroom, Zucchini Slices.
3. Strawberry, Ham Dice or Round Disc, Apple Slice,
   Melon Wedge, Ham Slices.
4. Mock Truffle, Star Mushroom, Carrot Tiger Lily,
   Boston Lettuce Leaves.

MOCK TRUFFLES

Yield: 12 1-oz. truffles
Ingredients

Used Coffee Grounds	1/2 lb.
Kitchen Bouquette	1/3 cup
Plain Gelatin, powdered	1–2 oz.

Method

Mix coffee grounds and Kitchen Bouquette. Heat
over a waterbath. Add gelatin slowly and mix
well. Chill slightly and roll in round balls. Set
on a parchment paper and chill.

Vegetable Flowers (left to right):
*1. apple bird; 2. turnip rose; 3. carrot
tiger lily; 4. leek daisy.*

Carrot Flowers

Carrot flowers lend a colorful note as part of a floral centerpiece or as an accent on a buffet platter. To make flowers, first peel carrot, then slice lengthwise. Flower will require five thin pieces, 3 to 5 in. long.

1. Cut lines through carrot slices and shape as shown in diagram.

2. Fold first carrot slice over as shown in diagram and insert toothpick to hold it together.

3. Fold next carrot slice and place on same toothpick. Repeat with next two slices. Roll fifth slice and stick on top of carrots.

4. As final step, place a round slice of carrot (ball) into the center of flower to hold it all in place. Place carrot flower into cold water until sides curl.

5. Carrot flower and fish sculptured from butter highlight tray of Whole Smoked Trout decorated with chaud-froid circles.

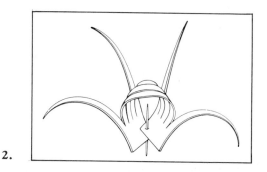

1.

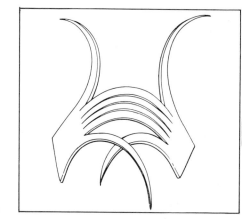

2.

3.

4.

5.

Among the possibilities are flowers, shoes, chains, fishnets, and other intricate designs.

Bouquet Arrangement—Fresh raw vegetables such as asparagus, string beans, or any other vegetables that can be cut in julienne, are usually blanched and marinated, then trimmed (each piece cut to an exact size), and assembled in bunches or bundles. Those that are "loose" (peas, sliced carrots, or other diced vegetables) can be assembled in bunches or bundles by "cradling" them in pastry shells, artichoke bottoms, or other carved foodstuffs. The carving can be kept quite simple or, when more elaborate designs are feasible, baskets or readily identifiable objects such as shoes or fish can be produced.

NOTE: The uses for fresh raw vegetables in food decoration, as have been explained, can be duplicated with fresh cooked vegetables and canned or marinated vegetables.

How are vegetable flowers made?

Vegetable flowers pictured on pages 176 and 177 are colorful, easily made and can be held for 3 to 4 days in a refrigerator when covered with cold water or wrapped first with a moist cloth and then with plastic wrap.

To make turnip daisies follow these steps:

1. Peel turnip and cut into 1/3-in. thick slices.
2. Using star cookie cutters in graduated sizes, cut stars from turnips. Cut two or three stars for each flower.
3. Use parisian scoop to form carrot center for daisy.
4. Take an 8- to 10-in. chinese skewer and put through largest star and one or two smaller stars. Add carrot center last.
5. Push a green scallion stem over skewer.
6. Cut bottom off raw Idaho potato so it stands flat. Push skewer topped with daisy flower into potato.
7. Use skewers of varying lengths for bouquet.
8. Cut leaves of varying sizes from green leek stems. Put toothpick through stem of leek leaf, then push leaf into potato. Use as many

leaves as are needed to accompany flowers.
9. Container pictured is carved pumpkin with handle fashioned from bread dough.

How is fruit used in food decoration?

Fresh raw fruit can be used in exactly the same way as fresh raw vegetables, except that pieces need not be blanched and/or marinated. However, they should be thoroughly washed, as the fruit is always used unpeeled, and sometimes the peel alone is used.

Large pieces of fresh raw fruits can be carved and used as containers from which other foodstuffs are served. For example, a watermelon can be carved in the shape of a baby carriage and filled with fruit salad. Or a watermelon might be carved into a fish from which shrimp cocktail would be served.

Canned and candied fruits are mostly used "en bordure" (i.e., along the edge of a platter or a container made by carving out fresh raw fruits or vegetables, as described earlier).

How are fresh herbs used in food decoration?

Generally herbs are used to add to the design, the color, or the texture (relief) of a surface to be decorated. Whole leaves are used mostly, although sometimes the stems can also be used. Fresh herbs work well in the design of trees, flowers, or other floral motifs.

How is aspic used in food decoration?

Although aspic (meat gelatin) is often thought of as a means of covering or wrapping foodstuffs, in food decoration this important material is also used to produce aspic sheets that can either be neutral or produced in a wide range of colors.

To make colored sheets of aspic, the aspic is mixed with natural food coloring (yellow from eggs, orange from pimento, green from spinach, black from truffles, red from tomato paste, etc.). The colored aspic is then poured into a metal or plastic tray in a thin layer and chilled until it sets into a solid sheet. When aspic is solid, metal cutters of various shapes and designs are used to

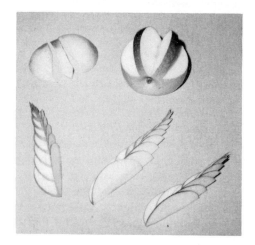

The apple bird, poised for flight on a pineapple perch, provides a conversation-making accent for any food presentation.

1. To make the apple bird, slice off 1/3 of an apple to be used later for the neck and head. Removing this much of the apple also provides a flat base for the bird to rest on. Next cut out small wedge from apple and start cutting slices around the wedge. Taco-shaped slices will become larger as more slices are cut.
2. Leaving a ridge of apple in place to provide a foundation for the wings and tail, continue to cut taco-shaped slices from either side of the two rims.
3. When enough slices have been cut away to assemble for the wings and tail, pieces can be laid out in the pattern shown.
4. Fit slices together, overlapping them slightly to form wings and tail.
5. Slice off 1/3 of the apple, if possible on the less colored side. Cut round apple disc in half, then into the bird's head (see drawing).

Apple Bird Head
1. Cut saved 1/3 of apple in half.
2. Fold together.
3. Cut, starting on x, following arrow. Make second cut starting on x and following other arrow.
4. Push toothpick at a 45° angle through neck.

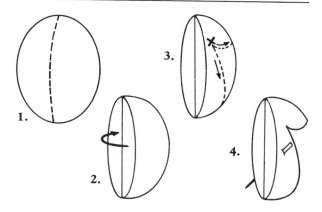

1.

2

3.

4.

5.

6.

Raw mushrooms to be carved must be firm.

1. *Holding the mushroom as shown, insert paring knife and slice off small wedge.*
2. *Slice from top to bottom.*
3. *When small wedges have been cut off all around the mushroom, press the tip of the knife into the top of the mushroom to make star.*
4. *To make flower, cut root off leek. Next cut 2-3 in. piece from white part of leek. Push toothpick about 1/2 in. into root end.*

5. *Holding the leek white by toothpick and root, slice thin strips (1/8 in.) to the center of the leek. Continue cutting similar strips all around the leek.*
6. *Push a thin carrot circle down over top of toothpick in center of leek. Then press leek lightly against surface of cutting board so strips spread out to create flower. Hold in cold water.*

stamp out decorations. (See basic recipe and illustrations, pp. 69–74.)

How are hard-cooked eggs used in food decoration?
Hard-cooked eggs can be used whole, as wedges, sliced, stuffed, or chopped (yolk and/or white). Eggs can be prepared in many ways to serve as decorative additions to platters.

How is fish roe used in food decoration?
Fish roe is used in food decoration primarily for color. However, the roe can also be used for texture, and in forming designs or patterns of all kinds. Of all the fish roe available, that of salmon (red caviar), sturgeon (black or grey caviar), or lobster (red coral) are usually favored by garde mangers.

How are baked goods and dairy products used in food decoration?
Baked goods can be used to contain other foodstuffs: "barquettes" (little boats), "tartelettes" (little tarts), or as an "en bordure" decoration such as "fleurons" (flower-shaped or leaf-shaped decorations).

Dairy products are mostly used when the application must be done with the help of a pastry bag (piping). The shape and pattern of the piped product will be determined by the type of metal tube that is set through the small end of the cone-shaped pastry bag. Note varied sizes of the cream cheese roses.

The tomato rose is an eye-appealing decoration and is simple to make. Peel the skin, with a little of the pulp (for added firmness), in a continuing slice from a firm, ripe red tomato. Roll this slice up into the shape of a rose and add stems made from the green end of leeks.

Pickles can make excellent buffet garnishes. The only tool needed is a paring knife.
1. *Cut pickle lengthwise in half.*
2. *Cut pickle half into spears.*
3. *Remove pickle ends and cut into long slices.*
4. *Fan pickle ends.*
5. *Fan pickle halves.*
6. *Press fanned pickle halves with paring knife lightly to form a reef.*

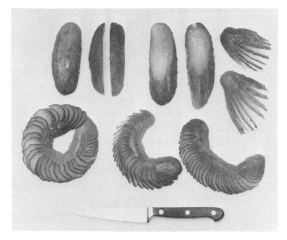

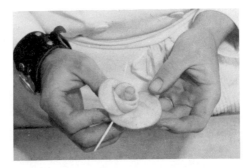

To Make a Turnip Rose

1. To make a turnip rose, slice one unpeeled, room-temperature turnip into paper-thin slices. (Do not store in water.) Roll one turnip slice into a tight roll and surround with other slices.

2. Use uneven number of turnip slices until desired flower size is achieved. Push two toothpicks through opposite sides to secure rose petals. Drop into cold water to stiffen.

NOTE: This rose can be made from red beets or rutabaga. If potatoes are used, deep fry.

Salmon mousse is piped into hard-cooked egg whites, making an attractive color combination. Stuffed eggs are presented on toasted croutons. Vegetable roses in center of tray are tinted. The star-shaped cherry tomato shells hold balls of salmon mousse topped with black caviar.

Set-up for making vegetable flowers, p. 171.

Push green scallion stem over skewer.

Put chinese skewer through vegetable circle, 1 or 2 small stars, large star, and carrot center.

Slice raw potato to use as base. Push flower-topped skewers into potato to make bouquet.

Cabbage Flower

1. You need three petals for each flower.
2. Stick prepared scallion into center as shown.
3. Keep flowers in cold water until use.

NOTE: For color change use savoy cabbage on loltite cabbage.

1. Remove the core.
2. Remove large leaves.
3. Cut oval shapes from the bottom of the leaf.
4. Turn upside down and trim excess stack paper-thin with a paring knife.
5. Cut white part of scallion (green onion) like leek flower without a carrot center (page 173).

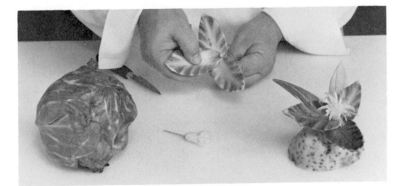

1. Cut thin carrot discs.
2. Push halfway down a toothpick.
3. And set oval cabbage petals in place.

CHAPTER FOURTEEN

COLD SAUCES-BUTTER AND CHEESE MIXTURES

The sauce should be the crowning touch for the dish it accompanies. It sometimes seems that there are as many sauces as there are menu items. However, a variety of sauces is especially important for garde manger foods.

Many of the cold sauces served as accompaniments for garde manger foods are derived from mayonnaise. Chaud-froid sauce (Chapter Four) should not be confused with the sauces described in this chapter, since chaud-froid is used as a coating while these sauces add a new complement of flavors to dishes they accompany. They are sometimes presented in separate containers.

How is basic mayonnaise prepared?
Commercially prepared mayonnaise may be purchased which usually eliminates the need to prepare mayonnaise in the kitchen. However, knowing how to prepare mayonnaise is valuable in many instances.

BASIC MAYONNAISE RECIPE

Yield: 1-1/2 pt.
Ingredients

Egg Yolks	4 to 5
Salt	1 tsp.
Cayenne Pepper	pinch
Prepared Mustard	2 tsp.
Oil	1-1/2 pt.
Wine or Unflavored Vinegar or Lemon Juice	1 tbsp.

Method
All ingredients should be kept at room temperature. Use a whip to prepare mayonnaise in order to ensure good emulsification. Pour oil slowly at the beginning to obtain perfect emulsification from the start.

In a stainless steel bowl, mix egg yolks, salt, cayenne pepper, and mustard. Slowly add oil, mixing with a whip. When thick, alternate oil and vinegar until all has been used. If sauce is too thick after all ingredients are used, add a small amount of lukewarm water to mayonnaise.

A mayonnaise that breaks down can be restored by following this simple method which proves to be successful most of the time: in a clean stainless steel bowl, place 1 tbsp. of cold water no matter what amount of mayonnaise is to be restored. Slowly whip a small quantity of the mayonnaise into the water in the bowl. The sauce will emulsify as it is whipped with the cold water and once emulsification starts, larger quantities of the broken mayonnaise may be added until restoration is complete.

NOTE: The use of sugar, food coloring or any other chemical ingredient in a mayonnaise should be avoided, since these will improve neither the taste nor appearance of the completed product.

SAUCES DERIVED FROM MAYONNAISE

Andalouse	Oriental
Chantilly	Remoulade
Devil's	Russian
Dijonnaise	Swedish
Gloucester	Tartar
or Piccadilly	Tyrolienne
Indian	Vincent
Marchand de Vin	Mousquetaire

Andalouse Sauce. Add to 1 cup of mayonnaise, 3 tbsp. of tomato paste and 2 tbsp. diced red pimentos, 1 tsp. lemon juice, dash of Worcestershire sauce.

Chantilly Sauce. To 1 cup of mayonnaise add 1/4 cup of unsweetened whipped cream. Season to taste.

Devil's Sauce. Reduce by two-thirds 1 cup vinegar, 2 chopped shallots, 1 tbsp. crushed peppercorns, 1 tsp. juniper berries. Strain this reduction and add to remoulade sauce. Season with 1 tsp. English mustard and a pinch of cayenne pepper.

Dijonnaise Sauce. A mayonnaise sauce combined with Dijon mustard, in proportions of 1 cup mayonnaise to 3 tsp. mustard.

Gloucester or Piccadilly Sauce. Add to 1 cup of mayonnaise, 1/2 cup sour cream. Season with 4 drops of Worcestershire sauce, 1 tsp. lemon juice and 1 tbsp. fresh chopped fennel.

Indian Sauce. Add 1 tbsp. curry powder, 1 tbsp. chives to 1 cup of mayonnaise.

Marchand de Vin. Blend 3 shallots with 1/3 cup of white wine, add to 1 cup mayonnaise with finely chopped parsley.

Mousquetaire Sauce. Add to 1 cup mayonnaise, 2 tbsp. chopped shallots cooked in 1/4 cup white wine and 1 tbsp. melted glace de viande.

Mustard Sauce. Add to 1 cup of mayonnaise, 2 to 3 tbsp. of prepared mustard.

Oriental Sauce. Add to 1 cup of mayonnaise, 3 tbsp. tomato paste, one pinch of saffron, 2 tbsp. diced, blanched green pepper.

REMOULADE SAUCE

Yield: 1-1/2 pt.

Ingredients

Mayonnaise	1-1/2 pt.
Capers	2 tbsp.
Cornichons (tiny sour gherkins)	2 tbsp.
Shallots	1 tsp.
Tarragon	1 tsp.
Parsley	1 tbsp.
English Mustard	1 tsp.
Filet of Anchovy, pureed	1

Method

Chop all ingredients fine and combine with mayonnaise. Season with mustard and puree of anchovy.

Russian Sauce. Combine 2/3 cup of mayonnaise with 1/3 cup of caviar. Season with 1 tsp. prepared mustard and the juice of one lemon.

Swedish Sauce. Use 2 cups thick mayonnaise to 1 cup applesauce flavored with white wine. Season with 1 tsp. lemon juice, 2 tsp. grated horseradish, 1/8 tsp. sugar.

TARTAR SAUCE

Yield: 1-1/4 pt.

Ingredients

Mayonnaise	1 pt.
Hard-cooked Eggs	4
Chives, chopped	1 tbsp.
Shallot, chopped	1

Tarragon, chopped	1 tsp.
Chervil, chopped	1 tsp.
Parsley, chopped	1 tsp.

Method

Put eggs through food mill. Combine with remaining ingredients and add to the mayonnaise. Flavor can be adjusted with salt, pepper, and lemon juice to taste.

Tyrolienne Sauce. To 1 cup mayonnaise, add 1 tbsp. chopped parsley, 1 tbsp. chopped chervil, 1/4 cup reduced, finely chopped tomatoes. Season with 1/3 tsp. black pepper, 4 drops Worcestershire sauce, 1 tsp. chili sauce.

VINCENT SAUCE

Yield: 1-3/4 pt.

Ingredients

Chervil, Parsley, Chives, Tarragon combined	2 tbsp.
Spinach	1 oz.
Watercress	1 oz.
Hard-cooked Eggs	3
Mayonnaise	2 cups
Worcestershire Sauce	5 drops

Method

Blanch all herbs. Cool, press all moisture out and blend together with eggs and 4 tbsp. mayonnaise. Add remaining mayonnaise. Season with Worcestershire sauce.

SAUCES NOT DERIVED FROM MAYONNAISE

Anchovy	Plain Horse-
Apple Horseradish	radish
Cranberry	Serbian Garlic
Cumberland	Vinaigrette
Frozen Horseradish	Orange Horse-
Gribiche	radish
Italian	Sauce Ravigote

Anchovy Sauce. Pound 4 hard-cooked eggs and 8 anchovy filets to a fine paste. Season with white pepper. Thin to desired thickness with oil and vinegar. Adjust seasoning.

Apple Horseradish Sauce. Peel and grate fresh apples. Mix with equal quantities of grated horseradish. Finish the sauce with a touch of oil, vinegar, salt, sugar, and a small amount of beef stock.

Cranberry Sauce. Pick over 1 lb. cranberries and wash in cold water; place in pot; cover with water. Add 8 oz. sugar and juice of 1 lemon. Bring to a boil. Serve cold.

CUMBERLAND SAUCE

Yield: 3/4 pt.

Ingredients

Red Currant Jelly	1 cup
Shallots, blanched, chopped	1 tbsp.
Orange and Lemon Zests, blanched	2 tbsp.
English Mustard	1 tsp.
Port Wine	1/2 cup
Orange	juice of 1
Lemon	juice of 1
Salt	1/3 tsp.
Cayenne Pepper	pinch
Ginger	pinch

Method

Melt red currant jelly; add blanched shallots, julienned orange and lemon peel (zests). Dissolve mustard in wine. Add to currant jelly. Simmer 5 to 10 min. Add lemon and orange juice. Season with salt, cayenne, and ginger.

NOTE: Oxford Sauce—Add grated orange and lemon peel to this recipe.

FROZEN HORSERADISH SAUCE

Yield: 1 pt.

Ingredients

Whipped Cream	1 pt.
Horseradish, grated	2 to 3 tbsp.
Vinegar	1 tbsp.
Salt	1/2 tsp.

(continued)

Frozen Horseradish Sauce (continued)

Sugar	pinch
Black Pepper, ground	1/2 tsp.

Method

Combine whipped cream with horseradish and vinegar. Gently mix all ingredients. Roll into greased parchment paper and freeze. At service time, cut into slices. This sauce may be served with beef, ham, corned beef, and tongue.

GRIBICHE SAUCE

Yield: 1-1/4 pt.

Ingredients

Hard-cooked Eggs	3
Prepared Mustard	1/2 tsp.
Capers, chopped	1 tbsp.
Sour Pickle, chopped	1 tsp.
Chervil, chopped	1/2 tsp.
Tarragon, chopped	1/2 tsp.
Parsley, chopped	1/2 tsp.
Vinegar	1-1/2 tsp.
Oil	1 pt.
Hard-cooked Egg Whites, julienned	2

Method

Put three hard-cooked eggs through sieve. Mix in mustard, capers, pickles, and herbs. Mix in oil and vinegar. Add 2 julienned egg whites.

ITALIAN SAUCE

Yield: 1-1/4 pt.

Ingredients

Sweet Almonds	1/3 oz.
Pistachio Nuts	3/4 oz.
Bechamel Sauce, cold	1 oz.
Egg Yolks	3
Oil	1 pt.
Salt, Pepper, combined	1/2 tsp.
Tarragon, Chives, Parsley, Chervil, combined	1 oz.

Method

Puree pistachio nuts and almonds together with Bechamel sauce. Mix in egg yolks and oil as in preparing mayonnaise. Season with salt and pepper and finely chopped herbs.

PLAIN HORSERADISH

Yield: 1-1/2 pt.

Ingredients

Fresh Horseradish	2 cups
Raw Apple	1 cup
Lemon Juice	few drops
Salt	1/2 tsp.
Pepper	pinch

Method

Peel apples and horseradish; grate fine. Add lemon juice, salt, and pepper.

SERBIAN GARLIC SAUCE

Yield: 1/2 pt.

Ingredients

Garlic	4 cloves
Salt	1/2 to 1 tsp.
Egg Yolks	2 to 3
White Pepper	pinch
Oil	1 cup
Lemon Juice	a few drops

Method

Mash the garlic with salt; add egg yolks and pepper. Mix in the oil as for mayonnaise. Finish with lemon juice.

VINAIGRETTE SAUCE

Yield: 2 pt.

Ingredients

Wine Vinegar	1 cup
Oil	3 cups
Parsley, Chives, Tarragon	2 tbsp.
Onion	2 oz.
Salt	1 tsp.
Pepper	pinch

Method

Combine oil and vinegar. Add finely chopped herbs and onion. Season to taste.

ORANGE HORSERADISH SAUCE

Yield: 1 pt.

Ingredients

Apples, fresh, grated	1 cup
Fresh or Prepared Horseradish	1 cup
Lemon	juice of 1/2
Orange, grated zest	1
Sugar	1/3 tsp.
Orange	juice of 1

Method

Mix all ingredients and marinate for 2 hours.

RAVIGOTE SAUCE

Yield: About 2 cups

Ingredients

Fresh Parsley, minced	2 tsp.
Fresh Chervil, minced	4 tsp.
Fresh Tarragon, minced	2 tsp.
Fresh Chives, minced	2 tsp.
Vinaigrette Sauce (use Basic French)	2 cups
Small Onions, diced	1-1/2
Minced Capers, well drained	2 tbsp.
Prepared Mustard	1 tsp.

Method

Combine all ingredients and blend them well.

USE OF COLD SAUCES

Cold sauces make good accompaniments for a large variety of dishes. The following chart can certainly be expanded but it is offered to help menu planners explore the many possibilities for cold sauces.

Asparagus, Artichokes
> Chantilly
> Vinaigrette
> Mustard

Egg Dishes
> All sauces derived from mayonnaise

Fish and Shellfish
> Andalouse
> Italian
> Russian
> Tartar
> Remoulade
> Vincent
> Gribiche
> Anchovy
> Serbian Garlic

Game
> Cumberland
> Oxford
> Cranberry

Meat
> Gloucester or Piccadilly
> Remoulade
> Tartar
> Tyrolienne

BUTTER AND CHEESE MIXTURES

Butter and cheese are combined with many ingredients to make spreads that can be used to create a large variety of canapes. The spreads thus produced enhance the flavor and taste of the canapes; they also provide a flavorful base for ingredients (shrimp, olive slices, etc.) that are used to top canapes to make their presentation more appealing.

The following list of butter and cheese mixtures can be extended to include various other types of butters; in fact, there is no limit to the variations that can be created.

Butters

Anchovy Butter. Blend 12 filets of anchovies with 4 oz. sweet butter, then put through a fine sieve.

Caviar Butter. Blend 2 oz. fresh caviar with 4 oz. butter and put through a fine sieve.

Cayenne Butter. Mix 1/4 oz. cayenne with 1 lb. butter.

Crayfish Butter. Blend 2 oz. cooked crayfish tails with 4 oz. butter and put through a fine sieve.

Curry Butter. To a very small onion, finely chopped and cooked in butter, add 1 tsp. curry powder. Simmer 2 min., remove from stove and let cool. Add 1 cup butter; mix and put through fine sieve.

Egg Butter. Blend 12 egg yolks with 8 oz. butter and a few drops of olive oil. Put through a fine sieve and add salt and cayenne pepper.

Foie Gras Butter. Blend 4 oz. cooked foie gras with 4 oz. butter and put through sieve.

Garlic Butter. Blend 5–6 cloves of garlic with 1 lb. butter and put through a fine sieve.

Herring Butter. Blend 2 desalted filets of herring with 3/4 lb. butter and put through a fine sieve.

Herring Roe Butter. Blend 3 oz. herring roe which has been poached in white wine with 4 oz. butter; add a pinch of mustard and put through a fine sieve.

Horseradish Butter. Mix 2 oz. scraped horseradish with 1 lb. butter.

Langouste Butter. Follow procedure for lobster butter below.

Lobster Butter. Blend 4 oz. lobster coral and liver with 8 oz. butter and put through a fine sieve.

Montpellier Butter (*Green Butter*). In a saucepan containing boiling water, put an equal quantity of watercress leaves, parsley, chervil, chives and tarragon (about 12 sprigs of each), two sliced shallots and 12 spinach leaves. Boil for about 2 min., then drain, let cool, and press dry in a towel. Blend this with 15 anchovies, 2 tsp. capers, 6 small pickles, 1 clove of garlic, and 8 hard-cooked egg yolks. Add 1/2 lb. butter, pepper, salt, and a little nutmeg. Blend together with 1/2 pt. olive oil and 1/4 cup tarragon vinegar. Put through a fine sieve.

Moscovite Butter. Blend 8 oz. butter with 4 oz. caviar and 6 hard-cooked egg yolks and put through a very fine sieve. Season with salt and cayenne.

Mustard Butter. Mix 1 tbsp. English mustard with 1/2 lb. butter. (This can be made with prepared mustard.)

Nutmeg Butter. Blend 2 nutmegs with 1 lb. butter and put through fine sieve.

Paprika Butter. To a very small onion, chopped and cooked in butter, add 1 tbsp. paprika and simmer a minute or two. Remove from heat, let cool, and add 1 cup butter. Put through fine sieve.

Perigourdine Butter. Blend 4 oz. butter with 4 hard-cooked egg yolks and 2 medium-sized truffles. Put through a very fine sieve. Season with salt and cayenne pepper.

Pimento Butter. Blend 1 oz. red pimentos with 3 oz. butter. Put through a fine sieve.

Portuguese Butter. Blend 3 hard-cooked egg yolks with 5 oz. butter. Add 1 tbsp. tomato paste, salt, and pepper. Put through a fine sieve and add a little red color.

Ravigote Butter. Blend in a mortar equal quantities of chervil, parsley, tarragon, chives, and pimprenelle (all these herbs to be blanched) with an equal quantity of butter. Put through a fine sieve.

Smoked Salmon Butter. Blend 1/2 lb. smoked salmon with 1 lb. butter and put through a fine sieve.

Sardine Butter. Blend 12 sardines, without bones, with 3/4 lb. butter and put through a fine sieve.

Shrimp Butter. Blend 2 oz. grey shrimps (cooked) with 4 oz. butter and put through a very fine sieve.

Butter for Snails. Blend in a mortar 1 oz. garlic, 3 oz. shallots, 2 lb. butter; add 2 oz. chopped parsley, salt, and pepper.

Tarragon Butter. Blend a handful of blanched tarragon leaves with 3/4 lb. butter and put through a very fine sieve.

Tunafish Butter. Blend 1 oz. tunafish with 2-1/2 oz. butter and put through a sieve.
NOTE: Whipped cream may be substituted for butter but the mixing must be carefully done to prevent curdling.

Cheeses

Crab Cheese. Follow procedure for Langouste Cheese below.

Langouste Cheese. Blend the meat of 1 langouste with 1/2 lb. gruyere cheese and 2 oz. butter. Put through a fine sieve and finish with heavy cream and brandy.

Lobster Cheese. Follow procedure for Langouste Cheese above.

Salmon Cheese. Blend 4 oz. cooked salmon with 4 oz. gruyere cheese and 1 oz. butter. Put through a fine sieve and finish with heavy cream and a little port wine.

Truffle Cheese. Blend 4 oz. truffles with 2 oz. gruyere cheese and 2 oz. sweet butter. Add 1/2 oz. brandy, spices to taste and put through a fine sieve.

Tunafish Cheese. Blend 8 oz. tunafish with 8 oz. gruyere cheese. Put through a fine sieve and finish with heavy cream.

CHAPTER FIFTEEN

COLD FOOD PRESENTATION

The menu items created in the garde manger are largely classified as cold foods. The successful preparation and presentation of cold foods depend on the methods and rules explained here:

- Poultry to be coated with aspic or chaud-froid must be thoroughly cooled, otherwise aspic or chaud-froid sauce will not adhere to it.

- Before applying chaud-froid sauce to food, a coat of aspic must be applied.

- The chaud-froid sauce must be firm and cold before the decoration can be applied.

- All ingredients to be used as decorations must be dipped into cold, liquid aspic before they can be arranged on the main piece. The aspic will prevent the decorations from falling off the large piece (gross piece) when aspic is poured over it.

- It is essential that all decorated pieces be coated with crystal clear, light-colored aspic. This will permit the full color of the decoration to shine through. The aspic should be neither too cold nor too warm when applied; the best temperature is either ice cold but

not congealed or when aspic is the thickness of heavy cream.

- When working with fish, it is important to cool it thoroughly and make sure fish is dry before applying the decor and aspic.

- A whole decorated fish should never be arranged on a platter smaller than the fish. A shallow tray or a platter especially designed for fish is best. Crystal clear aspic—diced, finely chopped, or in croutons—always gives a pleasing effect.

- If decorated silver skewers are necessary, only edible food should be used to decorate them and it is important that the foods used blend with the taste of the main ingredient of the display they are presented with.

- Display foods can be served on mirrors, or on plastic, wood, china, metal, or silver platters. If the service requires the use of silver or metal trays, it is helpful to cover the surface of the tray with a coat of aspic. This will prevent discoloration of the foods, as may happen, for example, when eggs are placed on silver trays. When metal trays are used, the

To carve a capon for chaud-froid (cold set-up): Remove breast and fill cavity with a mousse of liver (Chapter Ten). Slice breast into thin slices; place slices in sequence on a tray so they can be replaced in order on the chicken. Put slices of capon back into the breast cavity, starting at the top of the capon, overlapping slices.

To carve a chicken for chaud-froid: Slice breast of chicken into even slices. Stuff cavity of bird with a chicken mousse (Chapter Ten) and place breast slices back on the chicken in sequence as shown; coat with clear aspic.

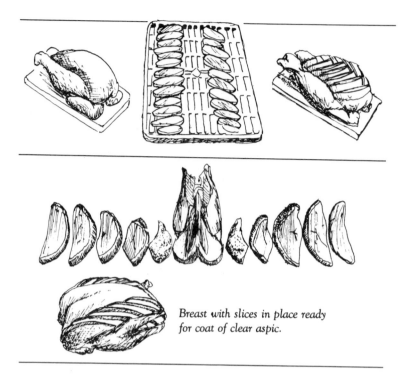

Breast with slices in place ready for coat of clear aspic.

coat of aspic will prevent the development of undesirable metal flavor.

- The proportion of the garnish should be balanced in relation to the food item it is used with. The garnish should not be larger than the main piece. The garnish is designed to call the diner's attention to the food it is used on, not just to the garnish.

- It is important to plan and sketch the decoration and arrangements of the main food trays carefully. Planning ahead keeps the work cleaner as there are fewer errors made. It is also easier and faster to arrange food and decoration according to a plan. It is important to remember that if foods are handled too often, they may be damaged. Too much handling can also contaminate foods. *Once the food has touched the tray, it should not be removed until it is served.*

NOTE: According to chefs and gourmets, amateur and professional alike, chaud-froid dishes are not as popular today as they were many years ago. This decline in popularity can be traced to a shortage of skilled labor as well as to the time required to make the dishes. This book suggests a method of chaud-froid preparation that makes it possible to create these dishes faster and more economically in the hope that one day, they will again become as popular as they once were.

While the shortcuts suggested may seem obvious, if they are followed by the kitchen staff, producing artistic and beautiful food trays for the buffet table can be justified both from the time and cost standpoint.

FOOD DECORATION

Practical Suggestions for Show and Practical Food Platters

1. Divide platter into 6 or 8 equal parts as indicated in the diagrams.
2. The centerpiece should never cover more than two spaces.

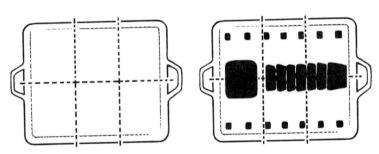

Suggestion 1.
Centerpiece and tranches. Pate, roasts and hams.

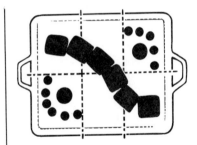

Suggestion 2.
Tranches without centerpiece.
Galantines, smoked salmon
and roast beef.

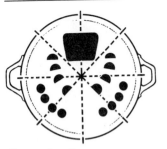

Suggestion 3.
Centerpiece sliced and reset; any style poultry saddle items.

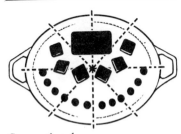

Suggestion 4.
Centerpieces and slices.
Poultry, galantines and tongues.

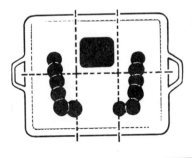

Suggestion 5.
Centerpiece and tranches.
Lobster, galantines and
various roasts.

Suggestion 6.
Centerpieces and tranches.
Fish pieces, different roasts and
poultry.

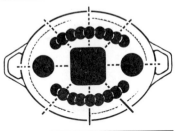

3. The proportion of the centerpiece to the garnish should be 2 to 1.
4. The star-shaped diagram can be used for round and oval-shaped food platters.

Basic Food Arrangement

1. Most foods shown on buffet platters have three elements:
   a. The centerpiece which is cut and displayed whole.
   b. The cut slices, or tranches, draped artistically to one's own taste.
   c. The garnish set in proportion to the cut slices or tranches.
2. The selection of the food tray (silver, mirror, or any other material) is achieved by the proportion of the size and space available.
3. "Less is more"; in other words, allow enough space between the food elements.
4. The foods should not touch the frame of the tray anywhere.

To make these Vegetable Snowmen, using a parisian scoop, cut 8 round balls from turnips. Put balls together with toothpicks. Use whole cloves for eyes and buttons and a bit of raw carrot for a nose. The scarf is a strip of blanched leek and the hat is cut out of whole wheat bread and toasted.

Pate of Chicken Noel uses a circle of pate slices to frame a snowman on mock mistletoe leaves. Sparkling diced aspic accents the row of slices. The mistletoe leaves are cut from blanched leek leaves. Several smaller snowmen are an added seasonal touch. Orange slices in port wine accompany pate.

NOTE: There are various options in the arrangement of practical or show buffet lines. These hints should be practiced as otherwise the danger of losing points or customer appeal is great.

Hints for Food Tray Arrangements

1. Selected tray should not be too small for food arrangement.
2. Garnishes should not be too large or too high.
3. Meat pieces roasted to rare and glazed with aspic take on an unnatural red color.
4. Do not use chopped aspic. If used, the aspic should be diced (croutons).
5. If an aspic mirror is used (silver platter covered with aspic), the aspic should be light brown and must be crystal clear.
6. The use of unnatural aspic, such as red, green, or blue, is not permitted.
7. Food slices or tranches should be placed exactly in line according to divided tray sections.

NOTE: For further information see American Culinary Federation Rules and Guidelines for Food Shows.

Arresting face that presides over this platter of roast turkey slices is molded from mashed sweet potatoes that have been mixed with aspic. When face is completed, coat with aspic. Blanched leek roots can be used for hair. Pickled corn and parsley outline figure. Cranberry relish is favorite accompaniment for Roast Turkey Party Style.

Elaborate decorations made from figures cut from sheets of aspic are limited only by the imagination. White chaud-froid provides an excellent background to set off these designs. If desired, display designs like these may be prepared in advance and stored in freezer.

CHAPTER SIXTEEN

SALADS

The only limit to the number of salads that can be created is the imagination of the chef. However, before experimenting with untested combinations, chef–salad makers should perfect their presentation of the established salad favorites. A large variety of salads, attractively displayed on a buffet, will be a drawing card for most patrons.

Salads are usually served with appropriate dressings, although sometimes, instead of having a dressing added, the salad ingredients are marinated in oil, vinegar, lemon juice, or other liquids. Marinated salads can be preserved for several days. Selecting the right dressing is an important element of salad preparation.

MARINADES AND DRESSINGS

BASIC FRENCH DRESSING
(called vinaigrette in France)

Yield: 1 qt.

Ingredients

Salt	1 tsp.
Wine Vinegar	1 cup
Olive Oil or Peanut Oil	3 cups
Pepper, freshly ground	1/4 tsp.

Method

Dissolve salt in vinegar, then add oil and pepper. Mix all ingredients well.

Variations of Basic French Dressing

Listed here are several popular ways to vary Basic French Dressing:

1. After mixing salt with vinegar, add 1 or 2 tbsp. good French imported mustard, mix well, then combine with oil and freshly ground pepper.
2. Mix 2 raw egg yolks with 2 tbsp. French imported mustard, season with salt and pepper. Add oil and vinegar. Mix well.
3. Put 3 hard-cooked eggs through a sieve, add oil and vinegar, season with salt and pepper. Beat until the sauce reaches a creamy consistency.
4. Blend 1 cup bleu cheese with Basic French Dressing.
5. Coarsely chop 3 hard-cooked eggs. Mix with Basic French Dressing, add 1 tbsp. chopped

parsley, 2 tsp. chopped tarragon, and 3 chopped shallots.

6. Combine 1 tbsp. chopped onion, 1 tbsp. chopped, crisp bacon, and 1 tbsp. chopped pimentos and mix with Basic French Dressing.

RUSSIAN DRESSING

Mix one cup of mayonnaise with 1/2 cup red chili sauce, add 2 tbsp. red peppers, one chopped hard-cooked egg, one dash of Worcestershire sauce, and one dash of hot sauce. Mix all ingredients thoroughly.

EMULSIFIED FRENCH DRESSING

(This type of dressing is very popular in the United States, although it is practically unknown to Europeans.)

Yield: 2-3/4 pt.

Ingredients

Eggs	2
Salt	1 tsp.
Fresh Garlic, crushed and chopped	1 clove
White Pepper	1/4 tsp.
Dry Mustard	1 tsp.
Paprika	2 tbsp.
Salad Oil	1 qt.
Cider Vinegar	1 cup
Worcestershire Sauce	1 tbsp.
Lemon Juice	1/4 cup

Method

Beat eggs with dry ingredients. Add oil slowly; when mixture has thickened, add a little vinegar. Alternately add oil and vinegar until it all has been used. Add Worcestershire sauce; finish with lemon juice.

GREEN GODDESS DRESSING

Yield: 2-3/4 pt.

Ingredients

Parsley, chopped	1 cup
Lemon Juice	1/3 cup
Tarragon Vinegar	1/4 cup
Mayonnaise	1 qt.
Sour Cream	2 cups
Garlic	6 cloves
Anchovies, drained	1 can
Chives	1/4 cup
Salt	2 tsp.
Black Pepper	1/2 tsp.

Method

Chop parsley, strain and save liquid to add as coloring. Blend liquid ingredients first, then add remaining ingredients.

THOUSAND ISLAND DRESSING

Combine equal parts of chili sauce and mayonnaise with heavy cream. Blend until mixture is thick.

VEGETABLE SALADS

TOMATO SALAD

Yield: 4 portions

Ingredients

Tomatoes, fresh, firm	2
Oil	3 tbsp.
Wine Vinegar	1 tbsp.
Onion, chopped	1 tbsp.
Chives, chopped	1 tbsp.
Salt	1/3 tsp.
Pepper	2 to 3 grinds
Oregano	a pinch

Method

Blanch and peel tomatoes. Slice 1/8 in. thick.

Prepare as Basic French Dressing: combine oil and vinegar, add onions, chives, salt, pepper, and oregano. Arrange tomatoes in ravier and cover with dressing. Allow to stand 30 min. Serve chilled.

CELERY SALAD NO. 1

Yield: 2 lb. or 10 portions

Ingredients

Celery	4 roots
Lemon	juice of 1
Basic French Dressing	1/2 cup
Thin Mayonnaise	1/2 cup
Parsley, chopped	to garnish

Method

Peel and cook celery with water and juice of 1 lemon. Cool and cut julienne; marinate in French dressing. Remove from marinade and mix with mayonnaise. Before serving, cover with mayonnaise, sprinkle with chopped parsley.

CELERY SALAD NO. 2

Yield: 4 portions

Ingredients

Celery	1 heart
English Mustard	1 tsp.
Heavy Cream	1/2 cup
Lemon	juice of 1
Mayonnaise	4 tbsp.
Salt	1/3 tsp.
Pepper, freshly ground	2 grinds

Method

Clean and peel celery stalks. Cut into julienne. Combine heavy cream, lemon juice, English mustard, mayonnaise, and seasonings and mix all ingredients well. Mix in the julienne of celery and marinate for 30 min.

CELERY SALAD NO. 3

Yield: 8–10 portions

Ingredients

Celery	2 hearts
Apples, medium, peeled	3
French Mustard	1 tbsp.
Heavy Cream	1/2 cup
Lemon	juice of 1
Salt	1/2 tsp.
Pepper, freshly ground	2 grinds

Method

Clean and peel celery, cut into small julienne. Peel and dice apples and combine with celery.

Mix heavy cream, French mustard, and lemon juice. Combine all ingredients and marinate a few minutes before serving.

ASPARAGUS SALAD

Yield: 4 portions

Ingredients

Asparagus Stalks	16
French Dressing	1 cup
Prepared Mustard	2 tbsp.
Parsley, chopped	1 tbsp.
Chives	1 tbsp.
Tarragon	1 tsp.
Salt	1/3–1/2 tsp.
Pepper, freshly ground	4 grinds

Method

Peel and cook asparagus, cut into pieces 2 to 3 in. in length. Marinate in French dressing made with mustard, parsley, chives, tarragon, salt, and pepper.

MUSHROOM SALAD NO. 1

Yield: 3–4 portions

Ingredients

Mushroom Caps	1 lb.
Oil	2 tsp.
Onion, medium, diced	1
Vinegar	1/4 cup
Oil	3/4 cup
Salt	1/2–1 tsp.
Pepper	1/3 tsp.
Tarragon Leaves, fresh, frozen, chopped	1/2 tsp.

(continued)

Mushroom Salad No. 1 (continued)
Method
Wash and slice mushrooms. In a saute pan, heat oil and cook onion and mushrooms; season.

Prepare Basic French Dressing, adding chopped tarragon. Marinate mushrooms in dressing for 1 hour.

MUSHROOM SALAD NO. 2

Yield: 4–5 portions

Ingredients

White Mushroom Caps	1 lb.
Lemons	juice of 3
Salt	1/2–1 tsp.
Pepper	1/3 tsp.
Soy Sauce	3 tsp.

Method
Wash and slice mushrooms very thin; marinate for 1 or 2 hours in lemon juice, salt, pepper, and soy sauce.

RED CABBAGE SALAD NO. 1

Yield: 8–10 portions (1 lb. 11 oz.)

Ingredients

Red Cabbage, medium	1
White Vinegar	1/3 cup
Onion, medium, diced	1
Salt	1/2 tsp.

Method
Shred cabbage. Mix onion and vinegar; add salt to taste. Marinate cabbage in mixture for 24 hours or more.

RED CABBAGE SALAD NO. 2

Yield: 8–10 portions (1 lb. 13 oz.)

Ingredients

Red Cabbage, medium	1
Vinegar	1/3 cup
Salt	1/2 to 1 tsp.
Pepper	1/3 tsp.
Oil	1 cup
Red Currant Jelly	1/4 cup

Method
Shred the cabbage fine and blanch for 3–4 min. in vinegar-flavored water.

Mix vinegar, salt, pepper, oil, and currant jelly and pour over cabbage. Marinate for 2–3 hours.

LEEK SALAD

Yield: 12–15 oz.

Ingredients

Leeks	1 bunch
White Stock	1 pt.
Basic French Dressing made with 1 tbsp. prepared mustard	1 cup
Hard-cooked Eggs, chopped	3

Method
Wash leeks and remove outside leaves. Cut leeks lengthwise, leaving 1 in. above the root uncut.

Tie leeks in a bundle and braise in white stock until cooked; drain carefully. Cut leeks into 2–3 in. pieces and combine with remaining ingredients. Serve sprinkled with egg.

MACARONI SALAD

Yield: 2 lb. 11 oz.

Ingredients

Macaroni	8 oz.
Mayonnaise	1 cup
Tomatoes, seedless, peeled and diced	2
Vinegar	2 tsp.
Green Pepper, diced	1 oz.
Red Pepper, diced	1 oz.
Salt	1/2 tsp.
Pepper	1/3 tsp.

Method
Cook macaroni in boiling, salted water for 10–15 min. Mix mayonnaise with remaining ingredients and combine with macaroni.

🙙🙚

GREEN PEPPER SALAD

Yield: 17 oz.

Ingredients
Green Peppers	1 lb.
White Vinegar	1/2 cup
Oil	1 cup
Sugar	1 tsp.
Tarragon, chopped	1 tbsp.
Chives	1 tbsp.
Salt	1/2–1 tsp.
Pepper	1/2 tsp.

Method
Wash peppers and cut in half. Remove seeds and cut into fine julienne.

Mix all remaining ingredients together and add to the peppers.

🙙🙚

BEET SALAD NO. 1

Yield: 15 oz.

Ingredients
Beets	1 lb.
Heavy Cream	1/2 cup
English Mustard	1 tsp.
Lemons	juice of 2
Sugar	1 tsp.
Salt	1–1-1/2 tsp.
Pepper	1/3–1/2 tsp.

Method
Wash beets and cook in boiling water till tender. Cool and slice.

Blend heavy cream, mustard, lemon juice, sugar, salt, and pepper and combine with beets.

🙙🙚

BEET SALAD NO. 2

Yield: 1 lb.

Ingredients
Beets	1 lb.
French Dressing	1 cup
Onion, medium, diced	1
Salt	1/2–1 tsp.
Pepper	1/3 tsp.
Worcestershire Sauce	1/2 tsp.
Parsley, chopped	1 tsp.

Method
Wash beets and cook in boiling water until tender. Cool and cut in medium julienne.

Mix remaining ingredients and combine with beets. Before serving, sprinkle with chopped parsley.

🙙🙚

BASIC POTATO SALAD

Yield: 2 lb. 12 oz.

Ingredients
Potatoes (not mealy)	2 lb.
Oil	1/4 cup
Vinegar	1/4 cup
Hot Chicken Stock	1/4 cup
Onion, medium, diced	1/2 cup
Salt	1 tsp.
Pepper	1/2 tsp.
Sugar	1/3 tsp.
Parsley, chopped	1 tbsp.

Method
Wash and cook potatoes in jackets. When done, cool potatoes and peel while still warm. Dice or slice.

Mix oil, vinegar, stock, onion, salt, pepper, sugar, and parsley. Marinate potatoes in this mixture for 1 to 2 hours before serving.

🙙🙚

GERMAN POTATO SALAD

Follow Basic Potato Salad recipe but add 1 diced, peeled apple and 1 tbsp. chopped chives.

🙙🙚

Potato Salad

DUTCH POTATO SALAD

Follow Basic Potato Salad recipe but add 2 tbsp. diced bacon and 1 diced herring, smoked.

☙ ❧

FRENCH POTATO SALAD

Yield: 2 lb. 6 oz.

Ingredients

Potatoes (not mealy)	2 lb.
Shallots, chopped	4
White Vinegar	1/4 cup
Oil	1/4 cup
Salt	1/2–1 tsp.
Pepper	1/2 tsp.
Parsley, chopped	1 tsp.

Method

Scrub potatoes, cook in boiling water until tender. Cool potatoes, peel and slice thin.

Mix sliced potatoes with chopped shallots, oil, vinegar, salt, pepper, and chopped parsley.

NOTE: All of the preceding types of potato salad can be mixed with mayonnaise.

☙ ❧

CARROT SALAD NO. 1

Yield: 15 oz.

Ingredients

Carrots, fresh (or a 14-oz. can of Belgian Carrots)	1 lb.
French Mustard	2 tbsp.
Garlic, finely chopped	1 clove
Oil	1/2 cup
Vinegar	1/4 cup
Salt	1/2–1 tsp.
Pepper	1/3 tsp.
Chives, chopped	2 tsp.

Method

Peel fresh carrots; cook until tender; slice. If using canned carrots, drain before using.

Combine all remaining ingredients and hold for 30 min. before serving.

☙ ❧

CARROT SALAD NO. 2

Yield: 1 lb.

Ingredients

Carrots	1 lb.
Basic French Dressing	1/3 cup

Prepared Mustard | 1 tbsp.
Lemon | juice of 1

Method

Peel carrots and grate. Mix Basic French Dressing, lemon juice, and mustard; add grated carrots and allow to stand in dressing for a few minutes before service.

BASIC CUCUMBER SALAD

Yield: 20–22 oz.

Ingredients

Cucumbers (10–11 oz.) | 2
Basic French Dressing | 1/2 cup
Parsley, chopped, or Dill | 1 tbsp.

Method

Peel cucumbers and slice thin. Marinate in dressing for a few minutes. Sprinkle with chopped parsley or dill.

ENGLISH CUCUMBER SALAD

Yield: 20–23 oz.

Ingredients

Cucumbers (10–11 oz.) | 2
Celery Stalks, cut julienne | 2
Heavy Cream | 1/2 cup
Lemons | juice of 2
Salt | to taste
Pepper | to taste

Method

Peel cucumbers and slice thin. Peel celery and cut into julienne.

Combine cucumbers and celery and add other ingredients; mix thoroughly and allow to stand for 1/2 hour before serving.

FRENCH CUCUMBER SALAD

Yield: 20–22 oz.

Ingredients

Cucumbers (10–11 oz.) | 2
Salt | 1 tsp.
Basic French Dressing | 1/2 cup
Parsley, chopped | 1 tsp.
Onion, medium, sliced thin | 1/2

Method

Peel cucumbers, cut lengthwise. Remove seeds, slice thin, and add salt. Place in bowl for 1/2 hour.

Place cucumbers in a clean towel. Squeeze out all water. Mix cucumbers with dressing and onions and sprinkle with chopped parsley.

RUSSIAN CUCUMBER SALAD

Yield: 24–26 oz.

Ingredients

Cucumbers (10–11 oz.) | 2
Mayonnaise | 1/4 cup
Sour Cream | 1/4 cup
Dill, chopped | 1 tbsp.
Lemon | juice of 1
Salt | 1/3–1/2 tsp.
Pepper, freshly ground | 2 grinds
Onion, medium, sliced thin | 1/2

Method

Peel and slice cucumbers. Combine mayonnaise, sour cream, lemon juice, dill, onion, salt, and pepper. Add cucumber to mixture.

HUNGARIAN CUCUMBER SALAD

Prepare Russian Cucumber Salad, then add 1 tbsp. chopped chives, 1/4 cup thin julienne slices of green pepper, and 1/4 cup thin julienne slices of pimento.

GREEN BEAN SALAD

Yield: 1 lb. 16 oz.

Ingredients

Green Beans, fresh or frozen	1 lb.
Basic French Dressing	1/2 cup
Pimento, diced	1/2 cup
Bacon, diced, cooked crisp	4 oz.
Garlic Powder	1/3 tsp.
Salt	1/2–1 tsp.
Pepper	1/2 tsp.

Method

If using fresh beans, cut tips from both ends and cut in 2-in. pieces. Cook beans in boiling salted water till done. Drain thoroughly and cool. If using frozen beans, cook according to directions. Combine pimento, bacon, and seasonings with dressing. Add cooked beans to dressing. Mix well.

BEAN SPROUT SALAD

Yield: 1 lb. 4 oz.

Ingredients

Bean Sprouts	2 cups
Soy Sauce	2 tbsp.
Sesame Seeds, ground	2 tbsp.
Pimento, diced	1/4 cup
Scallions, chopped	1/4 cup
Vinegar	2 tsp.
Garlic, chopped	1 clove

Method

Combine all ingredients and mix with bean sprouts. Refrigerate for 1 hour before serving.

ARTICHOKE SALAD PROVENCALE

Yield: 6 portions

Ingredients

Artichoke Bottoms	12
Tomatoes, medium	3
Anchovy Filets, canned	1 small can

Artichoke Salad Provencale

Lemon	juice of 1
Pepper	1/2 tsp.
Salt	1/2 tsp.
Chives	1 tsp.
Ripe Olives	6
Green Olives	6

Method

Quarter the cooked artichoke bottoms and deep fry a few seconds.

Quarter tomatoes and dice half of anchovies. Combine artichokes, tomatoes, anchovies, lemon juice, salt, pepper, and chives. Arrange on dish and decorate with remaining anchovy filets and ripe and green olives.

CAULIFLOWER SALAD

Yield: 20–25 oz.

Ingredients

Cauliflower, medium (16–20 oz.)	1
Basic French Dressing	1 cup
Prepared Mustard	1 tbsp.
Lemon	juice of 1

| Garlic, chopped | 1 clove |
| Hard-cooked Egg Yolks, chopped | 3 |

Method

Wash cauliflower and cook in boiling water until done. Cool and cut into small pieces.

Combine remaining ingredients and mix with cauliflower buds. Marinate for 1 hour in refrigerator.

CABBAGE SLAW, FARMER'S STYLE

Yield: 1 lb. 15 oz. (10–12 portions)

Ingredients

White Cabbage	1
Basic French Dressing	2 cups
Caraway Seeds	1 tsp.

Method

Shred cabbage and blanch for 2 min. Drain cabbage, then mix with dressing and caraway seeds. Refrigerate 1 hour before service.

INDIAN RICE SALAD

Yield: 2 lb. 6 oz.

Ingredients

Rice	1 cup
Smoked Fish	2 oz.
Tomatoes, blanched and peeled	2
Green Pepper	1
Basic French Dressing	1 cup
Salt	1/3 tsp.
Pepper, freshly ground	2 to 3 grinds
Worcestershire Sauce	1/2 tsp.

Method

Boil rice in 2-1/2 cups of salted water for approx. 20 min. When cooked, drain and cool.

Dice fish, tomato, and green pepper and combine with rice. Add salt, pepper, dressing, and Worcestershire sauce to mixture.

ITALIAN SALAD

Yield: 12 oz.

Ingredients

Celery Stalks	2 oz.
Tomatoes, blanched and peeled	2 oz.
Artichoke Bottoms	2 oz.
Apples	2 oz.
Olive Oil	1/2 cup
Lemons	juice of 3
Salt	1/3 tsp.
Pepper, freshly ground	2 to 3 grinds
Romaine Lettuce	1 leaf
Fennel, julienned	2 oz.

Method

Dice celery, tomatoes, artichokes, and apples. Mix oil, lemon juice, salt, and pepper and blend with diced celery, tomatoes, artichokes, and apples. Arrange on a leaf of romaine lettuce and top with julienned fennel.

WALDORF SALAD

Yield: 1 lb. 14 oz.

Ingredients

Apples	1 lb.
Celery	4 oz.
Walnuts	2 oz.
Mayonnaise	1/4 cup
Sour Cream	1/4 cup
Lemon	juice of 1
Salt, optional	1/3 tsp.

Method

Dice apples, celery, and walnuts. Mix mayonnaise, sour cream, and lemon juice. Blend apples, celery, and walnuts into mayonnaise mixture.

SAUERKRAUT WITH APPLES AND PINEAPPLE

Yield: 1 lb.

Ingredients

Sauerkraut, fresh	8 oz.
Apples, fresh	2
Pineapple, sweet, fresh	6 oz.

Method

Wash and drain sauerkraut and chop into coarse pieces. Peel and cut apple into small dice; cut pineapple into small dice. Combine all ingredients and serve on a bed of lettuce.

SALAD RACHEL

Yield: 24 oz.

Ingredients

Artichoke Bottoms	4 oz.
Celery	4 oz.
Mayonnaise	1 cup
Boston Lettuce	1 head
Asparagus Tips	8

Method

Cut artichokes and celery into julienne and mix with mayonnaise. Place mixture on a bed of Boston lettuce and arrange asparagus tips on top.

STOCKHOLM SALAD

Yield: 17 oz.

Ingredients

Celery, cooked, julienned	4 oz.
Beets, cooked, julienned	4 oz.
Dill, chopped	2 tbsp.
Vinegar	1/4 cup
Salt	1/3 tsp.
Pepper, freshly ground	2 to 3 grinds
Chantilly Sauce	1 cup

Method

Combine celery and beets with dill, vinegar, salt, and pepper and marinate for 24 hours. Drain liquid from vegetables and mix them with Chantilly Sauce.

RUSSIAN SALAD

Yield: 1 lb. 7 oz.

Ingredients

Beets, cooked, drained, diced	2 oz.
Potato, cooked, diced	2 oz.
Carrots, cooked, diced	2 oz.
Peas, cooked	2 oz.
Beans, cooked, diced	2 oz.
Mayonnaise, well seasoned	1/2 cup
Asparagus, cooked	5 oz.

Method

Combine all vegetables except asparagus tips with mayonnaise. Arrange salad on plate and top with asparagus.

NOTE: To give additional flavor, grated onions can be added to salad.

SALAD NICOISE

Yield: 10 oz.

Ingredients

String Beans, cooked	2 oz.
Potatoes, diced	2 oz.
Tomato Wedges, peeled	2 oz.
Basic French Dressing	1/2 cup
Salt	1/3 tsp.
Pepper	1/3 tsp.
Anchovies	2 oz.
Capers	1 tsp.
Ripe Olives	1 oz.

Method

Combine string beans, tomatoes, and potatoes with dressing. Add salt and pepper. Arrange mixture on platter and garnish with anchovies, capers, and olives.

HUNGARIAN SALAD NO. 1

Yield: 2 lb. 8 oz.

Ingredients

Ox Tongue, cooked	24 oz.
Pickled Cucumber	1
Pimento	2 oz.

Belgian Endives	2
Truffle	1
French Dressing	1 cup
Paprika	1 tsp.

Method
Cut ox tongue, pickled cucumber, pimento, endive, and truffle into julienne strips. Combine all ingredients with dressing and paprika and mix.

HUNGARIAN SALAD NO. 2

Yield: 8 oz.

Ingredients
Green Pepper	2 oz.
Red Pepper	2 oz.
Apples	2 oz.
Basic French Dressing	1 cup
Salt	1/3 tsp.
Boston Lettuce	

Method
Cut red and green pepper into fine julienne strips. Peel apples and cut into julienne strips. Mix all ingredients except lettuce with dressing; add salt. Place mixture on a bed of Boston lettuce before serving.

POLISH SALAD

Yield: 4–6 portions

Ingredients
Hard-cooked Eggs	4
Herring Filets	2
Potatoes, cooked	2 oz.
Gherkins	2 oz.
Beets	2 oz.
Carrots	2 oz.
Parsley, chopped	3 tbsp.
Tarragon	2 tbsp.
Salt	1 tsp.
Pepper	1/2 tsp.
Mayonnaise	1/2 cup

Method
Mix each ingredient separately with parsley, tarragon, salt, and pepper. Arrange each mound of ingredients separately on a silver platter, like a Bouquetiere. Serve mayonnaise separately.

SALAD MIGNON

Yield: 14 oz.

Ingredients
Shrimp, cooked	4 oz.
Artichoke Bottoms	2 oz.
Mayonnaise	1/2 cup
Heavy Cream	1 tbsp.
Cayenne Pepper	1/16 tsp.
Chicory	1 head
Truffle, optional	1

Method
Dice shrimp and artichoke bottoms. Mix mayonnaise with heavy cream and cayenne pepper. Mix all ingredients except truffle together and serve on bed of chicory. Julienne truffle and place on top.

SALAD MIMOSA

Yield: 8 portions

Ingredients
Boston Lettuce	2 hearts
Watercress	1 bunch
Basic French Dressing	1/2 cup
Hard-cooked Eggs, grated	3

Method
Wash and drain lettuce hearts and cut into quarters. Arrange on platter surrounded by watercress.

Pour dressing over greens and sprinkle half with grated hard-cooked egg yolks and the other half with grated hard-cooked egg whites.

SALAD MARIE-LOUISE

Yield: 2 portions

Ingredients

Banana	1
Celery	1 pc.
Apple	1
Truffle	1
Mayonnaise	1/2 cup

Method

Peel and slice banana; peel and quarter apple; peel and dice celery.

Combine all ingredients with mayonnaise and arrange on platter with a slice of truffle on top.

SALAD LORETTE

Yield: 9 oz.

Ingredients

Beets, cooked	4 oz.
Celery	4 oz.
Basic French Dressing	3/4 cup
Boston Lettuce	1 leaf

Method

Cut beets and celery in julienne strips. Combine with dressing; mix thoroughly. Place on leaf of Boston lettuce.

OXFORD SALAD

Yield: 1 lb. 14 oz.

Ingredients

Chicken, cooked, diced	1 cup
Sour Gherkins, sliced	2 oz.
Tomatoes, cut into wedges	2 oz.
Basic French Dressing	1/2 cup
Boston Lettuce	1 head
Tarragon, chopped	2 tbsp.
Truffle, finely diced	1 oz.
Hard-cooked Eggs, sliced	3

Method

Combine chicken, gherkins, tomatoes, and dressing and mix well. Place mixture on a bed of Boston lettuce and sprinkle truffles and tarragon over salad. Decorate with slices of hard-cooked egg around the salad.

ITALIAN VEGETABLE SALAD

Yield: 15 oz.

Ingredients

Carrots, cooked, diced	1 oz.
Green Beans, cooked, diced	1 oz.
Green Peas, cooked, diced	1 oz.
Tomatoes, peeled, diced	1 oz.
Salami, diced	1 oz.
Stuffed Green Olives, sliced	1 oz.
Anchovy Filets, small can	1
Mayonnaise	1/2 cup
Parsley, chopped	1 tsp.

Method

Blend all ingredients except parsley thoroughly and mix with mayonnaise. Sprinkle with fresh chopped parsley.

FISH SALADS

Fish to be used for salad is usually cooked first, then cooled and prepared as the recipe indicates.

Fish salads are seasoned with a variety of dressings, although mayonnaise is most frequently used.

The following recipes can be made using any leftover fish:

TUNAFISH SALAD NO. 1

Yield: 23 oz.

Ingredients

White Tuna, 14 oz. can	1
Mayonnaise	1/2 cup
Onion, chopped	1 oz.
Salt	1/3 tsp.
Pepper, freshly ground	2 to 3 grinds
Lemon	juice of 1

Tunafish Salad Plate
Decorated with Penguin Egg (page 96)
Cabbage Orchid (page 177)
Tomato Rose (page 174)

Worcestershire Sauce	1/2 tsp.
Parsley, chopped	1 tbsp.

Method

Flake tunafish. Combine mayonnaise and onions; season with salt, pepper, lemon juice, and Worcestershire sauce. Blend tunafish with mayonnaise mixture.

Arrange mixture in a dish and sprinkle chopped parsley over the top. There are many garnishes that can be used to enhance the presentation of the fish.

✧✧

TUNAFISH SALAD NO. 2

Yield: 24 oz.

Ingredients

Olive Oil	4 tbsp.
Onion, chopped	1 oz.
Garlic, crushed, chopped	2 cloves
Tunafish, 14 oz. can	1
Sweet Corn	4 oz.
Green Pepper, cut julienne	1 oz.
Red Pepper, cut julienne	1 oz.
White Wine	1/4 cup
Lemon	juice of 1
Salt	1/2–1 tsp.
Pepper	1/3 tsp.

Method

Heat oil in saute pan. Add onions and garlic; when lightly colored, add tunafish, corn, red and green pepper. Cook for 5 min., then add white wine and lemon juice. Season with salt and pepper.

Cook on low fire until vegetables are done. Cool and serve with marinated tomatoes.

✧✧

HERRING SALAD

Yield: 18 oz.

Ingredients

Bismarck Herring	8 oz.
Apples	2 oz.
Beets	2 oz.
Potatoes, cooked	2 oz.
Basic French Dressing	1/2 cup
Salt	1/3 tsp.
Pepper	2 to 3 grinds

Method

Soak herring in water. Dice apples, beets, and potatoes. Drain herring and dice.

Combine all ingredients. Add dressing, salt, and pepper. Refrigerate for 1 hour.

✧✧

SALMON SALAD

Yield: 15 oz.

Ingredients

Salmon, cooked	8 oz.
Basic French Dressing	1/4 cup
Salt	1/2 tsp.
Pepper, freshly ground	2 to 3 grinds
Cucumbers	2 oz.
Tomatoes	2 oz.
Mayonnaise	1/2 cup

Method

Season salmon with dressing, salt, and pepper. Arrange salmon mixture on a platter. Surround with tomato wedges and sliced cucumbers. Serve with mayonnaise.

LOBSTER SALAD

Yield: 21 oz.

Ingredients

Lobster Meat	8 oz.
Hard-cooked Eggs	2
Lemon	juice of 1
Mustard	1 tbsp.
Salt	1/3 tsp.
Pepper	2 to 3 grinds
Mayonnaise	1/2 cup
Lettuce	1 leaf
Parsley, chopped	1 tsp.
Lobster Coral	1 tsp.

Method

Dice lobster meat; combine with chopped egg.

Blend mayonnaise with lemon juice, mustard, salt, and pepper and combine with lobster and egg.

Place salad on lettuce leaf. Sprinkle with chopped parsley and coral.

KING CRAB SALAD

Use same procedure and amounts of ingredients as for Lobster Salad, except substitute crabmeat for lobster.

SALAD OF LEFTOVER FISH

Yield: 23 oz.

Ingredients

Shallots, chopped	1 tbsp.
Olive Oil	1/4 cup
Capers	2 tsp.
Green Olives, sliced	2 oz.
Cepes (wild mushrooms)	4 oz.
Garlic Cloves, chopped	2
White Wine	1/2 cup
Pickles, diced	2 oz.
Tarragon	1 tbsp.
Chili Sauce	1/4 cup
Salt	1 tsp.
Pepper	1/2 tsp.
Lemon	juice of 2
Fish, leftover, flaked	8 oz.

Method

Saute chopped shallots in oil, add capers, green olives, cepes, and garlic. Cook until transparent. Deglaze pan with white wine.

Add pickles, tarragon, chili sauce, salt, pepper, and juice from lemons. Cook for 5 min.

Pour sauce over fish, mix, and cool for 2 hours.

MUSSEL SALAD

YIELD: 9 oz.

Ingredients

Mussels, cooked, cleaned	4 oz.
Asparagus Tips	1 oz.
Green Beans, French-cut, cooked	1 oz.
Tomato, peeled, diced	1 oz.
Onion, chopped	1 tbsp.
Horseradish, grated	1 tsp.
Basic French Dressing	1/2 cup
Salt	1/3 tsp.
Pepper	1/3 tsp.

Method

Combine all ingredients, blend with dressing. Refrigerate for 1 hour before serving.

MEAT AND POULTRY SALADS

CALVES' BRAINS SALAD

Yield: 11 oz.

Ingredients

Calves' Brains	4 oz.
Vinegar	1 tbsp.
Bayleaf	1
Onion, sliced	1 oz.
Pepper	1 tsp.
Tarragon Leaves	1 tsp.
Parsley, chopped	1 tsp.
Chives	1 tsp.
Dill	1 tsp.
Mayonnaise, with 1 tbsp. mustard (or Ravigote Sauce)	1/2 cup

Method

Blanch calves' brains in salted water for 5 min. Water should contain vinegar, bayleaf, onions, pepper, and 1 tsp. tarragon leaves.

Cool and drain calves' brains. Slice brains. Sprinkle remaining herbs over brains and blend in mayonnaise with mustard or ravigote sauce.

↬ ↫

CHICKEN SALAD

Yield: 17 oz.

Ingredients

Chicken Meat	8 oz.
Celery, diced	4 oz.
Onion, chopped	1 oz.
Mayonnaise	1/4 cup
Salt	1/2 tsp.
Pepper	2 to 3 grinds
Worcestershire Sauce	1/2 tsp.
Leaf Lettuce	

Method

Dice chicken meat. Combine all ingredients and mix well.

↬ ↫

GAME SALAD

Yield: 17 oz.

Ingredients

Leftover Game Meat (venison, pheasant, hare, etc.)	8 oz.
Mayonnaise	1/4 cup
English Mustard	1 tsp.
Orange, julienned	1 tbsp.
Red Currant Jelly	1/4 cup
Walnuts, chopped	2 tbsp.

Method

Cut game into julienne strips. Mix mayonnaise with mustard, red currant jelly, and orange zest (grated outer layer, no white).

Combine all ingredients, and sprinkle with walnuts.

↬ ↫

AMERICAN SALAD

Yield: 24 oz. (5–6 portions)

Ingredients

Frankfurters	8 oz.
Swiss Cheese	8 oz.
Egg Yolks	2
French Mustard	1 tbsp.
Olive Oil	1 cup
Vinegar	1/4 cup
Shallots, chopped	1 tbsp.
Salt	1 tsp.
Pepper	1/2 tsp.
Chives, chopped	2 tbsp.

Method

Boil frankfurters and slice in 1/2-in. pieces.

Cut cheese into julienne strips. Mix egg yolks with mustard; incorporate oil, as for mayonnaise. Add sauteed shallots, salt, pepper, and vinegar to the sauce.

Combine frankfurters, cheese, and sauce. Mix all ingredients with chives.

ITALIAN MEAT SALAD

Yield: 24 oz.

Ingredients

Salami, Veal, or Bologna	8 oz.
Pickles	2 oz.
Apple	1 oz.
Mayonnaise	1/2 cup
Worcestershire Sauce	1/2 tsp.
Anchovies, chopped	1/2 oz.
Eggs, chopped	2
Pickles, chopped	1 tbsp.

Method

Cut salami, veal, or bologna in fine julienne strips. Cut pickles and apple into julienne. Combine these ingredients with mayonnaise, blend well. Add Worcestershire sauce and chopped anchovies.

Mix all ingredients well; decorate salad with chopped egg and chopped pickle.

BEEF SALAD NO. 1

Yield: 19 oz.

Ingredients

Beef, boiled or roasted	8 oz.
Onion, chopped	2 oz.
Basic French Dressing	1/4 cup
Salt	1/3 tsp.
Pepper, freshly ground	2 to 3 grinds
Hard-cooked Eggs, sliced	2
Tomato, sliced	1

Method

Cut beef into julienne strips or dice. Combine with onion and dressing. Add salt and pepper.

Marinate salad for 24 hours, then arrange in bowl. Decorate by alternating slices of egg and tomato.

BEEF SALAD NO. 2

Yield: 1 lb.

Ingredients

Beef, cooked	8 oz.
Pickles	1 oz.

American Salad

Tomatoes	1 oz.
Celery	1 oz.
Basic French Dressing	1/4 cup
Salt	1/3 tsp.
Pepper	1/2 tsp.
Garlic Powder	1/3 tsp.
Prepared Mustard	1 tbsp.
Parsley, chopped	1 tsp.
Tarragon, chopped	1 tsp.
Chives, chopped	1 tsp.
Green Olives	1 tbsp.
Hard-cooked Egg, sliced	1

Method

Cut beef, pickles, tomato, and celery into julienne. Marinate in dressing containing salt, pepper, garlic powder, prepared mustard, parsley, tarragon, and chives.

Before serving, decorate dish with sliced egg and sliced olives.

SWISS SALAD

Yield: 24 oz. (5–6 portions)

Ingredients

Shallots, chopped	2 tbsp.
White Wine	1 cup

Langostino Salad. *This salad is a combination of langostinos, diced apples and celery blended with mayonnaise, catsup and finely chopped fresh dill. Salad is decorated with langostinos, hearts of artichokes, sliced radishes and chopped eggs. Marinated green beans are used as a border.*

Basic French Dressing	1/2 cup
Hard-cooked Egg Yolks, chopped fine	1 oz.
Heavy Cream	1/4 cup
Ham, julienned	8 oz.
Swiss Cheese, julienned	4 oz.
Celery, julienned	2 oz.
Hard-cooked Egg Whites, julienned	2 oz.
Tomato, diced small	1 oz.
Salt	1/2–1 tsp.
Pepper	1/3 tsp.
Tarragon, chopped	1 tsp.
Parsley	1 tsp.
Chives	1 tsp.

Method

Reduce shallots and white wine to 2/3 of original amount; cool and combine with dressing and finely chopped egg yolk. Add heavy cream.

Combine ham, cheese, celery, egg whites, and tomato. Mix all ingredients together, season to taste.

Sprinkle each portion of salad with chopped tarragon, chives, and parsley.

FRUIT SALADS

SALAD ALICE

Yield: 4 portions

Ingredients

Lemon	juice of 1
Apples, medium	4
Almonds, sliced, toasted	3 tbsp.
Red Currant Jelly	6 tbsp.
Heavy Cream, whipped	1/4 cup
Salt	1/3 tsp.
Sugar	1/3 tsp.
Lettuce	4 leaves

Method

Cut tops, leaving stems attached, from the apples and set aside; remove all pulp from inside using a parisian scoop. Remove all seeds from apple and squeeze juice of one lemon over pulp.

Dice apple pulp and mix with toasted almonds, red currant jelly, and whipped cream; season with salt and sugar. Fill hollowed apples and put the tops over them. Serve whole topped apple with stem on a bed of lettuce.

SALAD MONTE CARLO

Yield: 5 portions

Ingredients

Oranges, medium	5
Pineapple, small	1
Maraschino Cherries	1/2 cup
Heavy Cream, whipped	1/2 cup
Lemon	juice of 1
Salt	1/3 tsp.

Method

Wash oranges and cut off tops. Scoop out fruit from inside of oranges. Reserve shells. Peel pineapple and dice fruit. Combine fruit from 1/2 orange with 1/2 pineapple.

Add maraschino cherries and whipped heavy cream; season with lemon juice and salt. Fill empty orange shells and replace tops. Serve on crushed ice.

SOUTH AMERICAN SALAD

Yield: 6 portions

Ingredients

Bananas, large	3
Apple, medium	1
Celery	1 pc.
Seedless Green Grapes or Blue Grapes	4 oz.
Mayonnaise, flavored with lemon juice	1/4 cup
Pistachio Nuts	1 oz.

Method

Cut bananas in two lengthwise; peel and save skins. Peel apple; remove any strings from celery. Slice bananas, celery, and apple in 1/3 in. pieces. Combine grapes with fruit. Blend mayonnaise into mixture.

Fill half a banana skin with the mixture and sprinkle peeled pistachio nuts over it.

MACEDOINE OF FRUITS

Yield: 60–65 oz.

Ingredients

Apples	2
Pears	2
Peaches	2
Pineapple, medium	1
Bananas	2
Oranges	2
Sugar	as needed
Walnuts	1 oz.
Pistachio Nuts	1 oz.

Method

Peel fruit and cut into slices or dice. Combine all fruit and mix well; add sugar if necessary.

Serve chilled in crystal bowl or in individual portions in champagne glasses. Top servings with chopped walnuts and pistachio nuts. Maraschino brandy can be added.

FRUITS STUFFED WITH SALADS

STUFFED CANTALOUPE

Yield: 4 portions

Ingredients

Cantaloupe	2
Peach Halves	4
Langostino Tails	8 oz.
Salt	1/3 tsp.
Lemon	juice of 1
Madeira	1 oz.
Chantilly Sauce	1/2 cup

Method

Cut cantaloupe into halves, scoop melon from shells, and slice lengthwise in thin slices.

Slice peaches and cut langostinos in half. Mix melon, peaches, and langostinos and marinate with salt, lemon juice, and Madeira. Blend Chantilly Sauce into mixture.

Fill melon shells with mixture and serve well chilled.

CANTALOUPE STUFFED WITH CHICKEN, LOBSTER, OR CRABMEAT

Yield: 4 portions

Ingredients

Cantaloupe	2
Chicken, Lobster, or Crabmeat	8 oz.
Pickles, diced	4 oz.
Mayonnaise	1/2 cup
Lemon Juice	1 tsp.
Tarragon, chopped	1 tsp.

Method

Cut cantaloupe in half, remove melon from shells.

Dice melon and combine with chicken, lobster, or crab and pickles. Combine mayonnaise, lemon juice, and chopped tarragon and blend into mixture.

Fill melon halves with salad, chill and serve on crushed ice.

STUFFED PEACHES

Yield: 8 portions

Ingredients

Peach Halves	4
Lobster Meat	4 oz.
Pears	4 oz.
Salt	1/4 tsp.
Pepper, freshly ground	4 grinds
Orange Juice	1/4 cup

Method

Dice lobster meat and pears. Season with salt and pepper. Mix above ingredients, adding orange juice.

Stuff peach halves with mixture and chill. Serve with mayonnaise and lemon juice.

STUFFED TOMATOES (*Variation I*)

Yield: 6 portions

Ingredients

Tomatoes, medium-sized, cut in half and scooped out	6
Chicken Meat	4 oz.
Pineapple	2 oz.
Chutney, chopped	1 oz.
Chili Sauce	1 oz.
Oil	2 tbsp.
Lemon	juice of 1
Salt	1/3 tsp.
Pepper	1/3 tsp.

Method

Dice chicken and pineapple, then combine with remaining ingredients. Stuff tomatoes with mixture and serve cold.

STUFFED TOMATOES (*Variation II*)

Yield: 6 portions

Ingredients

Tomatoes, medium-sized, cut in half and scooped out	6
King Crabmeat	12 oz.
Mushrooms, cooked	6 oz.
Oil	1/4 cup
Lemons	juice of 2
Chili Sauce	2 oz.
Salt	1/3 tsp.

Method

Dice crabmeat and mushrooms. Season with oil, lemon juice, chili sauce, and salt.

Stuff tomato halves and serve cold.

STUFFED TOMATOES (*Variation III*)

Yield: 8 portions

Ingredients

Tomatoes, medium-sized, cut in half and scooped out	4
Artichoke Bottoms	4
Green Beans	8 oz.
Basic French Dressing	1/4 cup
Parsley, chopped	1 tbsp.
Tarragon, chopped	1 tsp.

Method

Cut artichokes into julienne strips. Combine with beans and season with dressing.

Stuff tomato halves and sprinkle with tarragon and parsley.

꿎 ꮏ

STUFFED TOMATOES (*Variation IV*)

Yield: 12 wedges

Ingredients

Tomatoes, firm, red, ripe, small	3
Egg Yolks	5
Butter	4 oz.
Prepared Mustard	1 tsp.
Paprika	1/2 tsp.
Worcestershire Sauce	1/2 tsp.

Method

Cut tops off tomatoes and remove all seeds. Set aside.

Mix egg yolks with butter and season with mustard, paprika, and Worcestershire sauce.

Fill tomatoes with egg yolk mixture. Allow to cool for 1 hour.

Slice filled tomatoes or cut into wedges.

꿎 ꮏ

STUFFED TOMATOES (*Variation V*)

Follow directions for Variation IV except to the egg yolk mixture add: 1 tbsp. fresh chives, 1/2 oz. parsley, 1/2 oz. spinach that have been pureed together.

꿎 ꮏ

CHAPTER SEVENTEEN

CHEESES

Knowing what various kinds of cheeses taste like and how they are made is essential for two reasons:

1. To blend each kind of cheese successfully with other ingredients in cooking.
2. To select the proper cheese as the finishing touch for a successful dinner.

Cheese is made from the curds of milk from various domestic animals—cows, sheep, goats. The curds are separated from the whey by the action of the rennet and of certain bacteria or mold spores. After the curds are separated, the whey is molded into different shapes and sizes which are ripened into cheese, according to the tradition of the region where it is produced.

What are whey, rennet, and curd?
Whey is the fluid that separates from the curds when milk coagulates. Rennet is an extract taken from the fourth stomach of newly born calves. The curd is the main factor in cheese making. It is formed during the coagulation of the casein which occurs when rennet is added to separate the water from the milk.

Why are bacteria used?
Bacteria or mold spores are added to the rennet to give the cheese its individual characteristics. When using these bacteria, or, in trade language, starter cultures, the utmost care is required.

Mold works in different ways. The blue mold develops inside the cheese and forms blue or sometimes green veins like bleu cheese or Roquefort cheese. The white mold makes a layer on the surface of the cheese (like brie or Camembert).

The most frequently used bacteria are the lactic acids. These are the bacteria that develop as milk sours. These bacteria influence the texture and consistency of the cheese and they are the source of the enzymes that break down the proteins in the cheese. The greater the breakdown of protein, the better the flavor and aroma of the cheese. Cheese is classified according to its fat content.

Cheeses are made to preserve the most valuable constituents of the milk and to add special aromas and flavors to foods to which they are added.

Among the many cheeses that may be used in the garde manger department are: 1. *Cantal (French Cheddar);* 2. *Bleu de Bresse;* 3. *Comte;* 4. *Emmenthaler;* 5. *Beaumont;* 6. *Fromage au Marc de Raisin;* 7. *Port Salut;* 8. *Chabichou;* 9. *Reblechon;* 10. *Roquefort;* 11. *Brie de Meaux;* 12. *Valencay (Pyramid Goat Cheese);* 13. *Selle sur Cher;* 14. *Baron de Provence;* 15. *Baguette d'Avenes;* 16. *Colomiers;* 17. *Poivre Deux;* 18. *Triple Creme (Boursin);* 19. *Livarot;* 20. *Ascot;* 21. *Saint Maure;* 22. *Camembert;* 23. *Petit Suisse;* 24. *Montrcal;* 25. *Belletoile Triplecreme;* 26. *Chaource;* 27. *Brillat-Savarin;* 28. *Muenster;* 29. *Fromage de Cure;* 30. *Guerbigny;* 31. *Angelot;* 32. *Gervaise;* 33. *Edam;* 34. *Tomme de Savoie;* 35. *Reblechon.*
(*Courtesy* Foods of France.)

Every country and, as a matter of fact, in many countries every district, has its own unique cheese. Many local cheeses have become famous as menu items and are considered "kings" in their own right. Among the "kings" of cheesedom: the Cheddar, an English cheese that was first made in a village named Somerset; the Emmenthaler cheese named after a Swiss valley, the Emmenthal Valley in the Canton of Bern; or the Roquefort, a cheese from France, named after a town in the Saint-Affrique district.

As time has passed, however, many of these cheeses, although originally only made in a specific place, are being made elsewhere. For example, today, there are American cheddars and bries from Wisconsin and bleu cheese from Denmark. These cheeses are known as variants of the originals and sold as such.

What are the varieties of cheeses?
1. Fresh cheese (unfermented, made from raw curds)
2. Fermented cheeses, usually divided into two types:
   a. Soft cheese (Brie)
   b. Hard cheese (Cheddar)
3. There are also cheeses made from scalded curds (Emmenthaler or Parmesan). These cheeses are also called rennet cheeses.
4. Semi-soft cheese (Bel Paese, Muenster)
5. Blue mold cheese (Roquefort, Stilton)
6. White mold cheese (Camembert)
7. Sour milk cheeses
   a. Fresh sour milk cheese (cream cheese)
   b. Stored sour milk cheese (basket cheese)

The following is a list of the kinds of cheese most often used:

Bel Paese (semi-soft Italian cheese)

Bleu Cheese (made in Denmark)

Brie (called the King of cheese)

Camembert (perfected in 1790 by Mme Marie Harel)

Cheddar (an English cheese)

Cream Cheese (an American cheese)

Edam (famous Dutch cheese)

Emmenthaler (named after a Swiss Valley)

Gruyere (Swiss cheese)

Liederkranz (the only original cheese made in America)

Roquefort (famous for its flavor)

Stilton (an English cheese)

Bel Paese. This Italian cheese is semi-soft in consistency and of mild flavor.

Brie. It is a French white mold cheese, with a soft consistency and a fine, mild aroma. The cheese is round and flat, about 1 to 1-1/2 in. thick and sold on a straw matting. Brie remains in perfect condition for only a short time during which the rind is firm and thin and the inside mellow and soft in texture.

Camembert. It is a white mold cheese from Normandy; however, a similar cheese is produced and sold under the same label in this country. This cheese reaches maturity after one month. The consistency is waxy and semi-soft. The crust is white. As the cheese continues to ripen the skin becomes brownish red.

Cheddar. This cheese is generally available in large cylinders, weighing 50–100 lbs. It is wrapped in cheesecloth and stored at a low temperature for 6–12 months. A good cheddar should be uniformly colored, free of holes and there should be no cracks in the rind.

Danish Bleu Cheese. It is made from cow's milk and looks somewhat like roquefort but the taste is sharper and the consistency smoother. Danish Bleu Cheese ripens very quickly. It must always be listed as bleu cheese.

Edam. All of these Dutch cheeses have a characteristic appearance. They are spherical in shape with an outer covering of red wax and weigh 2–4 lbs. A smaller variety, weighing 1 lb., is known as Baby Gouda. It is slightly flattened in shape and wrapped in red cellophane. Edam cheese is light golden in color. The taste is mildly sour and rather salty. Storage time 2 to 4 months.

Emmenthaler. It originated in Switzerland but is now produced in this country and the rest of the world. Emmenthaler cheese takes from 7–12 months to ripen. When ripe it has a firm, dry texture with large tunnels or holes that contain a clear liquid. Cheese is made in the shape of wheels that measure about a yard in diameter and weigh up to 200 lbs.

Gruyere. It closely resembles Emmenthaler cheese, but is made in smaller sizes. It is stored in cellars having high humidity and as a result a putty-like layer is formed on the outer surface, giving the cheese a strong flavor and aroma. The period of aging is 8–12 months.

Parmesan. A cheese that belongs to the group of Italian Grand Cheeses and is only used for grating. The storage period is 2–5 years; the texture is hard and brittle. The flavor is mild but pronounced. The surface is black since it is smeared with oil containing lamb fat.

Roquefort. This French blue-veined cheese is made from sheep's milk. A salty cheese, it is stored in caves near the town of Roquefort under special conditioning of temperature and humidity. The cheese is cylindrical in shape and wrapped in tin foil.

Stilton. It is a blue mold cheese of high fat content with a brown wrinkled surface and a whitish yellow inside. The flavor is strong, aromatic, and salty.

Storing Cheese

All cheeses require cool storage, because if the room is too warm and moist, cheeses ripen too fast; if it is too dry, they become hard. Small pieces of cheese may be stored under cheese covers or rolled aluminum foil or a damp cloth. Larger pieces of cheese should be folded in cheesecloth that has been soaked in a strong brine.

Soft cheeses, like brie or camembert, are difficult to store. These types of cheeses should be bought when just ripe and should be used as soon as possible. Leftover pieces that have become hard can be grated, ground, or dried and stored in a screw-top jar in the refrigerator and used in salads or other dishes.

How should cheese be served?

Man invented cheese by accident, but ever since it has served faithfully as a nutritious food as well as a food that refreshes the palate. Today, cheese is still in demand on most buffets and in a la carte set-ups.

If cheese has been stored in the refrigerator, it must be taken out at least one-half hour before serving to give it a chance to breathe. The cheese is always served before the dessert. Cheeses should follow the main course or be served with the salad. Cheese is served on separate plates, if served individually, or for variety or more dramatic presentation it can be served on a cheese board.

Butter can be served with the cheese, however, connoisseurs will reject it. Among the breads that are excellent as accompaniments for cheese are Russian pumpernickel, Knaeke-Brot, various crackers, rye bread, toast, croutons, and

French or Italian Bread. For extra color and flavor, radishes and celery can be added to cheese servings. Sticks of celery, tomato wedges, olives, or bulb fennel also make very good accompaniments for cheese as do all kinds of fruit except citrus fruits.

What wines should be served with cheese?
Cheeses, especially strong ones, can be served with all wines, except sparkling and sweet wines. Strong cheeses demand red wine; lighter cheeses demand light wines.

CHEESE RECIPES

ROQUEFORT CHEESE STUFFING FOR CELERY

Yield: 16 oz.

Ingredients

Roquefort	1/2 lb.
Butter	1/2 lb.
Paprika	to garnish

Method
Mix together into a fine paste. Pipe to fill pieces of cleaned and peeled celery. To add color, sprinkle some paprika over filling. Chill before serving. Serve on folded napkin.
NOTE: Grated cheddar cheese may be substituted for roquefort cheese.

DEEP-FRIED CHEESE

This dish can be made from swiss cheese or camembert. For the swiss cheese version, medium-thin slices of swiss cheese are dipped into beaten eggs and then are breaded with white breadcrumbs and baked in butter. For the camembert version, camambert wedges are cut in half, dipped in beaten eggs and breaded with white breadcrumbs and deep fried. Serve on doily-covered plate with deep-fried parsley.

BELGIAN ENDIVE WITH BLUE CHEESE

Yield: 14 oz.

Ingredients

Belgian Endives, washed and trimmed	2
Hard-cooked Eggs	4
Blue Cheese	3-1/2 oz.
Butter	3-1/2 oz.

Method
Put egg yolks through sieve; add cheese and butter; beat together until creamy. Stuff endive leaves with the mixture. Garnish with grapes and rings of green pepper.

CHAPTER EIGHTEEN

NONEDIBLE DISPLAYS

Although food holds the spotlight in all buffet presentation—and the objective of buffet planning must be to achieve visual beauty both in the artistic presentation of each item of edible food, as well as in the arrangement of the many dishes on the buffet table—nothing heightens the beauty of the buffet more than an outstanding centerpiece, made of ice, tallow, or other nonedible material.

The guest should be able to identify the theme of the buffet at a glance, just by observing the nonedible decorations that provide an eye-catching background for the presentation.

A nonedible decorative display piece should be a work of art, always in good taste, whether the figure is made of ice, sugar, tallow, or any other material.

The garde manger staff can use various methods and materials to enhance the presentation of a buffet. The list of possibilities would include:

1. Ice carvings
2. Tallow displays

3. Decorative touches created with miscellaneous items which may be either made or assembled (flowers; styrofoam figures; boats made of bread, fruits, and vegetables; candles; wine bottles; flags made of wax leaves and similar items). China, posters, items from antique shops can also be rented to achieve the objective of a buffet.

ICE CARVING

The ice sculpture is the highlight of any buffet, the artistic touch, the focal point. Ice can be carved in any shape, size or figure that fits the theme or occasion; as an example, for Christmas, there could be a Santa Claus; for an anniversary, a heart; or for an Easter Buffet, a bunny.

Before starting an ice carving, the following items should be assembled:

1. A 100- to 300-lb. block of ice, 40 in. high by 20 in. wide by 10 in. thick. Blocks like this can be purchased.
2. A pair of ice tongs—for moving and handling the ice.

Telling Touches for Showcase Presentation
Nonedible item is used very effectively in this eye-catching food presentation. Butter sculpture of a native dancer focuses attention on Smoked Beef Tongue Taj Majal.

3. An ice shaver with 3 to 6 prongs—used to carve out the details and do the small cutting on the block of ice.
4. An ice pick—used to split the block into smaller pieces.
5. A hand saw—used to remove large cuts of ice or to make rough outlines.
6. Wood chisels—ranging in size from 1/2 to 2 in.
7. A compass—for drawing circles.

8. An electric chain saw; when working with this type of saw, it is important to have the saw grounded to prevent accidents.
9. A template made on graph paper of the shape of the ice carving that is to be made.

The best temperature for ice carving is 28°F. or less. An ice block will melt at the rate of 1/2 to 1 in. per hour under normal conditions (room temperature).

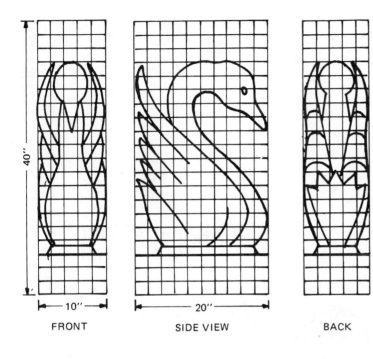

40"

FRONT   SIDE VIEW   BACK

10"   20"

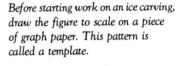

Before starting work on an ice carving, draw the figure to scale on a piece of graph paper. This pattern is called a template.

NOTE I: Each ice carving must have a base that is at least 4–5 in. high; in other words, when planning the carving, deduct 5 in. from the total height for the base. Be sure to draw the template accordingly.

NOTE II: If a piece of ice breaks off, dip each broken piece into salt and press pieces back together for a few minutes; the length of time will depend on the size and weight of the broken pieces. With the salt added, the broken pieces will freeze together and hold.

How to Display the Ice Carving on a Buffet

1. The table used for the carving must be sturdy and strong enough to support the weight of the ice.
2. The carved ice block should be placed in a specially constructed metal pan, wider than the base of the carving; wooden blocks should first be placed in the bottom of the

pan and the carving should rest securely on top of the blocks.
3. Colored rotating lights can produce a dramatic effect as they play over an ice display; this is especially effective when the lights themselves cannot be seen.
4. The pan under the ice sculpture should be covered with a linen cloth, flowers, ferns, or other decorative material.

(For additional assistance in planning and producing ice carvings, refer to the book *Ice Carving Made Easy* by Joseph Amendola.)

TALLOW DISPLAYS

When deciding on the selection of a pattern for a tallow display piece, it is essential that the display piece chosen match the theme of the buffet; however, it is even more desirable to select a pattern that may also, later on, fit into the decor theme of several other buffets. Creating an eye-

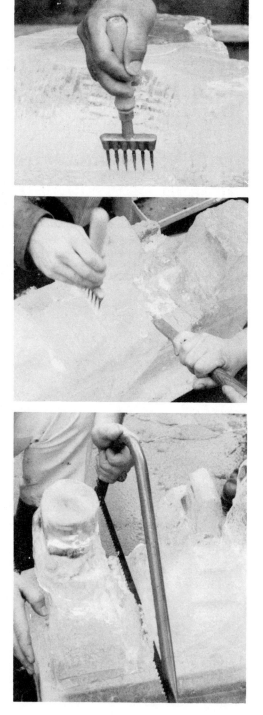

An ice carving provides an elegant centerpiece to heighten the beauty and set the theme for a buffet. Proper lighting can enhance the effectiveness of a carving. Here is the swan produced from the template on page 221.

Two tools essential to producing a professional ice carving are the 6-pronged shaver and the 1/2-in. chisel. The correct techniques for their use are pictured at right, top and center.

To prepare a large piece of ice for a carving, a hand saw is recommended as used at right, bottom.

This 3-dimensional tallow piece reproduces a wide variety of cheeses. Chef/Co-Author Nicolas stands beside his striking tallow display.

catching tallow piece is always time-consuming and should be planned well in advance.

A French restaurant serving a French buffet would add effectiveness to the presentation by displaying a bust of Napoleon or Escoffier or the Eiffel Tower. Such displays can be used over and over, but they should be covered with transparent wrap when not in use as dust tends to stick to them.

Pictured are several tallow displays executed by the authors, with the assistance of students. All have been made at The Culinary Institute of America and were displayed on buffets, at exhibitions, and at private parties.

To be successful in the execution of a tallow display, it is essential that certain rules be followed. The person making the tallow display should have a photograph or model of the piece to be made. This is especially helpful in creating busts as it helps to keep the proportions right. Architectural blueprints and photographs have been used by the authors to reproduce accurately in tallow the proportions of the Eiffel Tower, the Leaning Tower of Pisa, and the U.S. Capitol Building.

The composition of the material used in making a tallow display depends upon the piece to be made. In general, a formula made up in the following proportions works well in tallow displays, except for tall pieces like the Eiffel Tower, a Chinese Pagoda, or the Leaning Tower of Pisa:

1/3 beeswax
1/3 paraffin
1/3 beef fat

These ingredients should be melted together in a pot. The beef fat can be freshly diced fat, cooking fat, or other fat that solidifies when cold. The quantity of fat can be increased if a more pliable and workable mixture is needed, especially if the working area is cool, i.e., below 65°F. Most of the tallow illustrations in this book have been made with the above formula and can stand temperatures up to 90°F.

Preparing the Tallow
In a large pot, melt:

5 lb. of beeswax
5 lb. of paraffin
5 lb. of beef fat

The preferred method of melting the mixture is in a waterbath although that is not absolutely necessary; it is, however, dangerous to melt paraffin over a flame. When the wax and fat are

Tallow animals amuse young and old diners. Rabbit with extra-long whiskers captures everyone's attention.

Presiding over a Hawaiian buffet, this seated Buddha was placed on a mirror-topped riser. The formula was prepared in proportions of 1/3 paraffin, 1/3 beeswax, and 1/3 beef fat.

melted, pour mixture into empty milk cartons or other containers that can be opened. Allow to cool at room temperature, not under refrigeration. When tallow is completely cold, figures can be carved from the solid block. Great care should be exercised while carving as the tallow is brittle and may break.

The tallow can also be grated as it can then be molded like clay. When grating large amounts, use the coarse plate of the meat grinder.

A solid structure and base for the tallow piece must be created, especially if the finished piece has to be transported. A wooden base with dowels and a rough structure made of styrofoam have both been used in the following illustrations.

NOTE: The latest development in nonedible food sculpturing is salt dough, a mixture used by the 1976 and 1980 United States Culinary Olympic Teams. The method of working with it is the same as that for working with tallow.

Formula

Water	16 oz.
Cornstarch	12 oz.
Popcorn Salt	32 oz.

Method

Combine water and cornstarch and bring to a boil, or to a thick paste. Mix with heated popcorn salt. Store in plastic bags until needed.

Salt dough mixture can be colored with powdered spices and herbs.

ADDITIONAL DECORATIVE TOUCHES

These illustrated directions show how aluminum foil frills can be made for roasts and chops to be

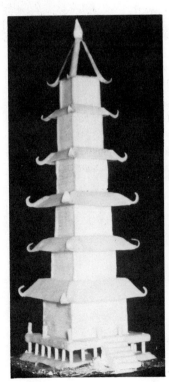

Unusually tall pieces like this pagoda are made of tallow that is half paraffin and half beeswax. Mixture is melted and poured on trays; figure is shaped while tallow is still hot.

Donkey playing violin adds light-hearted note to buffet presentation.

Tallow Sculpture (Sherlock Holmes) International Culinary Cooking Competition 1976

displayed as part of a buffet presentation. Ways to fold napkins into interesting shapes are also pictured.

1.

2.

To fold napkin into decorative shape, first lay flat and then fold each of the four corners into the center.

3.

4.

Fold each of newly made corners into center again and turn napkin over so smooth square is available for next step.

Fold corners into center again. Next pull out tabs from other side of napkin. (Note picture for position.) Arrange tabs in petals.

Now open corners from other side of napkin to make square as shown to serve as background for napkin flower.

Frills add a decorative finishing touch to many cuts of meat such as ham, chops, and crown roast. To make a frill fold the aluminum foil in half, shiny side inside, and cut strips with scissors.

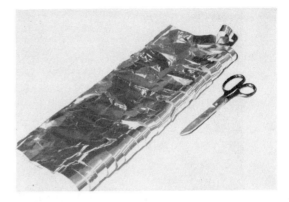

After cutting strips, reverse foil so shiny side is outside. Roll foil around bone as shown to crown decorated ham.

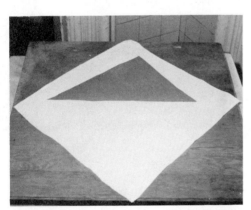

1.

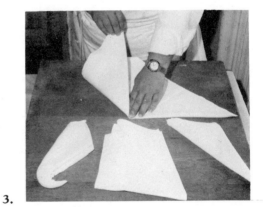

3.

2.

To make a napkin into a swan, first cut a piece of aluminum foil or brown paper into a triangle. Place triangle in center of napkin.

Fold napkin into triangle around foil or paper. Determine center of triangle, fold left corner to center, making sure edges are patted down.

Fold right corner to center.

(continued)

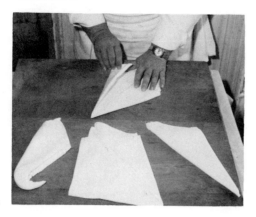

4.

5.

Swan Napkin (continued)

Fold newly made corners into center.

Wrap folded napkin in another cloth with open side toward you.

Set a weight on cloth, pull weight toward you firmly to form swan's head; crease napkin.

6.

CHAPTER NINETEEN

LOW CALORIE BUFFETS

Because of our health-conscious public's persisting demand for low calorie foods, many food-service operations have and will feature low calorie menu items. However, the difficulty for the chef is not creating and featuring these dishes on the daily a la carte menu, but in merchandising and arranging these foods for buffets. As we know, the temptation of eating food from buffets is great and people tend to overeat, especially if the buffet is self-service. But the saying of Brillet Savarin, "It is a cook's duty to tempt the appetite, and it is the guest's duty to curb it," can only be partially applied to today's health-conscious food world. Now it is impossible not to respond to the demand for low calorie foods.

This chapter will not cover the depths of "how and why," as this information is available in specialty books. But advice and some recipes will be presented in order to assist in preparing buffets and food arrangements more to the public's liking.

1. The basic principles of cooking must be followed while preparing low calorie foods.
2. Low calorie foods should be well-decorated,

have the correct portion size, and should be arranged in full view of guests.
3. Portion size can be controlled by service personnel with proper service utensils.
4. Use these winning suggestions from the 5th International Kneip Dietary Cooking Competition, West Germany, 1981:
   USA
   Four Season Vegetable Appetizer
   Asparagus Soup
   Roast Beef Roti, Culinary Institute
   Potato Puff, Braised Cucumbers, Spinach Leaves
   Pepper Cauliflower .
   Yogurt Cream with Berries Poughkeepsie
   Denmark
   Salads of the Season from Vegetables
   Irish Broth with Asparagus
   Roast Loin of Beef Rote Copenhagen
   Galette Potatoes, Broccoli, Red Beets, and Fennel
   Yogurt Ice Cream
   Badworishofen
   Melon with Vegetable Salad Cocktail
   Cream of Asparagus

Roulade of Beef Worisana
Vegetable Roesti, Risolle Potatoes
Cream of Yogurt with Blackberries

These menu ideas and the recipes for low calorie foods in this chapter will help you stimulate your public's interest. Once you have achieved the proper food appeal, your guests will thank you by eating, happily, your buffet food creations.

CUCUMBER AND GRAPE SALAD

Yield: 1-1/2 lb.

Ingredients

Cucumber	1
Green Grapes	1 cup
Chopped Nuts	1 tbsp.
Onion	1
Chopped Dill	1 tsp.
Grated Lemon Zest	a touch
Salt and Pepper	to taste
Vinegar	to taste
Yogurt	1/2 container
Sour Cream	2–3 tbsp.

Method
Remove seeds and slice cucumber. Cut grapes in half. Dice onion. Chop nuts. Add lemon zest, vinegar, salt, and pepper. Toss. Add yogurt and sour cream. Add herbs.

MARINATED MOCK ARTICHOKES

Yield: 16 portions

Ingredients

Lettuce Cores	80
Water	3 qt.
White Vinegar	3 oz.
Coarse Salt	1/2 oz.

Method
Trim lettuce cores of excess leaves and trim to a cone shape. Combine water, vinegar and salt. Bring to a boil. Add trimmed lettuce cores and

simmer for 10–12 minutes. Drain liquid and rinse cores with cold water.

DRESSING
Ingredients

Carrots	3 oz.
Chopped Parsley	1/2 cup
Garlic, minced	1 clove
Italian Dressing	1 qt.

Method
Dice carrots Brunoise. Chop parsley and reserve. Mince garlic. Mix Italian dressing. Combine all of the above ingredients. Add cores and marinate for 12 hours.

RADISH AND BANANA SALAD

Yield: 2 lb.

Ingredients

Radishes, thinly sliced	1 lb.
Bananas, sliced	1 lb.
Boston Lettuce	for garnish

DRESSING
Ingredients

Orange Juice	1/2–1 cup
Lemon Juice	1/2–1 cup
Salt to taste	1/2 tsp.

Method
Combine the orange juice, lemon juice, and salt and mix well. Add dressing to radishes and bananas. Toss well and let rest for 10 min. Arrange on Boston lettuce and sprinkle with crushed black pepper.

STRAWBERRY AND RADISH SALAD

Yield: 5–6 portions
Ingredients

Radishes, white, mild	3 oz.
Carrots	2
Sour Apple	1

Strawberries	9 oz.
Boston Lettuce	1/2 head
Juice of Lemon	1
Olive Oil	2-3 tbsp.
Fresh Ground Black Pepper	to taste
Sugar	a touch

Method

Peel radishes and slice paper thin. Sprinkle with salt and rest until water forms. Peel apple and carrots and slice. Cut strawberries in half or quarters. Clean Boston lettuce.

Drain radishes well. Toss together all ingredients except lettuce. Outline a bowl with lettuce and top with salad mixture.

Health Food Suggestions

Other dishes low in calories that could be featured in a buffet for dieters include the following:

Artichokes. Fresh artichokes cleaned and cooked in water and lemon juice and served cold with 2 oz. cottage cheese per artichoke.

Asparagus. 4 oz. fresh asparagus, peeled and boiled, then marinated with 1/2 tsp. lemon juice and served with 2 oz. cottage cheese.

Bananas and Radishes. Cut two bananas in half; save the skin; cut banana meat into thin slices; slice an equal amount of radishes. Mix juice of a half orange with 1 tsp. lemon juice. (A mixture of 1 part each crushed strawberries, sliced bananas and sliced fresh radishes can also be used.)

Beet, Apple, and Horseradish. 4 oz. peeled, fresh beets cut into julienne strips, 1 oz. fresh apples cut into julienne strips, 1/2 oz. fresh horseradish cut into very fine julienne; mix with 1/2 tsp. lemon juice and 1/2 tsp. honey; serve on lettuce leaf. 3-4 sliced toasted almonds can be added.

Belgian Endive with Ginger. 2 oz. diced endive, 1/2 oz. diced tomatoes, 1/2 oz. diced fresh pineapple, 1 oz. fresh orange sections. Mix all ingredients with 1-2 oz. cottage cheese and 1-2 tsp. lemon juice. Sprinkle 1/3 tsp. powdered ginger over the dish. Serve on lettuce leaf.

Carrot and Apple. Peel six new carrots and grate; mix with 1 tsp. honey and 2/3 tsp. lemon juice; add one grated medium apple; toss together and serve in a glass dish on a lettuce leaf to provide contrasting background.

Celery. Take the center (sometimes called the heart of celery) and peel it, removing all leaves. Wash carefully and braise for 15-20 min. in some lemon juice and a little beef stock. Season with sea salt. Serve cold with cottage cheese.

Celery and Fresh Pineapple. Mix 4 oz. diced celery, 2 oz. diced apples, 1 oz. diced pineapple, and 1 oz. fresh mandarin oranges with 2 oz. plain yogurt and 2 tsp. orange juice. Decorate with celery leaves.

Cucumber. 4 oz. cucumber, peeled and sliced thin, mixed with 1/2-1 tsp. lemon juice; season with 2 grinds of pepper, 1/3 tsp. chopped dill, and 1/3 tsp. salt; serve on lettuce (salt can be omitted).

Melon. Mix 2 oz. cantaloupe cut into julienne with 2 oz. red peppers cut into julienne; add 1/2-1 tsp. of lemon juice.

Mushroom and Spinach. Mix 2 oz. spinach, cut into julienne, 1-1/2 oz. sliced mushrooms, and 1 oz. diced apple with 2 oz. uncreamed cottage cheese. Season with 3 tsp. orange juice and 1/2 tsp. honey.

Mushroom and Tomato. Mix 2 oz. sliced raw mushrooms, 2 oz. diced tomatoes, 2 oz. diced apples, and 2 oz. diced melon with 4 oz. cottage cheese, 2 tsp. orange juice, and 1 tsp. lemon juice. Garnish with watercress.

Radishes. 2 oz. fresh radishes sliced and mixed with 1/2 tsp. of lemon juice; serve on a lettuce leaf sprinkled with chopped parsley.

Red Cabbage. 4 oz. red cabbage cut into fine julienne and 1 oz. apple cut into julienne mixed

This buffet offers many items that calorie counters can enjoy. Unexpected twists in flavor and color keep patron ratings for these low calorie combinations at the same level that richer foods enjoy. On tray at left front: Grated Carrot in Orange Shell, topped with orange sections and chopped red pepper; Julienne of Beets and Apples, zipped up with fresh horseradish; Sliced Cucumber, Red Cabbage and Apple; Pear Halves topped with radish slices that have been marinated in dill-flavored lemon juice. Tunafish mold in center is flanked by lobster timbales. Tray at right holds apple slices, topped with a mound of grated carrot and a walnut half. Endive leaves are combined with mound of green grapes filled with low calorie cottage cheese. Fresh pineapple slices, diced tomato and yogurt sparked with diced red pepper is another unusual combination. Yogurt cocktails are garnished with thin wedges of cantaloupe.

Trays on center level present: Chicken Galantine with cherry tomatoes stuffed with cottage cheese, framed by cherry-topped orange slices; Poached Salmon, Galantine of Veal with tuna sauce in cantaloupe shell decorated with melon balls held in place by skewers. Top row: Roast Capon with medallions of capon filled with liver and yogurt; Roast Chicken with fruit and asparagus; Sliced Prosciutto Ham with melon wedges and gelatin-filled orange shells; Saddle of Veal with Vegetable and Yogurt Salad; Slices of Roast Turkey with fresh orange slices and gelatin-filled orange shells. While the number of calories was kept to the minimum, a maximum amount of imagination was used in planning and presenting this collection of low calorie foods. For other low calorie ideas, see p. 230.

together with 2 tsp. lemon juice and 1/2 tsp. honey.

Sauerkraut. Mix 1/2 part sauerkraut (fresh) with 1/4 part grated apple and 1/4 part diced fresh pineapple; serve on lettuce.

Spinach. Wash carefully and cut into julienne. Mix 1/2 part julienne-cut spinach with 1/2 part julienne-cut apple and a little honey and lemon juice.

Watercress. 2 oz. watercress, 1 oz. grated apple mixed together with 1/2–1 tsp. lemon juice added. A little sugar can also be added.

GLOSSARY

Aitchbone. The hip or rump bone; also, the cut of meat (usually beef or pork) containing the bone.

a la. According to the style of, such as: a la Francaise or according to the French way.

a la carte. Foods prepared to order: each dish priced separately.

al dente. Cooked just to the point of being done, especially pastas and fresh vegetables; cooked to retain crispness.

Allumettes. Potatoes, carrots, and similar items, cut into thin strips like matchsticks.

Antipasto. Italian hors d'oeuvre. Assortment of appetizers.

Appetizers. Beverages or assorted snacks served before a meal.

Aspic. A savory meat jelly, used to coat meat, poultry, or fish or in making molds of meat, fish, or vegetables. Served cold. Also cut in designs or chopped to use in decorating buffet displays.

au Naturel. Cooked simply.

Bain-Marie. A table having openings to hold containers of food over hot water in steam table. Double boiler can be used for same purpose with smaller amounts of food.

Barding. To cover (e.g., meat or game) with slices of bacon for cooking.

Baste. To pour liquid or drippings over meat while cooking to hold moisture and provide flavor.

Bean Sprouts. Mung beans from China. Sprouts are used when tiny, tender, and green in making Chinese dishes; also as a salad ingredient.

Beating. Regular lifting and stirring motion to bring mixture to a smooth texture. Often done for the purpose of making mixture fluffy by incorporating air into it.

Beignets. Fritters.

Belgian Endive. A variety of chicory having leaves in stalk that are pale green to white; used raw as a salad, or braised.

Bind. To cause to cohere, unite, or hold together, such as white sauce used to bind a croquette mixture.

Blanch.
1. To scald or parboil foods in boiling water or steam before cooking or freezing.
2. To dip in boiling water to facilitate the removal of skins from tomatoes, fruits, nuts, etc.

Blending. Thoroughly mixing two or more ingredients.

Bouchee. Small meat patty or pastry shell filled with meat, poultry, or lobster. Sometimes filled with fruits.

Bouquetiere. A variety of vegetables in season arranged around a dish or platter of meat, poultry, or fish.

Braise. To brown meat or vegetables in a small amount of fat and then cook covered in oven or on top of the range, adding liquid as needed to prevent scorching or burning.

Brazier. Heavy-duty stewing pan with tightly fitting cover.

Brine. Liquid of salt, water, and vinegar used for pickling meats or vegetables.

Brioche. A small pear-shaped roll of raised dough made with yeast, eggs, milk, butter, and flour. Very light. Sometimes filled for service as canape.

Brunoise. Cut in fine dice.

Buffet. Display of ready-to-eat hot and cold foods. Often self-service from table or tables of assorted foods.

❧

Canape. An appetizer prepared on a base such as bread, toast, or crackers.

Capon. Castrated poultry noted for its tenderness and delicate flavor.

Charcuterie. Cold cuts and meat dishes such as sausages. Also a delicatessen specializing in dressed meats and meat dishes.

Chaud-Froid. A jellied sauce used as a covering for meat, fish, or poultry; food covered with a chaud-froid sauce usually has been molded into shapes after cooking and is served cold. May be white or brown.

Chef. Chief of the kitchen. Person in charge of food preparation.

Ciseler. To shred finely; to make an incision in the skin of fish or meat.

Clarify. To make clear by adding a clarifying agent which removes suspended particles, such as in the preparation of consomme.

Cocotte. A small, shallow, individual baking dish usually with one or two handles.

Concasser. To chop coarsely. A coarse mince.

Coral. The cooked roe of a lobster.

Corn. To salt lightly by placing in brine containing preservatives, sweetening, and sometimes spices. Usually for meat.

Cornucopia (*horn of plenty*). A receptacle shaped like a horn or cone. For a buffet may be filled with choice fruits. May be carved out of ice. A pastry roll filled with whipped cream or meringue and nuts.

Court Bouillon. Fish stock, water, or other liquid in which fish is cooked, usually mixed with vinegar or wine, and savory herbs.

Croquettes. Chopped or ground food usually held together with a thick sauce, shaped and rolled in breadcrumbs or cornmeal and fried in a skillet or in deep fat or oven-baked.

Croustades. Baked forms or patty shells. Also hot patties filled with meat or liver paste.

Croutons. Small pieces of fried or toasted bread used in soups, in garnishing, etc. Also made of thick layers of aspic.

❧

Deglaze. To moisten a roast pan or saute pan with wine, vinegar, stock, or water in order to dissolve the caramelized drippings so that they may be incorporated into the sauce.

Dice. To cut into small cubes.

❧

Egg Albumen. The white of an egg.

Eggwash. Egg yolk diluted with water or milk. Used to give color and gloss to yeast dough or pastry.

Emulsification. The blending together of two incompatible liquids, such as oil and water. The blending is achieved by slowly adding droplets of one liquid to the other while beating constantly.

en Bordure. Bordered or ringed (as with rice or mashed potatoes) as a garnish.

en Croute. In a crust.

Farce. Stuffing, forcemeat.

Farci. Stuffed.

Fatback. Fresh pork fat.

Fennel. Vegetable resembling celery. It has a slight anise flavor.

Filet *(French).* A piece or slice of boneless lean meat or fish. To cut into filets.

Fleuron. Puff paste baked in a crescent shape used as a garnish.

Forcemeat. Chopped meats and seasoning used for stuffing.

Game. Edible wild animals such as bear, buffalo, deer, hare, opossum, squirrel, rabbit, and reindeer.

Garnish. To embellish platter or tray or food item to be used in displays; to decorate. Also used as a noun, referring to a foodstuff being used as a garnish.

Garnitures. French term for items used in garnishing: hard-cooked egg slices; timbales; aspic croutons; stuffed cherry tomatoes; filled fruits.

Gelatin. Colorless, tasteless, brittle substance made by boiling bones, hooves, and animal tissues. When granulated or powdered, gelatin is used to make jelly-like dishes such as aspics, desserts, molded salads, and mousses. Because gelatin has no flavor of its own, it makes a compatible ingredient for flavorful food combinations.

Gelee. Jelly or jellied.

Glace de viande. A meat glaze from white or brown poultry stock or brown meat stock. Boiled down, it is reduced to a syrup that jells when cold. Used to add flavor to sauces and soups.

Glaze. A liquid preparation (as sugar syrup, gelatin dissolved in meat stock) brushed over food (as meat, fish, pastry), which, after application, becomes firm and adds flavor and a glossy appearance.

Goujon. A small river fish of the catfish family.

Gourmet. A connoisseur of food and/or wine, as well as the proper combination of dishes on menus; one with sensitive and discriminating tastes in food and wine.

Herb Bouquet. Mixed herbs tied and used for seasoning.

Herbs. Cultivated plants that are combined with foods to improve flavor. Some, such as parsley, celery, basil, and chervil, may be used fresh. Most can also be used when dried.

Hors d'Oeuvre. Small appetizers or canapes served before a meal or as first course of a meal.

Julienne.
1. Potatoes: cut in long slices, thinner than for french fries, and served very crisp.
2. Soup: clear soup with thin strips of vegetables.
3. Poultry: cut in narrow 1-1/2-in. strips.

Kibbe. Ground lamb and wheat baked in a cake.

Kirschwasser. A dry, colorless brandy made in Germany, France, and Switzerland. It is distilled from the fermented juices of the black Morello cherry and has a bitter almond flavor.

Larding. Strips of salt pork inserted with a special larding needle through a good-sized piece of meat or fish which is to be roasted.

Lardons. Strips of salt pork used for larding and as a garnish. Also, julienne of bacon.

Leek. Mild form of onion with broad, long, succulent leaves. Used as a vegetable or an aromatic seasoning.

Liaison. A binding agent for sauces; usually cream and egg yolks.

Lox. Smoked salmon.

❧ ☙

Macedoine. Mixture usually of fruits or vegetables.

Maraschino Cherries. Large cherries preserved in true or imitation Maraschino liqueur.

Marzipan. A confection of crushed almonds or almond paste, sugar, and whites of eggs that may be shaped into various forms (fruits, vegetables, etc.).

Masking. To cover completely, as with frosting or sauce (aspic or chaud-froid).

Medallion, Medaillon. A small, round, or oval serving of food, usually meat filets.

Melting. Making liquid by application of heat.

Minced, Mincing. Finely chopped. Finely chopping, similar to grinding.

Mirepoix. A flavoring made from meat (ham or bacon), vegetables, herbs, and seasonings used chiefly in braising meat.

Mixing. Combining two or more ingredients.

Mousseline. A frothy sauce or puree made so by the addition of whipped cream or beaten egg whites; often hollandaise sauce.

❧ ☙

Noisette. A small, rounded morsel of food, such as a small piece of lean meat or a small potato ball browned in butter.

❧ ☙

Oeufs (*French*). Eggs.

❧ ☙

Paillettes. Straws, often of pastry.

Papillote. Cooked in parchment paper (or foil) to seal in flavors.

Parboil. To boil until partially cooked.

Parchment Paper. A highly grease-resistant and water-resistant paper with a gelatinized surface, often used as a food wrapper.

Parmesan Cheese. Italian type used for grating. Flavor, mild but pronounced; texture, hard.

Pastry Bag, Pastry Tube. A funnel-shaped container for holding soft food (mashed potatoes, whipped cream, cake frosting) from which the foods are forced through the pastry tube at the tip to make ornamental coatings or decorations.

Paupiettes. Thin slices of braised meat or fish rolled around forcemeat.

Pilaf, Pilau. Rice, usually combined with meat and vegetables, fried in oil, steamed in stock, and seasoned with any of several herbs (as saffron or curry).

Piping. Forcing dough or decorating icing through a pastry tube in a narrow stream.

Pimento, Pimiento. Sweet red pepper, cooked and canned for use as a garnish for salads or casserole dishes. The source of paprika.

Piquant. Spicy, highly seasoned.

Poaching. Cooking eggs, fish, etc., in water that is just below boiling temperature.

Profiteroles. Small balls of pate a choux used as a garnish; usually hold savory filling.

Prosciutto. Dry-cured, spiced ham.

Pud (*variation of pood*). A Russian unit of weight equal to about 36.11 lb.

Pumpernickel. A sourdough bread; made with rye flour as a dark variety, and with a mixture of rye and wheat flours for the lighter types.

Puree. Thick soup made of strained pulp of vegetables. May also refer to any vegetable or fruit pulp that has been mashed and sieved.

❧ ☙

Quenelles. Balls of forcemeat mixture cooked in boiling water or stock; used as a garnish for entrees and soups or may be served as a separate dish.

Quiche. A pastry shell sprinkled with bits of fried bacon and grated cheese, filled with onion-flavored custard and baked.

🙠 🙡

Rack. Market term for the unsplit forequarters of veal or lamb.

Ragout. Thick savory stew.

Ramekin. Shallow china dish in which food may be baked and served.

Ramequins (*See also ramekin*). Slices of bread covered with cheese and eggs and baked in a mold or shell.

Ravier. An oval container.

Reduce. To reduce volume by cooking or simmering.

Rendering. Melting fat out of suet or other animal fats to free it from connective tissues.

Rennet. Rennin is an enzyme found in the lining of calves' stomachs and is used in converting milk into junket or cheese.

Rillettes. Highly seasoned, potted pork.

Rissoles. Little turnovers of very thin puff paste with a filling of a highly seasoned mixture of ham or chicken or other delicate meat, chopped and moistened with white sauce. Dipped in egg and fried in deep fat.

Romaine. Lettuce with deep green, straight leaves and marked flavor.

Roti. Roast.

Roulade. A thin slice of meat rolled with or without stuffing and braised or sauteed.

Roux. Equal parts of fat and flour cooked; used to thicken sauces and gravies. Roux may be light-colored for light sauces; cooked until browned for darker sauces.

🙠 🙡

Sachet Bag. A small bag with selected herbs, used to season stock, soups, etc.; removed after cooking.

Saddle. Market term for the two unsplit hindquarters, as of lamb or veal.

Salami. Sausage of pork, beef, and seasonings. Dried. Usually contains garlic.

Saute. To cook quickly in a small amount of fat.

Shallots. Onion-like plant with clustered bulbs that resemble garlic but are milder. Used for seasoning soups, stews, salads, etc.

Simmer. To cook slowly just below the boiling point. Cooking time is longer than in poaching.

Skewer. A long pin of wood or metal for fastening meat to keep it in desired shape while roasting; also used to hold small pieces of meat and vegetables for broiling.

Skim. Using a skimmer or ladle to remove scum or grease accumulated on top of a soup, sauce, or stock.

Smorgasbord. Swedish appetizers or full meals arranged on a table like a buffet.

Steeping. To soak in liquid below boiling point, off heat, to extract flavor or color, as for tea.

Stock. The liquid in which meat, poultry, fish, or vegetables have been cooked. Brown or white.

🙠 🙡

Tallow. A waxy substance, such as paraffin, beeswax, or beef fat, used in making displays for buffets.

Template. A pattern or guide to be followed in making, for example, an ice sculpture.

Timbales.
1. A small pastry shell fried with a timbale iron and filled with a cooked timbale mixture.
2. A creamy mixture (as of chicken, seafood, cheese, fish, or vegetables) cooked in a drum-shaped mold or in individual molds or cups.

Tournedos. A small filet of beef, usually cut from the tip of the tenderloin and encircled by a strip of suet, salt pork, or bacon for quick cooking.

Trussing. To skewer or to tie wings and legs of poultry before roasting.

Try Out. To cook fat until oil is out. Render.

Turban. A dish (as a filet of fish) formed in the shape of a turban with a well in the center to be filled with a suitable accompanying mixture.

❦

Venison. Deer or reindeer meat.

Vinaigrette. A sauce made of vinegar, oil, onions, parsley, and herbs.

Vol-au-vent. Case made of puff pastry in which meat or poultry is served; usually covered with a crust lid.

❦

Waterbath. A vessel containing water, usually hot, over or in which food is processed. Also called a bain-marie.

Watercress. Plant of the mustard family whose crisp green leaves are used in salads, sandwiches, and as garnishes.

Whipping. Beating rapidly to increase volume by mixing in air.

❦

Zest. Piece of peel or of thin, oily outer skin of an orange or lemon; used to flavor.

❦

INDEX